By Suleika Jaouad

Between Two Kingdoms

The Book of Alchemy

THE BOOK
OF
ALCHEMY

THE BOOK
OF
ALCHEMY

A CREATIVE PRACTICE
FOR AN INSPIRED LIFE

SULEIKA
JAOUAD

RANDOM HOUSE
NEW YORK

Random House
An imprint and division of Penguin Random House LLC
1745 Broadway, New York, NY 10019

randomhousebooks.com
penguinrandomhouse.com

Contributor credits are on pages 289–305.

Library of Congress Cataloging-in-Publication Data
Names: Jaouad, Suleika, author.
Title: The book of alchemy / by Suleika Jaouad.
Description: New York, NY: Random House, 2025. |
Identifiers: LCCN 2024049036 (print) | LCCN 2024049037 (ebook) |
ISBN 9780593734636 (hardcover) | ISBN 9780593734650 (ebook)
Subjects: LCSH: Diaries—Authorship.
Classification: LCC PN4390 .J36 2025 (print) | LCC PN4390 (ebook) |
DDC 808/.06692—dc23/eng/20241028
LC record available at https://lccn.loc.gov/2024049036
LC ebook record available at https://lccn.loc.gov/2024049037

Printed in the United States of America on acid-free paper

1st Printing

First Edition

BOOK TEAM: Production editor: Andy Lefkowitz • Managing editor: Rebecca Berlant • Production manager: Richard Elman • Copy editor: Caroline Clouse • Proofreaders: Pam Feinstein, Megha Jain, and Mimi Lipson

Book design by Ralph Fowler

The authorized representative in the EU for product safety and compliance is Penguin Random House Ireland, Morrison Chambers, 32 Nassau Street, Dublin D02 YH68, Ireland. https://eu-contact.penguin.ie

For Jon,
who infuses creativity into
every corner of life

Live the questions now.
Perhaps then, someday far in the future,
you will gradually, without even noticing it,
live your way into the answer.

—Rainer Maria Rilke

CONTENTS

CHAPTER 6: **On the Body** 143

CHAPTER 7: **On Rebuilding** 171

CHAPTER 8: **On Ego** 197

THE WAY IN

I've kept a journal for as long as I can remember. It has been the keeper of my memories and yearnings. I've used it to mark the biggest thresholds, to ride the roughest waves, to traverse the liminal space between no longer and not yet. As a teenager, I journaled through various heartbreaks and growing pains, and I journaled in the days leading up to momentous, anxiety-provoking transitions, like going off to college and finding my way after graduation. The throughline in all these journal entries was an orientation toward the future, toying with the question, "What am I going to do with my life?" I filled pages with endless permutations and possibilities, a sliding-doors-esque exercise in what all my alternate lives could look like—whom I'd wake up next to, whether I'd be a lawyer or a novelist, whether I'd raise human children or canine ones, and everything in between.

Journaling went from a favorite pastime to a lifeline when I was diagnosed with leukemia at age twenty-two. Though I knew my diagnosis was grave—my doctors told me my chance of long-term survival was only 35 percent—I approached treatment with youthful naïveté. I expected a short stay in the kingdom of the sick: a few weeks of chemo in the hospital, followed by a bone marrow transplant, then back to life as I knew it. Into the cancer unit I brought knitting needles and yarn, with the goal of becoming an expert scarf maker by the time I was discharged. Perhaps even more delusionally, I packed a thick stack of tomes like *War and Peace,* cheerfully telling my parents I planned to use my time there to read through the entire Western canon. I had always been ambitious, and I thought I could maintain my pre-diagnosis level of productivity.

But time and calamity have a way of dispelling our illusions, and by the end of the summer, all of mine were gone. After weeks locked in isolation in a hospital room, poked and prodded with needles and endless questions, suffering the brutal side effects of chemo, I learned that the standard treatment was not working. Far from being eradicated, the leukemic blasts in my bloodstream had more than doubled. I was going into bone marrow failure, and my only option was a phase II clinical trial. An experimental trial that had not yet been proven safe or effective meant terrifying uncertainty at a time when I desperately wanted the confidence of a cure. Over the next few months, the new chemo drugs went to work, slowly and effectively nuking the leukemia, paving the way for the transplant, all the while taking more of a toll than I ever could have imagined.

By that point, I had spent the better part of a year in and out of the hospital—for treatment and also for dangerous complications ranging from neutropenic fevers to sepsis. My immune system was nonexistent, and I wasn't allowed to go to restaurants or movie theaters or any other crowded public spaces. Whenever I stepped out the door, I had to wear gloves and a mask. My doctors warned me that something as basic as a cold could be lethal. Being confined to a hospital bed, unable to do anything unassisted—even things as basic as taking a shower—sent me into a deep depression. My central preoccupation was no longer *What am I going to do with my life?* but *Who am I and what really matters to me?* I was unrecognizable to myself, and the idea of knitting a scarf or reading anything, much less *War and Peace,* struck me as not just naïve but silly. I felt like my life was over before it had even begun.

What pulled me out of that despair was a 100-day project, an endeavor that originated with the designer and Yale professor Michael Bierut in which you perform one creative act daily for one hundred days—a sketch, a poem, a photograph, whatever medium calls to you. The point of the project is to use discipline as a vehicle for creative inspiration. As Bierut says, "It's easy to be energized when you're in the grip of a big idea. But what do you do when you don't have anything to work with? Just stay in bed?"

In my defeated state, left to my own devices, my answer to that question would probably have been *yes.* The 100-day project had come at the suggestion of a college friend who proposed we all do this together—to help us stay connected during that difficult time. My parents were desperate to find something to anchor our days, something to think about besides impending bad news, and they immediately hopped on board. My dad wrote a daily memory from his childhood in Tunisia (though in a nod to *The Arabian Nights,* he insisted on penning 101). My mom painted a ceramic tile every day and, once finished, assembled them into a shield and hung it above my bed as a kind of protective talisman. Their enthusiasm was contagious, and so despite my reluctance, I agreed to take part. And for my creative act, I chose the thing that had always given me comfort in times of turmoil: journaling.

It often wasn't easy to make my way to the page, but the 100-day project offered much-needed structure, accountability, and most important, a container for my restless mind. I began using my journal like a reporter's pad, recording snippets of overheard nurses' conversations or things I saw through my hospital window: tiny people in suits hustling to work; teenagers making out on benches; the trees in the park a burnished gold, then bare of leaves, then fanged with icicles. I kept rage diaries, where I vented against my situation, against my body and its betrayals, against the well-meaning exhortations from others to "stay positive" and to "keep looking for the silver lining." I recorded my fever dreams. I doodled. I made lists. I explored things I couldn't say out loud, that I hadn't been able to admit to others or even to myself. At times what I wrote felt unbearably heavy, but afterward, I always felt relief, like a burden had been lifted. And for every sad moment I recounted, I began to notice beautiful and even funny ones unfolding at the same time.

Journaling through illness gave me a productive way to engage with my new reality. Rather than shutting down or surrendering to hopelessness, I could trace the contours of what I was thinking and feeling and gain a sense of agency over it. And once I figured out how to contend with my circumstances on the page, it became possible to engage with people around me and to speak the truth of how I really was. In turn, they began to do the same, and together we accessed new depths of intimacy and love. It taught me that if you're in conversation with the self, you can be in conversation with the world. This became quite literal about a year after my diagnosis, when I turned those journal entries into fodder for my first writing job: a weekly *New York Times* column where I chronicled the experience of being a young adult with cancer. It was called Life, Interrupted.

And yet, what had happened to me was not an interruption—something I learned only much later. The word *interruption* suggests a brief pause before you continue on with whatever you were doing. My illness was not brief, and I wouldn't be able to pick up and continue on with my same old life. I spent four harrowing years in treatment before I was declared cancer-free and left the relentless fluorescence of the hospital. Having dreamed for so long of that day, I expected a swift and happy return to my life before cancer. Instead, my body was battered, my heart fractured into a thousand pieces, and the gap between my expectation and my reality was unacceptable to me. I was lost in transition, stuck between a haunted past and a future I couldn't yet imagine.

In that lost year after I finished treatment, I stopped journaling. I felt like I had nothing to say, and at the same time, too much to say. The events of my life had trained me to not trust that anything would go according to plan, so whenever I tried to journal about my stuckness and to dream about what my next steps might be, the voices of doubt and fear immediately chimed in. *But what if you're not well enough?* they said. *What if some known or unknown danger upends the plan? What's the point of rebuilding only to have the ceiling cave in again?*

I do this sort of tango with fear perhaps more often than most people because of illness, but we all do a version of this, don't we? You go through a bad breakup and swear off romance because you feel like you won't be able to survive that kind of heartache again. You get a rejection letter, and the sting is such that you vow to never put yourself out there. You want to try something new, but you worry you'll be bad at it—you fear you'll humiliate yourself—and so you never start. But I knew that a fear-driven life was one where I never made plans, where I stopped myself from dreaming ambitiously. It meant living safe and small, always hedging against the worst-case scenario. Instead, I wanted to live boldly.

I wanted to hold the best-case scenario at the forefront and have that guide my decisions and actions.

And so I concocted the wildest plan I could muster: a new 100-day project in the form of a fifteen-thousand-mile solo cross-country road trip, where I visited strangers who had written to me while I was in the hospital, offering stories of their own reckonings, their own wisdom and insight. That trip put me in motion, quite literally, but it also gave me new grist for the page. My modus operandi became this: to trust and find ways to delight in the mystery of how things unfold, even if it's not what you had planned, even if it's far from ideal, and to believe that facing the thing you fear brings you exactly what you need. In my journal I wrote: *It is possible to alter the course of my becoming.*

When I returned home to New York City, I quickly realized I needed a change. After months of living on the road, communing with its vast landscapes and strangers turned highway angels, my old life no longer fit. The city rattled my nervous system. My small apartment, with its old demons lurking in corners, began dimming my newfound perspective. I had also been granted what felt like no small miracle: a book deal, my first. To conjure into words all that I'd seen and lived would require space and focus. So five years after my initial diagnosis, on the verge of turning twenty-eight, I packed up my things, sublet my apartment, and decamped to a log cabin in Vermont to write.

It was summer when I arrived, and the view was a sloping hillside fringed by woods, its canopy an impossibly vivid green. Near the bottom of the hill were two apple trees, and from time to time, deer would wander out to nibble fallen fruit, or a black bear would amble across the meadow. Aside from my scruffy terrier mutt, Oscar, I was alone. My solitude was punctuated only by phone calls from friends like Max Ritvo, a brilliant poet who was in the midst of experimental treatment for his advancing Ewing sarcoma. For the most part, I had only my mind's chatter for company, and without anything to distract or direct my thoughts, my head was a cacophony of confusion and doubt.

There, in the quiet of the cabin, I was plagued with all kinds of big life questions—most pressingly about writing a memoir and what it might reveal, about how to begin such an epic undertaking—but had no clue where to start. I vowed to set a daily word count goal and muscle through. I rose at five A.M., made a pot of coffee, lit a fire in the wood stove, and sat down at the kitchen table to write. But there's nothing quite like creating a fresh Word document titled "Book," typing the words "Chapter 1," and staring at the merciless blink of a cursor to summon every fear of being exposed as a hack, every insecurity about seeing a creative endeavor through, every internal groan of "Who even cares what I have to say?"

So I returned to the journal. I began doing "morning pages," a practice popularized by Julia Cameron in *The Artist's Way*. The concept is this: Upon waking, before brushing your teeth or drinking coffee—before your inner critic is roused—you write three longhand, stream-of-consciousness pages. In my morning pages, I wrote about everything. About the trees and the deer, about childhood secrets, about loneliness, about dreaming. About things I'd seen and done on my road trip, about the imposter syndrome that my book deal had ignited, and the terror of writing my own story only to be misunderstood or criticized—or maybe worst of all, ignored. I wrote a lot about the wreckage of cancer and how it had metastasized to my relationship with my ex, and the hurt and regret I felt over how our relationship had ended. I wrote about the compounding grief of losing so many fellow patients turned friends to this brutal disease—including Max, who died a few weeks after I arrived at the cabin. I wrote about my grief; I wrote about his poems. I wrote about the musician I had started seeing and my fear of opening myself up to new love. I wrote about the person I wanted to become and the distance between me and her.

Rather than waking up anxious or afraid, I began to feel a clear—if humble—sense of purpose: All I had to do was write my three pages. The goal of writing three pages felt like a challenge, but one I could keep up. It became my morning meditation, sweeping out the clutter in my mind. It freed me from the bondage of perfectionism and allowed me to get loose and limber before diving into the rest of the day's work.

But as weeks passed, I learned I needed more than morning pages to get me there. Certainly, I got better at transcribing the chaotic jumble of my mind, but when you're stuck in your life, you can also get stuck in a solipsistic chamber of your own thoughts. That was me. I wasn't breaking through the same tired patterns. I got caught in repetitive loops. I began dropping my pen when my energy flagged, when I found myself rehashing the same old grievances, or when I exhausted myself with yet another rambling soliloquy about my ex. I was officially bored by the sound of my own voice.

In search of a new way in, I sought out the voices of other writers who had famously kept journals, like Sylvia Plath, Susan Sontag, and Isabelle Eberhardt, before cracking open my own journal each morning. To prompt myself—to push myself *beyond* myself—I would read a page or even just a paragraph, often selected at random.

The experience was kaleidoscopic. A sentence, an idea, an anecdote could turn the barrel, refracting and reframing my perspective. Plath is so often reduced to her pain story, but in her journals, she was funny and quick and made me want to write more playfully. Sontag was searching and rigorous, and I found myself digging deeper, looking for meaning beneath the surface of my stories. Eberhardt's travel diaries were full of wild escapades—about the lovers she took, the drugs she experimented with, the gender roles she flouted—and they gave me permission to write into parts of myself I previously deemed off-limits.

I have long believed that journaling allows you to alchemize isolation into creative solitude. As it happens, reading also enacts that shift. Rather than feeling trapped and alone with your thoughts, you're in conversation. You've got company. That summer, I dipped my toe into the gorgeous stream of Annie Dillard's nonfiction. Her loving attention to the natural world showed me that I was not alone in the woods of Vermont— on my daily walks, the fallen logs, the fungi, the ferns became friends. To gain insight on my own corporeal limitations after cancer, I read Virginia Woolf's "On Being Ill," Audre Lorde's *The Cancer Journals,* and the hybrid art journals of Frida Kahlo. So often, the hardest part of living in the in-between is feeling alone—like you're the only person who has ever struggled or felt lost in that particular way. Suddenly, I was in dialogue with these women, sharing our experiences with the physical body—its desires and its suffering. Their words threw off sparks, kindled fresh questions, and sent me in surprising directions. They twisted the cylinder, and the light fell differently. I beheld new visions.

I wasn't used to being prompted in this way. When I began writing professionally, I had not formally studied writing, and if I had been instructed to write to a prompt, I would have said, "Absolutely not." Even now, a writing prompt on its own can feel like homework. For example, if I'm told, "Write about a time you had a change of heart," my mind goes blank. The poet Craig Morgan Teicher described this kind of prompt as the equivalent of sticking your finger in a goldfish pond: All the goldfish scatter to dark corners.

But reading someone else's words before I write always stirs something new in me. It's such a natural way in to keeping a journal. Sometimes I respond to an insight, an image, a turn of phrase. Sometimes it's the fact that the person's experience feels so familiar. Other times, the writer's perspective is so unlike my own that I'm completely bewildered by it, and I write into that bewilderment. Someone else's words awaken a different train of thought, a new energy. A synapse fires that, moments earlier, was dead asleep.

The years following my time in Vermont were full of change. I returned to New York City and made a number of big life moves. After feeling in limbo for so long, I started a path forward. I fully committed to my new relationship, and my boyfriend, Jon, and I moved in together. I went to graduate school and started teaching creative nonfiction. I began learning to accept my body and its limitations, and I celebrated my thirtieth birthday by running a half-marathon. And after many stops and starts and bleary afternoons on the floor of my office in the fetal position, I finally turned that years-long dream of writing a book into a finished manuscript of my memoir, *Between Two Kingdoms*. It had taken years, but I finally felt like I had rejoined the greater gathering.

Eventually, I came to believe I had made it to the other side of my turbulent twenties. I thought I had finally reached a place of stability, and that the going would be relatively smooth from there on out. Of course, that's not how life works. The most ferocious storms were yet to come, like the pandemic, and then learning my leukemia was back. When the ceiling caved in, I knew what to reach for—my journal.

This time, I invited strangers from all around the world to join me.

—⁂—

When the pandemic hit in 2020 and everyone went into lockdown, we all found ourselves in what was, for me, an eerily familiar place: canceling all foreseeable plans, quarantining at home, stocking up on face masks, feeling hypervigilant about each hug or handshake, worrying that if we encountered the wrong pathogen at the wrong moment, it could be the end. All across the internet, I saw people asking the same questions: *What do we do? How do we get through? How do we stay connected? How do we remain hopeful and grounded in the face of so much uncertainty and fear?*

I didn't feel quite that same sense of disorientation. In fact, I felt uniquely prepared for exactly this kind of apocalyptic isolation—a talent no one would want but I had nonetheless spent much of my adult life honing. During treatment, I had lived a version of what we were now experiencing on a global scale, and it occurred to me that the creative tools I'd developed for navigating life's upheavals might be helpful to others—maybe even in the form of a 100-day project.

In late March, I was hunkered down in my childhood home in upstate New York with my quaran-pod—my brother, Adam, my partner, Jon, and my friend Carmen. One day, as Carmen and I were doing a little yoga, stretching out in parallel downward dogs, I blurted out to her, "I have an idea." I then began daydreaming out loud about a daily journaling project, delivered in newsletter form, that might help people cope with the fear, loneliness, and uncertainty of lockdown. Carmen replied, "Go write that down now—before you forget it."

It wasn't a great time for me to start something new. In addition to sanitizing doorknobs and groceries and learning how to cohabitate with new roommates, my final edits for *Between Two Kingdoms* were due at the end of the month. I have a friend who describes the ill-timed arrival of a new creative idea as a mistress doing the dance of the seven veils. But I couldn't get it out of my head. My niche experience was no longer niche, and I felt compelled to share what I'd learned with others.

And so I launched a project that combined all of the elements that had helped me: a daily journaling practice, done communally, with a short essay for inspiration and a prompt to get started. I reached out to the most remarkable people I knew, asking them to contribute an essay and an accompanying prompt. On April 1, 2020, I started a newsletter and sent out the first dispatch inviting readers to begin journaling each day for one hundred days and, if they felt so moved, to share their entries. I called it the Isolation Journals.

The response was astonishing. By the end of the first month, there were more than eighty thousand of us—a number that eventually grew to hundreds of thousands—of all ages and walks of life, journaling, searching, making sense of our lives together. What was meant to be a small, short-lived side project became a phenomenon, and by the end of quarantine, Carmen had quit her job to help me steward this creative community. It was call-and-response, reverberations begetting reverberations. Through these essays and prompts, which were interpreted in so many ways beyond the typical pen-and-paper diaristic entry—from daily sonnets to songs and drawings—the alchemical properties of journaling showed us how to turn isolation into creative solitude, confinement into connection, and confusion into clarity and calm.

This book was born of that project. Designed to be a companion through life's transitions and challenging times, *The Book of Alchemy* explores the art of journaling and all it can contain. Though I write about the creative process, this is not a craft book. Though the emphasis is on journaling, this is not a guided journal. Instead, I share everything I've learned about how this life-altering and even lifesaving practice can help us tap into that mystical trait that exists in every human: creativity. It's a gathering of hard-won wisdom and one hundred essays and prompts that serve as touchstones in which we might find a flash of recognition. In these stories, we hear echoes of our own.

Above my desk, I keep a Post-it of a quote attributed to Viktor Frankl, the Austrian psychiatrist and Holocaust survivor: "Between stimulus and response, there is a space. In that space is our power to choose our response. In our response lies our growth and our freedom." *The Book of Alchemy* is designed to expand that space, to give us ideas and inspiration for how to choose our response. It provides tools to engage with discomfort, to peel back the layers, to uncover your truest, most laid-bare self—and in doing so, to distill kernels of insight, to dream daringly, to learn to hold the brutal and the beautiful facts of life in the same palm.

What comes next is simple. Think of *The Book of Alchemy* as your own 100-day project: Read an essay and prompt each day, then sit down to journal. You'll hear from a range of voices—from beloved authors, Olympians, and iconic musicians to a man reentering the world after a long prison sentence to a young mother on the verge of widowhood. These stories are a way into a dialogue with fellow seekers meditating on the central questions of life. They can also be a mirror, showing you things about yourself—what you're holding on to, what you're resisting, what you're longing for, who you want to become next.

And with that, let's begin.

THE BOOK
OF
ALCHEMY

CHAPTER I

ON BEGINNING

N ot long ago, I was invited to a conference billed as a gathering of
fifty of the world's most innovative thinkers. Each day, there were
lectures by everyone from leading scientists and tech CEOs to
pioneering artists and actors and Arctic explorers. Afterward,
we'd meet up in breakout sessions to discuss and debate the implications
of their ideas. In these smaller groups, people would often start the conversation by identifying their field, then asking, "And what do *you* do?"

It's that oh-so-human need to categorize, to sort by type, but as a
writer, I've come to dread answering the question. I know the follow-up
will be: "What kind of writing?" Much of my work has lived in the
realm of memoir, which is often characterized (unfairly, I believe) as
navel-gazing and lacking rigor, especially when the author is a young
woman. In certain company, I sometimes feel tempted to beef it up, to
make it sound more "serious." Rather than saying, "I wrote a column
about being a young adult with cancer," I find myself wanting to say, "I
used to write for the *New York Times* science section."

So imagine my inner panic when, in the middle of this group of intel-
lectuals, business scions, and Nobel-winning scientists, I was asked, "A
writer, huh? So what is it you're working on now?"

I was working on this book—this distillation of a practice that has
saved my life. "A book about journaling," I replied. I watched the answer fall flat, just as I'd feared. In that knee-jerk way, I felt I needed to

justify it. To explain that, though journaling is sometimes dismissed as a childish pastime you do in a pretty diary with a tiny lock, its physical and mental benefits have been extolled in study after study—everything from reducing symptoms of depression and anxiety to improving working memory and strengthening the immune system. "It's something everyone could benefit from," I wanted to shout, "maybe especially you!"

I didn't say that. Instead, I quickly changed the subject back to them and their pursuits. I have always thought of journaling as serious—it has had very serious applications in my life—but I've never been very good at the one-sentence pitch. If I could go back and explain why I feel called to share my particular approach to journaling, I would say this: *I do this work because I know it works—and it's necessary.* The studies may be useful to sway the skeptics, but they're just confirmation of what I already know on a soul level.

This is not just true in my own life. I have heard from more people than I can count testifying to how transformative this practice has been. A fifty-year-old woman who was stuck in a soul-sucking corporate job used these tools to realize her lifelong dream of becoming a writer: Her journal entries turned into prize-winning essays; she wrote a memoir, got an agent, and quit her day job. A mother reeling from the loss of her daughter began making art from these prompts, which allowed her to feel connected to her daughter and begin to process her grief. An oncologist who saw the health benefits of this approach to journaling has literally prescribed these prompts to over a hundred patients. I could fill pages and pages with stories like these.

Journaling as a process is utterly alchemizing, with practical applications in every area of one's life and work. The journal is like a chrysalis: the container of your goopiest, most unformed self. It's a rare space, in this age of hypercurated personas, where you can share your most unedited thoughts, where you can sort through the raw material of your life. Day by day, page by page, you uncover the answers that are already inside of you, and you begin to transform. And yet, at the same time that it offers transcendence, there's nothing more humble than the journal. As long as there has been literacy, people have turned to it to catalog the everyday, which the word's etymology makes clear. It comes from the Old French word *jurnal,* which has its roots in the Latin *diurnalis,* meaning "of a day." If you trace the origin of the word *diary,* it's the same. The oldest journals we know of were for recordkeeping, like the Diary of Merer, the ancient Egyptian papyrus logbook that recorded the transport of limestone to Giza, where it was used as cladding for pyramids.

Over the years, the form evolved from simple cataloging to include much more: everything from Marcus Aurelius's private musings turned guide to life, *Meditations;* to the "pillow books" of the women of the Japanese court around A.D. 1000 (so named because they hid the diaries beneath their pillows), which detailed their public lives as well as fantasies and fictional tales; to the scientific notebooks of Leonardo da Vinci and Charles Darwin.

In the twentieth century, we get Anaïs Nin's most intimate thoughts about her sexual and political awakenings and Virginia Woolf journaling about her reading and writing life. We get the diaries of individuals grappling with their private lives against the backdrop of repressive regimes, like Alice Dunbar-Nelson, who gives us an unadulterated look into the life of an early-twentieth-century woman of color in America, and Anne Frank, who famously documented her experience as a young Jewish girl in hiding under Nazi persecution.

Journals have become important historical artifacts, giving us glimpses into the past and providing insight into what our fellow humans lived through, be it illness or war or some other crisis, and how they managed to endure. As Anaïs Nin wrote, "When we go deeply into the personal, we go beyond the personal. We achieve something that is collective."

The journal is capacious. It can be an aid to memory, a reliquary of major life events, a place to let off steam, rattle off lists of dos, don'ts, and dreams, or conjure something beautiful and wild and unexpected. It's where we can go to cut through the noise, where we take stock and discover meaning, where we tap into the subconscious and our free-flowing stream of intuition. The journal is where we seek out and find our highest, most liberated, most creative self.

But whether you're a longtime journaler or new to the practice, you've likely experienced that moment when you behold the blank page and are stricken with the question: *How do I begin?*

For me, it starts with the journal itself. Whether it's a classic composition notebook from the drugstore or a leather-bound beauty, I always personalize it in some way. I adorn the cover or write myself a creative contract on the flyleaf or tuck a favorite old photograph into the opening pages—anything that amplifies its appeal and encourages me to return. I also keep handy a stock of my favorite pens.

The physical, tactile nature of journaling by hand is important to me. I love the interaction between paper and palm, how the pen glides across the page, how the letters emerge as images—swooping up, looping back, charging forward. "There is a state of mind which is not accessible by thinking," writes Lynda Barry in her creative workbook and graphic memoir, *What It Is*. "It seems to require a participation with something, something physical we move, like a pen, like a pencil, something which is in motion—ordinary motion, like writing the alphabet." Virginia Woolf also extols the joy of writing by hand; after spending many months revising a manuscript on her typewriter, she returned to pen and paper, and in her journal, she wrote: "How I should like . . . to write a sentence again! How delightful to feel it form and curve under my fingers."

If you're feeling resistant to the idea of writing by hand, what I'll say is this: I myself find it useful, both because I like the unfurling of ink on the page and also because I'm less likely to self-edit that way. But we all have different needs, and you should feel free to journal in any way that makes sense for you—be it on a laptop, on your phone, or on a legal pad with a pencil stub.

Often, when I get to the page, several self-sabotaging thoughts rear their heads: "I have nothing to say" and "I don't feel inspired to write one word, much less fill three pages" and "I'm never going to be able to do this consistently, so what's the point?" I've concocted a number of tricks for pulling my mind out of those ruts, but one of my favorites was shared with me by the poet Marie Howe: "Whenever I can't do the practice, I'll get a composition book, and I'll write three pages a day, but I write it with my nondominant hand, so it's a big scrawl," she said. "Or I'll write, 'I don't want to write about . . .'" and then just write into that—so there's a release in it."

And yet sometimes, the resistance is deeper. Once, in a journaling workshop I was teaching, a participant asked me, "Any advice for someone who can't journal without feeling cringey? I think it has something to do with the fact that my mother used to read my journals growing up and nothing was private. Now I feel like I cannot put anything personal to paper." I was grateful for her question, understanding that others were likely to be carrying similar baggage. With the input of other attendees, we came up with seven tips for breaking through deep resistance:

1. *Tell yourself you can burn it afterward.*

2. *Try writing in the second or third person to distance yourself from your inner censor.*

3. *Write in lists, or in sentence fragments so it feels more like "jotting down thoughts" instead of journaling.*

4. *Maybe call it the un-journal. Loosen the rules and claim it your way.*

5. *When stuck in past events, tell yourself, "That was then. This is now," and then feel right now, and write into that.*

6. *Store your journal in a lockbox, safe from prying eyes.*

7. *May I suggest that you write directly to your mother?*

The last suggestion may or may not have been a joke, but it brings to mind an exercise that the singer Stacie Orrico Johnson shared with me a few years ago as a way to silence those critical voices. It goes like this:

Close your eyes and imagine the last time you tried to create. Who appeared? What did you hear? Maybe it was a critical parent, a competitive classmate, a teacher's thoughtless remark, or a line from a rejection letter. Maybe it was a voice of unknown origin that you hear on loop: It's too late, you're not good enough, you'll never get there. *Write an eviction notice to whoever or whatever hinders your creative joy. Name them. Call them on their bull. Firmly usher them out the door.*

Another common challenge is developing consistency. There are a few different things I've found helpful for building what my friend Lisa

Ann calls a "sticky" practice: You fold your journaling into a nonnegotiable part of your existing routine, you build in some kind of accountability, and you lower the barrier to entry.

Try to sit down at roughly the same time each day, ideally alongside a favorite habit. For me, journaling revolves around my first cup of coffee. I wake up, let my dogs out, then head straight to the kitchen to grind the beans and turn on the kettle. In the five minutes it takes for my French press to steep, I read a short passage and let the words wash over me. Then I sit down at the kitchen table with my journal and start. Maybe for you this happens when the house is quiet and your children are asleep. Maybe it's on your subway commute, or in the parking lot before you step into the office. I've found fifteen minutes to be the golden increment of time I need to write through the fog and to get somewhere unexpected and interesting. But if all you can spare is five minutes, that's more than enough.

The times when I've journaled mostly consistently are when I've committed to a daily practice of some specified duration with friends or family—like my mom, who is far more disciplined than I am. She journals first thing each morning no matter what, both in words and a quick watercolor, while she drinks her tea. Often, she'll send me a photo of her notebook next to her favorite ceramic mug, which spurs me to get to it and to send a photo of my own journaling setup back to her. I love that kind of positive peer pressure—the way we draw energy from each other.

Consider inviting a loved one to read and write through this book alongside you. Or if you prefer a solo experience but want accountability, mark off each day you journal on a calendar for a visual tally. This book contains a total of one hundred essays and prompts, but if a 100-day journaling project feels daunting, commit to ten days and see how it builds from there.

When I embarked on my first 100-day project, I lowered the barrier to entry by making three firm rules for myself:

1. *Write every day.*

2. *Aim for three pages, but any amount will do. A paragraph. A sentence. A word.*

3. Let your thoughts unspool, going in any direction they want, and once you're done, you never have to look at them again.

However you approach your journaling, at whatever time and in whichever form, there is no right or wrong way to do it. But the lower the stakes—the less precious the process—the more likely you are to return to it.

This is not polished, I'm-penning-an-opus writing. You do not need any prior experience. Just let the words pour from your pen, without restraint, without a goal, without self-censoring, without editing or concern for grammar or punctuation. If a particular prompt doesn't speak to you, maybe write about why, or let your words take you in a completely different direction. This writing is for you; tailor it to suit your needs.

Not long ago, I had the chance to interview Michael Bierut, the designer who formalized the 100-day project as an assignment for his graduate students at Yale. We spoke of how he came up with the idea and the many incredible projects that emerged from it. One story he shared was of a young woman whose project was putting one hundred paint chip cards into a box, then fishing one out every day and writing something about that color—something poetic, or something quick and dismissive, sometimes just a single word, sometimes a long essay. Michael liked a lot of things about her project, including the fact that it had the perfect combination of constraint and variability built into it. It also invited consistency, because as soon as she dipped her hand into the box, she was committing to one more day. But what he liked most was how it was a microcosm of the human experience, which is full of uncertainty, marked by chance, coincidence, and happenstance. When she pulled the paint swatch from the box, did she get the color she was hoping for? Did she feel elated and think, *Oh, today I get to write about this bright yellow*? Or was she disappointed to find herself holding a muddy gray?

"If you take it to another level, life is like that," Michael told me. "Sometimes it's the thing that you were hoping for, sometimes it's the thing you were dreading, and your ability to react to it in a human, authentic way is how we survive."

I don't believe going through something hard makes us wiser or stronger or braver by default. But the transitional moments in our lives offer the possibility for a new beginning. May these first ten essays and prompts welcome you into this light-giving practice. May they spark something new and beautiful and true. Let your pen fly. Follow your curiosity and intuition.

HERE GOES NOTHING

Dani Shapiro

To begin, begin, Wordsworth said. So simple in theory, and yet so elusive in practice. The writer facing the blank page has her toes curled around the edge of a high board. Perhaps she doesn't know how to dive. Perhaps she doesn't even know how to swim. Perhaps the pool below has been drained of water. To launch herself into something new—whether a novel, a memoir, a story, an essay—she must first gather up an unreasonable, unearned confidence bordering on lunacy.

It doesn't matter how many books she's written. When it comes to this new piece of work, she is in uncharted territory. Voices emerge from every part of her: *Who are you to think you can pull this off? You know this has been done by (fill in intimidatingly brilliant author) already, right? This time, you're going to fall flat on your face.* If she's just starting out, she might be subject to a younger, halting tirade that finishes each sentence with a question mark. *Maybe you should have gone into marketing? I mean, come on, how many social media followers do you have? You do know that's what matters?* If she's been writing for a long time, she might hear a noxious whisper: *You're done, honey. You have nothing left to contribute. Hang it up.* Whatever the voice says, make no mistake: It is not here to help you. Its aim is the total annihilation of the creative process.

On my computer desktop, amidst a clutter of folders containing the quotidian, one folder is filled with short pieces I've written over the last decade. Essays, craft talks, keynote addresses, book reviews, short stories. Some of these were assignments. Some began with my own exploration. But all started with the same three words: *Here goes nothing.*

Those words spring from a feeling that there really should be a complicated German word for, a combination of desperation and abandon. This is how I feel when I finally set out. But before I get to that phrase, that high board, first I must navigate a fallow period—either blessedly brief or mercilessly long—in which I get in my own way. Eleven books into my writing life, and I still haven't managed to avoid it, which leaves me with the reluctant belief that it must be fertile in its own fallow way. It might look like doing laundry, checking email, filling out health insurance forms better saved for a time when my brain is already fried. Or it might look like falling into various fascinating rabbit holes in the name of research, or politics, or the Instagram shopping algorithm that knows me so well. Regardless, when it goes on long enough, it leads to a state very close to despair.

This despair-adjacent state is when things get interesting. A while back, I had been hard at work on my memoir, *Inheritance,* when I realized the two hundred pages I had accumulated were nothing more than a false start. "I know I would tell anyone in my circumstances this is creative despair," I told my husband. "But it just feels like despair." I was pretty close to hitting bottom, which is the exact spot where true beginning happens. To get to *here goes nothing,* first a writer must feel she has nothing to lose. And truthfully, what is there to lose? *To begin, begin.* What's the worst thing that will happen? You'll get it wrong? Write pages that make you cringe the next day? Ball them up and toss them out? To begin, begin again.

For writers, a day spent writing is a good day—always. A day spent writing is de facto better than a day spent avoiding writing. It means a writer has successfully silenced the voices, summoned that wild confidence, transmuted it into courage, and faced down the contents of her deepest interior, because that is where our sentences are formed. And if we put together a string of days like this, eventually we will notice that we have begun.

THIS IS YOUR PROMPT:

What would you write if you weren't afraid? Set a timer for ten minutes. Don't worry. No one's going to read a word. You can shred it. You can burn it. You can keep it. It's entirely up to you. Ready, set, go! Begin.

JUST TEN IMAGES

Ash Parsons Story

I spent my early years in a rural village in Zaire, Africa, in the 1980s, and when our family moved back to the United States, I didn't fit in. Fortunately, my parents gave me my first diary, complete with a little gold lock and key, as a "welcome home to the home that doesn't feel like home" gift. Lonely and confused about this new version of a village, I poured everything into those pages. I never missed a day, and each year I started a new one. Understanding my life by writing it down became a practice I carried into adulthood, married life, and motherhood.

Then we adopted our third son. Zion was born three months premature and weighed two pounds. The first time I saw him, wires and tubes came from his body like octopus legs, and the beeping alarms of the NICU screamed at me. But the sight of him gave me the same feeling as when I gave birth to my other two sons: It was like coming home. I spent the next six weeks holding Zion inside my shirt, skin to skin, watching him grow. Life as a NICU mom was all-consuming and not conducive to writing. There's only so much you can do when you're holding a fragile, football-sized human in your arms.

So I started to make mental notes of images:

- The scrub room at the NICU entrance, where I'd lather my hands at the wide metal basins, using my foot to control the faucet.

- The flashing red number that signaled his oxygen saturations were dropping as he lay in his incubator, and how they came back up to normal as soon as I held him.

- The way he furrowed his brow like an old man when he was hungry, pursed and wrinkled his lips as he gave out a little squawk.

I carried these images in my mind's back pocket and wrote them down when I got home. Without even realizing it, I was finding a way to write my life—even when I had "no time or energy to write."

Zion is nine now and life hasn't gotten any less complicated. Mothering a critically ill child with disabilities is the most wild gift. It's a life of surprises, delights, and never-ending interruptions, and that's just before breakfast. But writing is how I translate my life to myself. It's my sense-maker. So in the middle of it all, I have embraced a writing life of Ten Images. That's it, just ten.

I think of ten moments, mental pictures, scenes, objects that pop up when I recall the last twenty-four hours, and then I write them down. They range from the mundane to the exceptional—it doesn't matter. The value doesn't lie in the image, but in my attention to it. Sometimes one of those images jumps out at me and says, "Let's go somewhere together . . ." and I find myself writing an entire chapter or essay. True story: I'm currently writing a memoir this way. But most of the time I look at my list and exhale with a great sense of accomplishment: I have lived another day. I have seen what I've seen. And I have given my life a voice by writing it down.

THIS IS YOUR PROMPT:

Your life might look nothing like mine, but maybe you also feel that you lack the time, the emotional space, or the presence of that saucy minx, "inspiration," to write. Maybe you can't sit down and write multiple pages or hundreds of words, but I bet you can come up with ten images from the last twenty-four hours. Give it a try.

One of my favorite things is going back through my Ten Images pages from the last year and seeing what I saw. No matter what is going on in the world, within or without, I know I can find a home in these pages.

THE ART OF DAILINESS

Michael Bierut

In the wake of 9/11, I began making a drawing every day inspired by a photo in *The New York Times*. Like a lot of people, and as a New Yorker particularly, I felt deeply disoriented. It was a chaotic time, and I wanted to engage with current events, but on my own terms, in a meditative way. I didn't realize that consciously in the moment. I just thought that drawing was nice, and that it'd be nice to have an excuse to draw every day, and also that doing it daily would take the pressure off. Maybe you screw it up one day, then the next you draw something pleasing—that seemed appealing to me.

I began my daily drawings on January 1, 2002. My rule was simple. I would get that day's paper and choose a picture—something I thought was funny or interesting or provocative, or something I wanted to look at longer than anything else in the paper that day—and use that as my source material. It might be a politician making a speech or a photograph from a conflict zone. Something that inspired me regularly was a feature the *Times* began running that February called Portraits of Grief, where every day they published life sketches of people who died on 9/11, along with a photograph of each—usually a snapshot shared by the family. Some days I found myself in the mood to luxuriate in the drawing, and I would spend three hours on it. Other days I would say, "I won't take another breath until I've finished." I gave myself permission for both of those responses to be equally valid. Also equally valid was whether I actually captured a likeness or not. The practice had less to do with the output and more with getting myself in a proper frame of mind for the rest of my day.

It was a ritual I continued throughout the entire calendar year. This was before the omnipresence of social media, and it wouldn't have occurred to me to share these images with anyone—it was just something I was doing privately. However, at the time I was teaching graduate students in the graphic design program at Yale, and the director of the program somehow learned of this project and suggested I assign something like it to my students. The idea of the class undertaking something together—but picking their own subject matter, instead of doing the same thing—appealed to me immediately. The question then was, of what duration? I looked at the calendar and saw I was scheduled to teach two classes that year, one in the fall semester and one in the spring semester, and they happened to be exactly one hundred days apart. It was a coincidence, but it felt meaningful, the way a year had felt meaningful with my own project. It was almost as if that round number was telling me exactly what to do. So I wrote up a brief, and at the top, I typed "The 100-Day Project"—capitalizing every word to make it feel as if it was official. Then I wrote a simple prompt, very unstructured and open-ended: *Starting tomorrow, do one creative act that you can repeat for 100 days.*

For the next five years, I assigned that brief on the first day of class. As the students meditated on what their project might be, I would go around and talk to them and give feedback on the practicality of their ideas. For example, a student might say they wanted to take a picture at the same street corner near campus every day, which would prompt me to ask them, "Are you going away for the holidays?" They'd answer, "Yeah, to Phoenix, to see my parents." So I'd tell them to figure out something portable—something that would also work in Phoenix. In time, I came to see that there was a sweet spot between specificity and open-endedness. There needed to be some constraints, but it was also important that they could make a choice, however small. But even when people hemmed themselves in, even when they came to me on day twenty-two and said they never wanted to do their particular creative act again, I'd say, "Make your resistance the thing. See how that works."

Mainly I tried to encourage my students to do things they wanted, and I was amazed again and again by what they came up with. One student took a well-known poster from the 1950s and made a visual variation of it every day. There was one young woman whose preacher grandfather always gave the same very long sermon about heaven and hell, and she spent fifteen minutes every morning memorizing it, and at the end of the hundred days, she delivered that sermon from memory in front of the class. Another put on the song "Here Come the Warm Jets" by Brian Eno and began designing; when the song ended, the piece was done. One of the most memorable projects was by a student named Ely Kim, who filmed himself dancing to a different song in a different place every day. At the end, he edited all hundred clips into a seven-minute video called "Boombox," which jumped between him dancing in the stairwell of the art building, in his apartment, and back home in Las Vegas, where he was from, and dozens of other locations, too. It went viral and led to invitations to perform all over the world.

With something like the 100-day project, there's no right way to do it, and there's no wrong way to do it. The reason this project works is the reason anything like this works: You can do it on your own terms, in your own way. It has nothing to do with any expertise that I or anyone else would profess to have about it. It's that old saying: The only way out is through. You somehow have to work your way through the whole thing, and even if you hate 95 percent of the things you did, if you've made it to one hundred days, congratulations—that's amazing in and of itself.

Of course, not everyone makes it to the end, and that's okay, too. I had students who dropped off quickly, some at two weeks, others after a month. Once people got about halfway, they had so much personal investment, and they had internalized the process enough, that there was a good chance they'd make it to the end. But even the ones who dropped out at two weeks would say, "I got so much out of it—even just doing it for fourteen days."

I'm always amused when I get credit for coming up with the 100-day project, because part of what makes it interesting is that there's nothing original about it. It's what we all do every day. We do routine things, and we do things that require acts of imagination that we're never going to do again, whether it's naming a goldfish or responding to a stranger tripping over a curb. Toggling between such routine experiences and unique ones are what, in the aggregate, constitute life.

THIS IS YOUR PROMPT:

Write about a time when you began doing something daily, be it a creative endeavor, a new course of study, or a form of exercise. What prompted you to start it? What obstacles got in your way? When you felt resistance or missed a day, what called you back? Now reflect on what you gained from it and how you might apply that knowledge to a new daily creative practice.

BE SLOW

Rachel Schwartzmann

As I write this, I'm sitting at my desk surrounded by three machines: phone, laptop, and desktop computer. They flash with a deluge of reminders, each notification a gateway to multiple lists filled with the day's tasks. Everything is syncing up and fueling the inevitable question that many of us face when looking at our to-do's:

Where should I begin?

For a long time, this question was enough to send my mind into overdrive. But in my line of work as a writer, I get to ask a lot of questions. Recently what's seemed the most urgent is the question of our collective relationship with pace and its influence on how we live, work, and create in our digital age. It's a tough one to tackle even in a landscape that provides easy and immediate answers—many of which can be found within the four corners of a screen.

But as we've all slowed down this year, I haven't been as satisfied with the answers we've been given. And instead of searching for more online, I've spent time looking at what's right in front of me: Above my machine-laden desk hangs an oil painting stretched on canvas. To the right, perched and at the ready, is the corkboard I use to create monthly mood boards. Below that, a stack of papers and a vintage globe sit atop a filing cabinet. There are noticeable divots, creases, and cracks in all of these things. The globe, in particular, is faded and covered in a thin layer of dust. As I reach over and give it a twirl, I think about all of the people in the world—spinning, asking questions, searching for answers.

Unlike the click of a button, these objects don't provide immediate answers, but they refocus the blurred lines between physical and digital, real and obscured. They create opportunities to look more closely, to listen more carefully, to consider more honestly: *What do I want to make? Where do I want to go? Who do I want to be?*

Our work will always be there; it will be ongoing. But during this rare opportunity to truly slow down, I silence my alarms, put my phone away, and ask myself: *Where should I begin?*

THIS IS YOUR PROMPT:

Set your timer for five minutes and do nothing. Stare at the desk or the wall or the dust motes in a slice of sunlight. Then write about the thoughts, the questions, and the answers that came up in that moment of slowness, of stillness.

JOURNEY AND JOURNAL

Pico Iyer

I had never thought of keeping a journal when I stepped onto a bus in Tijuana, at the age of eighteen, to bump for a hundred days down to a city in Bolivia named for peace. Surviving school hadn't encouraged introspection, and being surrounded by more than a thousand other boys—only boys—had made me think of writing to and for myself as not much more valuable than muttering to myself. But how could I not wish to catch the thick foliage of the jungle in Guatemala as night fell— and I tumbled into a deep ditch? How might I not wish to preserve the sensation of riding on a runaway horse up to a deserted hillside in Colombia to stare at a pre-Columbian statue almost as worn as myself? How could I stop myself from writing when the blinding sunlight of Rio greeted me out of the blue, and I thought of the school from which I had narrowly escaped?

Fifty years on, I see a journal very differently. Every morning I walk to my desk and step into what feels like a cabin in the woods. Sometimes words come out of me that I can share with others; often memories or intuitions arise that may be useful only to me. But the process of sitting alone in a quiet space and hearing what lies on the far side of my thoughts is the closest I'll ever get to meditation: It clears the beehive of my mind, it dispels the tangles that can never be truly answered, and it allows me to step back out into the clamor as refreshed and directed as if driving down from a monastery.

I've come to feel that it hardly matters what happens to the writing. The joy and clarity come in the doing of it. And I'm no stickler for form;

I haven't had a bound, pretty journal since those teenage years. Most of the time I just reach for the nearest scrap of paper, or a tiny black notebook that fits inside my pocket. But writing, more than anything, takes me away from surfaces and into the heart of essentials. If you're at odds with a loved one, if you don't know what you think about the world, if you've become an overflowing stream in the throes of love—open your diary and share the moment with your future self.

The result, almost always, is pure wonder.

THIS IS YOUR PROMPT:

What is the moment—the place, the person, the activity—that has moved you to forget the time, to lose yourself, and to return to what can feel like forgotten depths (or heights)? And how can you begin to get back there, as early as tomorrow?

HOW ARE YOU REALLY?

Nora McInerny

"How are you?"

The person asking the question was being sincere. They had tearstains on their flushed cheeks and used tissues wadded up in their hands. I had a toddler on my hip and my husband's ashes in a wooden box next to me. I hadn't slept in weeks and wouldn't sleep properly for months to come. I was anxious, depressed, and struggling with what I now know was post-traumatic stress disorder.

I hugged them. Smiled.

"Fine," I said, lying between my teeth.

I was not, of course, fine. Are most of us? When we're regularly chugging from a firehose of human suffering on all of our screens and involuntarily taking extra servings of stress and responsibility even though our plates are plenty full?

"How are you?" is a question lobbed at us by our closest friends and the checkout person at the grocery store. We ask and answer this question mostly on autopilot, and most of us just say "fine"—because fine is expected. Fine is acceptable. Fine is . . . fine. Except, of course, when fine is a lie that you're drowning in and the truth could be a life preserver.

Months into my young widowhood, I was sobbing in the front seat of my sister's car. I was also screaming. At her. At the world. At how everyone, it felt, had disappeared, left me all alone. She did what she always does: She listened and scratched my back, and when I'd fully exhausted myself, gently reminded me that I was the person who had told everyone I was fine.

I had no idea I was such a convincing actress, and no idea that "fine" was not a little white lie, but a brick wall I'd placed between me and the people who loved me. Because I wanted to *be* fine. Because I was too afraid to look at my own pain and need, let alone share it with another person. Because I was afraid that if someone saw the truth, it might be all they could see.

Small talk has its place, of course. The checkout person does not get paid enough to hear the truth, and there are people in our lives with whom it's not safe for us to share our tenderest truths.

But among the people who matter most to us, why do we relegate such a fruitful question—*How are you?*—to shallow small talk? And what would happen if we didn't?

In my household, which now includes a blended family of four children and a second husband, the only f-word is "fine." When I ask how you are, or how your day was, you can say anything . . . except fine. And if you ask me, I'll trust you with the truth.

THIS IS YOUR PROMPT:

How are you really?

RADICAL RECEPTIVITY

Marie Howe

When my mind is cluttered with the never-ending list of daily tasks and I am longing to write into something deeper and more surprising, I turn to this practice:

First, I clear my desk or table (which is often as cluttered as my mind), then I open a fresh new notebook—or gather a big pile of white printing paper. I sit down, take a few deep breaths, and set a timer for two or three or five minutes. Then I pick up a pen or a pencil and place that pen in the fingers of my nondominant hand. Now write with that hand, without stopping to think, until the timer dings.

Why the big pile of paper, or the fresh notebook? To write freely and legibly, I need to write *big* and to use a *lot* of paper. I'll start with a line that might lead me somewhere I might not want to go: "I don't want to write about . . ." Or somewhere I do want to go: "I want to remember." Or I start with the physical day: "Just now I see that the night sky has turned a washed shade of pale blue." Whatever is at hand.

The promise and practice are to keep writing. No matter if the mind is rushing ahead of my hand—keep writing, sometimes only four or five big words to a page, as children scrawl. After the timer dings, I'll read through the words and clarify what isn't instantly legible. Then I'll set the timer again.

And wonderfully, sometimes, if I continue to write with the non-dominant hand, things begin to slow down. Things become relaxing and interesting. Often, by the time my hand catches up to what my mind was so intent on writing, something else appears. That's the joyful part—when the racing, willful mind gives up, and I get to watch what the hand is writing. This is the surest way I know to move more quickly to the unconscious, to listen to what wants to speak, what has been waiting, underneath.

THIS IS YOUR PROMPT:

Set a timer for two or three or five minutes, and begin to write with your nondominant hand. Start with one of the following: "I don't want to write about," or "I want to remember," or a description of the day. Keep writing until the timer dings. If you'd like, restart and go again.

INSIDE SEEING

Lou Sullivan and Alexa Wilding

My six-year-old son Lou is no stranger to isolation, which I can't help but think is partly responsible for his wonderfully wild imagination. At one year old, he was diagnosed with a rare form of pediatric brain cancer. After four years in remission, Lou relapsed in the spring of 2019 and we spent the next year cooped up in a hospital room, gloved, gowned, and masked, so bored we were talking to the Purell dispensers. During the worst of it, when Lou could barely move and I couldn't write a word, he came up with a game called Inside Seeing that saved us both.

"Close your eyes," he said, "and tell me what you see!"

"Ugh, nothing?"

"No, Mama, really look. Inside!"

We lay together in the hospital bed closing our eyes until shapes and light flecks began to form behind our eyelids. "I see fireworks," I said.

"I see a monster," Lou said, "but he's actually nice."

After our journeying, Lou would draw what he saw, and I scribbled down ideas, amazed that my bald six-year-old was now my personal shaman and writing coach.

"What's it called when stars make pictures?"

"Constellations?" I guessed.

"Yes! I see constellations. The lines are a jungle gym, and we're going to climb all the way back home."

A few months later, we did make it home, and eventually Lou joined his twin brother, West, back at school, only to have Covid-19 force us back to a way of life we know all too well. We played a lot of Inside Seeing to pass the time. Lou thinks you should try it, too.

THIS IS YOUR PROMPT:

Okay, close your eyes. Maybe lie down so you're cozy? A blanket is nice. Okay. What do you see? At first, it's dark in there. But if you really look, you will start to see pictures. Maybe it's a bear with claws, or an ice-cream cone, or a memory. Like, cuddling your mom. Maybe it's words, like *love* or *dancing*. Sometimes it's just tickly lights. Whatever you see, write about it. Really explain it until it becomes a story. I like to draw what I see, too.

FIRST LINES

Erin Khar

You'd think that as a memoirist I'd always have plenty of stories to draw upon—after all, it's my life. But as I was writing *Strung Out,* where I delved into my fifteen-year struggle with heroin addiction, I dealt with my fair share of writer's block. I've had to develop different ways of getting creatively unstuck. Sometimes it's zooming in on a specific sense—noticing the air around you, the temperature, what your arm or shoulder or hair smells like. Other times, to get myself going when I feel blocked, I start by pulling one sentence from a favorite book or essay and using that as a starting point. A few of my favorite lines:

From Dorothy Allison's *Two or Three Things I Know for Sure:*

"Let me tell you about the women who ran away."

"Behind the story I tell is the one I don't."

"Two or three things I know for sure, and one of them is that change when it comes cracks everything open."

From John Irving's *The Hotel New Hampshire:*

"Keep passing the open windows."

"Sorrow floats."

"I thought he had rather delicate hands for a revolutionary."

From Lidia Yuknavitch's *The Chronology of Water:*

"Little tragedies are difficult to keep straight."

"When morning came, even the sun looked wrong."

"I am learning to live on land."

"We raged by and through one another."

THIS IS YOUR PROMPT:

Choose a line from a book—you can grab the nearest one and flip it open to a random page, or pick an old favorite you've memorized by heart. Whatever grabs your attention; whatever intrigues. Use it as the opening sentence for today's journal entry, and let the words flow from there.

I BEGIN AGAIN

Aura Brickler

My new beginning has yet to happen.

I don't know much about it, but I know it will come with a bang. I know it will hurt like hell even though I have braced myself for years. Some days it feels like I sit and wait for it, daydreaming about what it will feel like. It can show up like a slow-motion video of a head-on collision; as a family comes into focus I realize it is ours. Other times it looks like a storm way off in the distance, a disastrous cloud over an Idaho mountain range while we're being spared a few last rays of the sun's light. When it happens I will scream and cry and whisper to myself, "But you had so much time to prepare."

I will begin again in a suffocating state of mourning. I will smile at others and assure them that I am okay. I will agree that he's better off not suffering, that he is no longer laboring to find each and every single breath. I will hope with all of my might that there is an afterlife, one that has offered him eternal peace after so much pain. I will begin again wanting more than ever to believe in the narrative of heaven, because what else do you tell your young child about where her father goes when his body dies? I will likely tell her that he lives among the stars now, always hovering over her, and when the night sky is the darkest, she'll see him the most.

I will begin again as someone with a lot of regrets. The idea of living every day as if it is the last fades after 3,206 days of trying hard to do so. Cancer has a way of digging in and dragging along. It grabs you by your weaknesses and makes you beg for an ounce of strength. It gnaws at the foundation of your collective hopes and dreams, allowing despair to fill in the cracks. I will begin again and learn how to forgive.

I will begin again as a narrator, telling stories to keep him close to us. Telling tall tales that protect our daughter from the parts of the story that are too painful. I imagine being left in a fog of uncertainty, fear, and confusion. When the fog begins to lift, I will begin again as grateful— for what we had and what, of him, I still have. I will begin each day like I do now, with a cup of coffee. I will begin again as a widow.

THIS IS YOUR PROMPT:

Have you been bracing yourself for a new beginning? Perhaps one that is daunting yet inevitable, or maybe one that you've been hoping for and dreaming about. What will it take for you to get there? Who will be with you? What will it feel like when you get to the other side?

If you'd like, use the refrain, "I will begin again as . . ."

CHAPTER 2

ON MEMORY

When I was young, my family and I often spent summers in Tunisia. We lived in a house that my dad and two of his brothers built themselves outside of Gabès, their hometown, on a remote plot of land where the Sahara Desert meets the Mediterranean Sea. It was a simple, traditional structure, made of white plaster topped by domes, and rustic—no electricity, telephone, or internet. Neighbors were scarce. There were only one or two other houses like ours, a few fishermen's huts, and a nearby Bedouin camp.

There was very little to do. The sea was at our doorstep and I loved swimming, but given the scorching sun, we didn't go until late afternoon, after it had dipped low in the sky. I spent those early sun-bleached hours alternating between three activities. The first was household chores, like washing the laundry by hand, then hanging it to dry on a clothesline—a task I would've hated back home, but that there, with all of my aunts and cousins chatting and laughing, I actually enjoyed. The second was reading battered old paperbacks, mostly classics left over from my dad's undergraduate days at the University of Tunis. I would lie on my back on the tile floor, the coolest surface I could find, and get lost in sweeping, epic tales by Tolstoy, Dickens, and Flaubert.

The third thing, which will probably not come as a surprise, was journaling. I wrote and I wrote and I wrote and I wrote, filling up who knows how many composition notebooks. Around the house was an olive grove that my uncles Mounir and Jelani had planted, and one particularly large tree was only a stone's throw from the house. I would climb it as high as I could, and from my perch in the canopy, I wrote about the Bedouin neighbors coming over to build a mud oven and making tabouna, a flatbread you bake by sticking the dough to the oven's sides. About having my first café au lait, made for me by my aunt Fatima. (It was mainly sweetened milk with only the tiniest splash of coffee.) About the ritual of preparing my favorite breakfast food, bsisa, a traditional Tunisian dish made of ground barley, sugared and flavored with anise and fenugreek, then mixed into a paste with olive oil, topped with dates and nuts.

I also wrote about the heat, the sand, and the siroccos, which are desert winds that sweep in, lifting and swirling the grains of sand with growing intensity, forcing you to retreat inside, to pull the doors and shutters firmly closed. I wrote about the wraparound terrace on the second story of the house and how each night, my cousins and I would drag little pallets out to sleep in the cool night air; how my cousins and I whispered to one another, teased one another, played pranks that occasionally erupted into a pillow fight. I wrote about how we smoked pilfered cigarettes on the roof once all the adults had gone to bed and about the desert sky on those nights—how clear it was, how inky black, and how impossibly incandescent were the stars.

Those days remain in my memory in minute detail, especially the last full summer I spent there, the summer I turned eighteen. Nothing noteworthy happened, but I remember it viscerally. I was chronicling what I saw, smelled, felt, and heard—the daily happenings, the shifts in the desert winds and sky—but more than that, I was detailing my interior life. A huge transition was on the horizon. Soon, I would be off to college, which to me signaled adulthood. I remember imagining that new life, all my hopes for it and my fears, too, and at the same time mourning my childhood. I was keenly aware that it was the last summer our family would be together like that, likely the last summer of my life where I would be bored, and I felt the impulse to hold on to certain childhood things. Keeping a journal did that for me. Writing everything down crystallized it: the feeling of cool tiles against sticky skin, the view from the olive tree, the smell of the sea, that sense of impending change.

I still have those journals, and at times, I return to them. What usually makes it into our memory banks are the bigger things—the zeniths or the nadirs—so it's a kind of luxury to recall those sweet small moments, the ones that fade from view with the passage of time. It's fascinating to revisit who I was at eighteen, cringeworthy moments and all. (If only I had channeled the time I spent writing about boys into learning languages, I could've been a prizewinning polyglot.) As the writer Dani Shapiro once said to me, "To go back to my journals is a way to reach a hand out to that young woman, to dance with her a little bit. As opposed to remembering myself at that age, I actually *encounter* myself at that age."

This is one of my favorite things about the journal. It's a repository of memory, a place to catch moments as if in amber. At the same time, journaling can also be an act of recovery. Here I think of my dad, who wrote down his childhood memories as part of our 100-day project. A scholar of literature, he had long contemplated writing stories, but he'd never gotten around to it. However, my illness transported him to his own brush with serious disease when he was young. At the age of seven or eight, he contracted polio, and while he was sick, the women in his life sat around his bed telling him fantastical stories, both to distract him from his pain and to heal him, as they believed storytelling had magical power. By writing these childhood stories and sharing them with me, my dad hoped he could conjure such healing energy. And in a sense, he did. I got to know my father in a new way and to connect with him at a moment when I felt very isolated. As he later noted, writing those stories became "a form of journaling, an unanticipated therapy."

Excavating his memories also had a ripple effect. The more he dove in, the more memory begot memory, so much so that he is now writing his own memoir about growing up in Tunisia, *Until the Sahara Blooms Again*. "My memories appeared to me diffracted, at random, in different modes and forms: a sort of kaleidoscope of eclectic images, stories, snapshots, evocations, reminiscences, ruminations, sketches, portraits, ordinary and momentous events," he says in the introduction. "In the process of recovering these long-forgotten memories, I realized that, in fact, I was writing my body, remembering its sundered parts and reassembling them into a corpus, a bio-album." It's not a complete history, of course. Recovering memory is more like picking up shards of your past. But even that can be beautiful, because they can be reassembled as a mosaic, which, as the author Terry Tempest Williams says, is "a conversation between what is broken."

—⁂—

Maybe it seems I'm writing about memory through the rose-colored lens of nostalgia, as if all memories are cherished experiences. It's more nuanced than that—of course, not all memories are happy ones. Looking back is not always pleasant. In fact, it can be disorienting. How many times have we tried to remember, only to come up blank? Or felt a bad memory eclipse an entire period of time? Or had a seminal memory conflict with someone else's version?

In his memoir *Uncle Tungsten*, Oliver Sacks writes about a vivid memory of a bomb falling behind his house when the Germans were blitzing London in World War II. He recalled how the bomb burned with "a terrible, white-hot heat," how his father fought the fire, how his brothers helped by carrying in pails of water to douse it, but the water only made it burn hotter. "There was a vicious hissing and sputtering" each time the water hit it, Sacks said, "and meanwhile the bomb was melting its own casing and throwing blobs and jets of molten metal in all directions."

It was such a deeply held memory that Sacks couldn't believe it later when his brother Michael told him he was wrong—that he couldn't have seen it, because he wasn't there. The two of them had been sent to Braefield, a boarding school in the country, at the beginning of the war. But their older brothers had stayed home, and one had written them a vivid, dramatic letter detailing the event. Sacks had conjured the scene in his own mind and been so entranced that he adopted the memory as his own.

"It is startling to realize that some of our most cherished memories may never have happened—or may have happened to someone else," Sacks writes. He doesn't condemn himself for the mistaken account. Instead he does something far more interesting: He interrogates why. Why are our minds so open and porous? Why is it difficult for us to distinguish a real memory from a borrowed or blended one?

The conclusion Sacks comes to is that our memories may be fallible and imperfect, but they are also powerfully flexible and creative. We don't walk around like reporters, recorder in hand, taking careful notes and identifying sources. Instead, our imaginations allow us to experience the things we hear and see as if they were our own, which leads to powerful connections. "This sort of sharing and participation, this communion, would not be possible if all our knowledge, our memories, were tagged and identified, seen as private, exclusively ours," he writes. Our memories are made of not only our direct experiences, but also the experiences of others. They arise and exist in conversation, an ever-evolving dialogue.

This dialogue works in various ways. It can be a literal dialogue with another person, teasing out the facts and the fictions, as in Sacks's case. Or it can be a dialogue with someone who's no longer with us. I was once speaking to Marie Howe about her poem "What the Living Do," which is addressed to her brother Johnny, who had died a few years before she wrote it. It begins as a recounting of the everyday things—the clogged sink, the spilled coffee, the things that the living do, which Johnny doesn't do anymore. Then comes the volta, or the turn, which is where the energy shifts, where the poem answers itself (even here, a dialogue):

> But there are moments, walking, when I catch a glimpse of myself in
> the window glass,
> . . . and I'm gripped by a cherishing so deep
>
> for my own blowing hair, chapped face, and unbuttoned coat that
> I'm speechless:
> I am living. I remember you.

Marie repeated this last part to me, with emphasis: "I re-*member* him." She went on, "To remember somebody means to put them back together and to hold them within ourselves. As everybody knows—or will come to know—people who you can't live without die, and you keep living. But once they're dead, they can be with us all the time."

It's a powerful insight—though of course, remembering of this kind is not without pain. However, I've found that avoiding a painful memory does not make it go away. In fact, it's often the opposite. You can try to build a dam against it, but there's a watery element to memory, and inevitably it breaks over you, often when you least expect it.

I've found that it's not avoiding such memories, but consciously grappling with them that frees me from their grip. After putting them on the page, I'm no longer pinned by them, pinned to that moment, that feeling, that hurt. With a little distance, they are transformed from a trauma that I'm forced to continually relive into a record of my resilience, which lends me pride and confidence. They become a reminder to my future self: *See what you've been through. Look at what you survived.*

And to me, that may be the most useful dialogue—the one I have with my past selves, where I see my own evolution, my own growth and change. "I think we are well advised to keep on nodding terms with the people we used to be, whether we find them attractive company or not," Joan Didion wrote in her iconic essay "On Keeping a Notebook." "Otherwise they turn up unannounced and surprise us, come hammering on the mind's door at 4 A.M. of a bad night and demand to know who deserted them, who betrayed them, who is going to make amends. We forget all too soon the things we thought we could never forget. We forget the loves and the betrayals alike, forget what we whispered and what we screamed, forget who we were."

Excavating memory is how we identify and hold on to a principle of being. It's how we trace the throughline from our past, how we notice patterns that inform our present, that ripple out to our future. In the pages to come, you'll find ten essays and prompts that ask you to recount important lessons you've learned, exceptional meals you've shared, and unforgettable places you've traveled to. You'll revisit challenging memories and your best ones, too.

In all of them, you'll remember, as in: *re-member.* And that's the point. To return to Didion: "Remember what it was to be me: that is always the point."

MIND MAP

Carmen Radley

After the novelist Philip Roth died in 2018, I came across a short tribute Zadie Smith wrote to him. I'm not particularly a Roth fan, but I was charmed by the piece, especially the opening anecdote, where Smith recounted a conversation she had with Roth about swimming laps, something they both enjoyed. When Roth asked Smith what she thought about as she swam, she said, "I think, first length, first length, first length, and then second length, second length, second length. And so on."

His answer was wildly different: "I choose a year. Say, 1953. Then I think about what happened in my life or within my little circle in that year. Then I move on to thinking about what happened in Newark, or New York. Then in America. And then if I'm going the distance I might start thinking about Europe, too. And so on."

When I first read this, I couldn't imagine having such recall. Could I give that a shot?

In 1953, Roth was twenty. On a page in my journal, I wrote out the year I was twenty. From radiating spokes, I wrote: Austin (where I was attending college), and the name of my high school boyfriend (with whom I'd reconciled that spring), and Sour Lake (my hometown, where I returned for the summer, in part for the boyfriend).

Each new word conjured some words of its own, like from Sour Lake: Lamar University, the nearby college where I took summer classes; the inordinate amount of time I spent navigating sweltering parking lots; Tropical Storm Allison, which flooded the city of Houston, just eighty miles west of Sour Lake, and also my car. (I'd left the windows down, the interior was soaked, and a sour smell set in that never left.) With only slight pressing, I could remember outfits I loved and people I hadn't thought of in two decades. And in the course of remembering, I naturally moved to national and even world events. All to say, this mind map helped me recover long-forgotten details and took me to unexpected places.

I've found I can do this not only with periods of time, but also with people and places. I can do it with a favorite word, like pilfer: Immediately I'm three years old, at the grocery store with my mother, caught with a balloon tucked tightly in my fist.

The experience is strange and wonderful: spatial rather than linear. It's associative, surprising, even exhilarating. It mines the memory for things long buried—maybe to be used in fiction or memoir, maybe simply cherished as a recovering of the past.

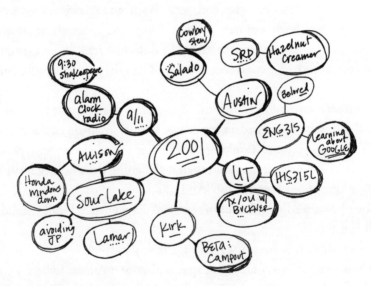

THIS IS YOUR PROMPT:

Create a "mind map." Choose a year, a place, a person, or a favorite word. On a page in your journal, write it down, and begin mapping out the web of associations and memories that appear in your mind. Follow it where it leads.

I HAVE BEEN EATING FIGS

Annie Campbell

I have been eating figs. Every day. The season has been extended by Whole Foods and Trader Joe's, and I try to buy enough for a couple of days at a time. They are delicious.

My husband has been mystified by this and I try to explain how good, how sweet, how satisfying they are. He bites into a fig and shrugs. Why are they so delicious only to me? Yesterday my friend Goldie wrote about plums and grief—and as she read, my tears, unshed, lit up behind my eyes. Suddenly I knew why the figs were so sweet.

There was a house in Jericho at the foot of the Mount of Temptation. It had been an ancient sugar mill. On the main level was a terrace shaded with bougainvillea and vined grapes. The veranda stood above terraced orange groves and date palms and had a view of the Jordan River and the Moab hills beyond. It was small, and in the open courtyard, stone steps wound up to the roof level, where there was an old spring-fed pool. "Weekend house" seems too grand a name for such a primitive spot, but that is what it was for us.

The water in the pool was cool and black. Once, we went to the house in the middle of the week and shepherds were bathing their sheep in the pool. This partly explained the dark, murky water. It didn't stop us. Into the water we dove, rising to tread water while reaching for the figs from the trees that grew around the pool. There were six of us in that water. Only two of us are left to tell the story.

I read my parents' letters about the war and the fighting and the refugee camps below our house. Yes, I remember all of that. But that is not what I remember when I eat figs. I remember my family, all of us, treading water in a murky pool and reaching up to the branches heavy with fruit.

I remember the celebratory call-and-response: "Tean," one of us would call out—the Arabic word for fig. The rest of us would respond with "Alhamdulillah." Thanks be to God.

THIS IS YOUR PROMPT:

What food evokes a transporting moment of time and place? Taste the moment and write down everything you can remember.

MY TEACHER, MRS. R—

Arden Brown

Mrs. R's first name is Ann. She teaches fourth grade.

She also runs marathons. She has run Boston and New York City.

Mrs. R hates the Jersey Turnpike and the drivers on the Jersey Turnpike.

She also dislikes metal water bottles, and the words "snow" and "satisfaction."

She doesn't like children needing to use the restroom or her cat, Otto, tripping people.

There used to be a very large tree in Mrs. R's yard. It was cut down.

Mrs. R has two sons. They are both single and both live in Colorado.

W is the younger one, B is the older one. One of them (I don't know which) is a designer or sometimes an architect.

W is bad at getting up in the morning. Mrs. R bought him an alarm. The alarm has a helicopter on the top. The helicopter flies off the alarm in the morning. Then it beeps until you put it back on the alarm.

Mrs. R's mother is in her nineties and dating again. She once made a very spicy soup. She added three times the spice called for. Mrs. R and her family had to eat it because they were poor.

. . .

Mrs. R speaks with an American accent with some British thrown in. She says VAH-ses instead of VAY-ses.

Mrs. R's husband is a surgeon. Mrs. R will faint if she sees blood. She makes him keep his papers out of the house.

Mrs. R is neat. Her husband is messy. He leaves things everywhere.

Mrs. R met her husband at a burger shop. She was an employee. He was a customer. Mrs. R loves burgers.

Otto once tripped Mrs. R's husband at the bottom of the stairs. Otto is a bad kitty.

Mrs. R says she is a rule follower but that she did some bad things in college. Her worst was driving a car without a seatbelt. The car didn't have seatbelts.

THIS IS YOUR PROMPT:

Write about a teacher, cataloging what you remember (good, bad, and otherwise) and how you saw them as a child. Then write about them as the student of life you are today.

SHORTENING THE NIGHT

Hédi Jaouad

Night falls suddenly and quite spectacularly in my native town of Gabès in southern Tunisia. The neighborhood would, seemingly in an instant, plunge into total darkness, except for our house, which was the only one connected to the town's rudimentary and erratic electric grid.

In those days of ambient superstition, nighttime and darkness were a real menace: It was when the forces of evil came out to taunt the weak and confound the unbeliever. People hastily retreated to the safety of their dwellings, and when they had to go to the bathroom—usually in a traditional outhouse tucked in some remote corner—or venture out of the family compound to tend to an emergency, they did so by candlelight, almost always with a companion or in a small group.

The moonless nights were particularly frightening to us children, for it was a time considered in our local mythology most propitious for the apparition of ghouls, djinns, and other demonic creatures. Every shadow and whisper became ominous. People groped their way in the darkness, murmuring in the foreboding stillness of the night the famous Ayat al-Kursi, or the Verse of the Throne, reputed as the most powerful verse of the Quran to ward off evil spirits and other maleficent forces and spells.

Before the coming of radio and television to Gabès, and apart from the occasional wedding in the family or neighborhood, the only evening entertainment was storytelling, especially during the long, cold winter months. At night, the temperature dropped, and the cold became biting. We'd huddle under heavy blankets around a kanoun, a clay brazier filled with embers, to listen attentively to haunting stories of sorcery, magic, and the supernatural. These stories completely mesmerized us until we fell asleep.

Three matriarchs, all in their seventies or older, were particularly gifted at telling stories. My aunts Oumi Zohra, Oumi Salha, and Oumi Fatma were all widows, lived by themselves, and were our surrogate grandmothers. Either my mother, one of my siblings, or I would beg them to come to our house to "shorten the night," the expression we used for passing time together, and they would often spend an evening of enchanting storytelling with us.

These women wove fanciful tales like they wove baskets. They always obliged our insatiable appetite with encores. My favorite storyteller was Oumi Fatma, who was almost blind. When she came, usually after many entreaties because she dreaded walking, it was a rare treat. On that special occasion, even the adults would stay to listen to her tales of witches, sorcerers, and magicians, for she had a knack for speaking of the uncanny.

With the advent of radio in Gabès in the early 1950s, such evenings began to lose their appeal. We gathered instead around the wooden box, listening to distant voices and alien tongues. When we quickly grew tired of the radio, the matriarchs were no longer there to tell us stories, and since we had no books to read—not even the Quran, as my older brother liked to joke—a vital link was forever broken. I look back and feel a sense of loss, not only for our matriarchs and their stories, but also for those long and dark nights when we saw things that didn't exist, when our imaginations were most alive.

THIS IS YOUR PROMPT:

What role did superstition play in your childhood? Was it indulged by the adults around you or scoffed at? Do any of those early beliefs still hold sway? Write about them, and why.

ENCAPSULATING EPHEMERA

Jenny Boully

When memories make themselves manifest, they alight like butterflies—fleeting, momentary, ineffable, seemingly uncapturable. The task of the writer then, having had the epiphany embedded within memory, is to relate not only the message from the dream embedded within the memory, but to also articulate, in language, that nebulous nature of the memory. How then do we encapsulate the memory in a way that also preserves its transitory nature?

THIS IS YOUR PROMPT:

Pick five items from the list below.

> *popcorn * lettuce * iceberg * cotton candy * puffs * sugar cubes * dandelions * buttercups * pallbearer * clothesline * National Geographic * fire ants * watermelon * sunflowers * ticket stub * campfire * satellite * fish scales * baby powder * quilt * brooch * barrette * tin can * bingo * Ferris wheel * Frisbee * legumes * lima beans * caterpillar * earthworm * mockingbird * wagon * shaved ice * envelope * rotary phone * silk glove * single shoe * postcard * diner * cheese * houseplant * canoe * sharpened pencil * glue * lunch box*

Then write one memory associated with each item—or write associations you have of this item—in two hundred words or less. Limit the use of "I." Refrain from stating any emotions. Like dreamscapes, rely on images to convey feeling. Assemble these memory fragments into a collage essay. Give it a one-word title.

Bonus: For the future, or to grow your memoir fragments, you can make your own lists of random words, pick words at random from various books and dictionaries, or have friends generate lists.

COLLECTING PLACES

Stephanie Danler

Long before I could admit to myself that I was writing a memoir, I was collecting places. I would often recall the second chapter of Thoreau's *Walden*, "Where I Lived, and What I Lived For," and think of how inextricable location and motive are from each other. Joan Didion, of course, is a master at this, echoing the psychological landscape with a physical one. In her case, those landscapes are often threatening. I would also think of Roland Barthes, who said in *A Lover's Discourse*, "Where there is a wound, there is a subject." As I remembered places from my youth, I found wounds that had been untended for decades.

In the case of my memoir, *Stray*, I would take an index card, and on the front, I'd write a place—"Laurel Canyon," for example. Then, on the back, I'd write any details that came to mind: landslides, traffic, Lily's coffee cart, squirrels stealing pomelos, care and threat, Fleetwood Mac, loneliness, losing the daylight. Another was "Owens Lake"—dust, a scab, my father, rattlesnakes, amnesia, mistrust of love, parched, the crime that created Los Angeles.

I had eighty of these cards, and most of them didn't make it into *Stray*. But some of them were shockingly complete scenes and became cornerstones of the book. I only had to go back and ask, *Why do you remember the rattlesnakes? Why is Owens Lake a scab? Why does loving Los Angeles, or loving my father, seem to depend on having amnesia?* In answering those questions, I wrote a book. And I later realized that with those cards I had made myself a map.

THIS IS YOUR PROMPT:

Meditate on places. If you're working on fiction, perhaps choose places from that fictional world. The easiest might be your childhood home, but it could be a restaurant, a street, a parking lot, a ferry station, a borrowed home in the Catskills where it rained for three days, or a stranger's glass penthouse where you once did too many drugs. Write down any images, details, or words that come to mind. Don't worry about complete sentences. Don't worry about describing the place as much as describing what it felt like.

This isn't research, or even a place to collect lines of dialogue or turns of story. It is simply to remember, to feel out for a tender spot, search your own memories for the surprising detail, the "punctum," which Barthes defined as "the accident which pricks me."

POV: MY HAT

Kiese Laymon

I often use the comic as a way into memories I'd rather forget. For example, last year I did a public conversation with Jesmyn Ward in New Orleans—and everyone who knows me knows I believe she's the world's most influential living writer. The event was amazing, and afterward one of the organizers gave me a ride back to the hotel. As I got out of her car, a gust of wind blew my hat off my head.

It's nine thirty on a Friday night and I'm in the middle of Canal Street with my hat on the ground. This might not seem like a big deal, but I have two arthritic hips that are bone-on-bone, and if I bend down to get that hat, there might be no getting up. But I don't want to be that guy in front of the event's organizer and all the folks on the street. Sigh. I bend down, I fall. From my knees, I put the hat back on my head. I try to get up again. The hat flies off once more. I fall again, busting my knee. Some beautiful Black boys walk by me. One says, "That dude drunk as hell," and they laugh. (I do not drink.) So there I am, bloody-kneed, still two feet from my hat. I see two police officers across the street, heading my way. I don't want to have to answer their questions. I don't want to need their help to get up. So, leaving my hat in the street, I crawl to the curb and pull myself up. I limp back over to my hat and start kicking it out of the street, over the curb, toward the entrance of the hotel. There, I lean on a column, put my grimy hat on my head, and shuffle up to my room.

I was too embarrassed to tell this story out loud until I considered it from the hat's point of view. To that hat, it must have seemed absurd, even slapstick. I could hear the hat's laughter, and that ushered me back into the moment, the memory, the scene.

THIS IS YOUR PROMPT:

What's the funniest thing that happened to you last year? Write a paragraph from the point of view of an inanimate object that bore witness to it. Could be your hat. Could be your wedding ring, a streetlamp, or the plant in the corner of the bar. Use as much sensory/sensual language as possible to describe the memory from that object's perspective.

FROM MY BED

Tamzin Merivale

It is my firm belief that true happiness in life is a rock-hard mattress.

From this flimsy hospital bed, the sterilized linoleum floor looks more inviting for a good night's sleep than this narrow, sagging, hot Mattress of Despair. It makes me think of all the beds I've ever slept in, and all the ones that I've forgotten. The beds that felt like home, and those that felt like hell. The beds I shared with friends, and others I shared with lovers.

It makes me think about my mattress at home, of how we struggled to buy it, in a new country and a new language, and about the air bed we slept on while we waited for it to arrive, which deflated every night.

It makes me think of my third apartment in Florence, living alone—at last—where I slept on an old sofa bed and woke to the sound of motorinos and the passionate arguments of my neighbors, which I eventually came to understand.

It brings back a hot and sweaty room that I can barely remember in northern Zambia, a hotel room in Harare shared with strangers, a bunk bed in a hut, a damp floor in Aden, another hospital bed—not so different from this one—in Marrakech. And a filthy room in Dakar, buzzing with mosquitoes, which I loved nonetheless, because I was seventeen years old and on my own in Africa.

I think of a blanket on the sand under the stars in Mauritania, bats flapping about. Of crawling into a tent in the Tuscan forest at dawn, after lying in the hot springs in the dark, sotto la luna. I remember "The Bus," a room with a view in Sana'a that belonged to a friend, where I woke to the gentle muezzin's call every morning—replaced, soon after I left, by the whistle and roar of bombs.

A cozy bed by the fire also floats into my mind, where every year with friends, after walking along the coast in the wind, rain, or sun, we laugh and talk for hours into the night. Never mind the beds where I've been violently ill while traveling—should've been more careful—or the beds that held me through sadness and grief, in their desperate grip. The bed where I woke to the sound of a church choir in Slovenia, holding beauty and mourning together in my heart.

My parents' bed, where I went for cuddles when I was little. Or the house on the cliff on an island in Spain, where I could breathe for the first time after a year of sorrow, and where, waking early, I stepped out onto the balcony to watch the sun rise over the sea, filling me up with color and light.

Waking, drifting, tossing, turning, dreaming, laughing, crying, bonding—so many beds, so many memories, and inshallah, many more that lie ahead.

THIS IS YOUR PROMPT:

Write about all the beds you've ever slept in—the beds that felt like home, those that felt like hell, the beds you can barely remember and those you'll never forget. What memories float up?

GHOST BREAD

Angelique Stevens

One Saturday afternoon over thirty years ago, on a weekend visit, my father said, "Today is a good day for you to learn how to make ghost bread."

My sister Gina and I were drinking coffee in his kitchen, and he took two big bowls from the cupboard and placed them in front of us, so we could each prepare our own batches of ghost bread—a type of Indian fry bread. He explained that the government gave Natives commodity foods like white flour, cheese, meats, and lard so they could live after being forced onto reservations. Then he scooped flour into our bowls. I was about to pour the water into mine when he snapped at me: "You're doing it wrong."

"I thought it was just bread," Gina said. He told us curtly that it wasn't just bread—that ghost bread is how we remember our ancestors, both the ones who died before us and those who are still connected to us.

This moment is part of a longer scene in my memoir-in-progress. I've been thinking lately about why it stuck with me for so long, why it was important for me to write about it. I tell my students that everything in their writing should bring with it some greater meaning: every word some greater depth, every character some greater representation, every object some greater symbolism. As writers, it's our job to make sure our words do some heavy lifting.

On a very literal level, the bread represents sustenance—and since bread in varying forms is a staple food in most cultures, it's universal.

That we are making it by hand represents some degree of self-sustainability; that our father is teaching us represents a legacy; that we are doing it together represents community; that we are angry as we do it represents discord. On a much larger scale, the ghost bread represents the conditions our ancestors endured: colonialism and repression and forced assimilation.

In trying to figure out the symbolism of the bread, I could get to the heart of this moment. I could understand what was at stake: the loss of my father, but also on a much larger scale, the loss of culture.

There is so much here in this ghost bread.

THIS IS YOUR PROMPT:

Write about an important first—where someone taught you how to use or do something. It could be anything: a cooking lesson, fixing a flat tire, learning to drive, helping a cow give birth, taking the swim test, riding a bike over a rooted mountainside, cutting in paint on a wall, or kayaking on the river. When you finish, consider all the greater meanings embedded in that moment.

PAST THE BREAK

Nathan Lowdermilk

I didn't always love the water. On a school field trip when I was about five, some kids told me that the swimming pool was shallow. Though I wasn't a strong swimmer, I jumped into the deep end, and it didn't go well. The lifeguard had to save me, and I was afraid of water after that.

But I spent every other weekend with my dad in Waves, a small stretch on the Outer Banks of North Carolina, about thirty miles south of where I lived with my mom. My dad was a serious surfer, and he took my older brother and me to the beach a lot. Because I was terrified of the waves, I'd sit on the shore and watch for hours as my dad and brother paddled out. Finally my dad started putting me on the front of his surfboard and taking me out. When we made it past the break, it felt like a whole different world. It felt like my safe zone. I was hooked.

I don't think I've ever been away from the water for more than two weeks at a time in my whole life. I've spent a lot of time in Central America and the Caribbean catching waves and surf guiding. Still, the Outer Banks is home. It's simple, just empty sand dunes on a two-lane road, barely any streetlights or stop signs, and never too crowded, because the waves are unpredictable. When the conditions are right, they're some of the most perfectly shaped shore-break waves you can find. But you have to be patient and pay close attention to the wind forecast and the tides.

As a surf instructor, I mostly work with kids. Our normal conditions are great for beginners—waves one to two feet, perfect size to start. Before we ever get in the water, I try to convey everything I'm thinking when I'm out there—everything from wind direction, swell, and rip currents to paddling and popping up—and then we head out. Some kids get pretty frothed up about catching so many waves; others want to chat me up about my life. Sometimes we end up in a lull between sets, and I ask them questions about theirs—like what their interests are, if they play sports, if they have any buzzer-beater wins. I tell them that when I'm hanging out and waiting for a wave, I think back to moments like that as a way to pass the time.

I don't really remember how I started it; I just know that's where my mind goes. Surfing is a sport that requires a lot of patience—to learn to read the movements of the ocean, to spot a set of waves coming in, to know where to be to catch the one you want. There's a lot of downtime, watching and waiting, often with no one to talk to. In those moments, I find myself thinking about going surfing with my nine-year-old niece, pushing her into waves. I think back to a handful of days surfing with my best friends at home, scoring the best waves of our lives.

Or I think about the best wave I ever caught, which was here in the Outer Banks. It was at a spot about an hour from where I live, near an old lighthouse where a wave breaks. I went with a friend who doesn't surf as much as I do, and I had paddled a little farther out by the time a giant set came in. I watched five waves explode on him, and he gave up and went back to shore.

Then this wave rose up, perfectly shaped, the length of a football field. I caught it, and I stood in three different barrels. Afterward, I looked around, and not one single person was there except my friend. Had he not been, maybe no one would have believed it. I sometimes can't believe I'm so lucky—to surf perfect waves right where I live.

THIS IS YOUR PROMPT:

Imagine you're out past the break, waiting for the perfect wave. All you can see is water and sky and a distant shore. All you can hear is wind, the waves, the seagulls calling overhead. Now call to mind your best memories—times with family or friends, places you've visited, small moments that mean something to you but maybe you don't often think about—and write them down.

You can do this whenever you want. It's a deep ocean. Memories often spark other memories.

CHAPTER 3

ON FEAR

To say I was afraid of mice is to put it mildly. For years, I was utterly terrified of them, not only the way they looked, or the way they scuttled along a baseboard, but also what they portended. This began in the spring of 2011, when after months of failing health and misdiagnoses, I spent a week in a hospital in Paris, where I was living at the time. Doctors ran tests for everything from cat scratch fever to HIV but found nothing conclusive. Eventually, they diagnosed me with burnout syndrome and sent me home with a script for a month of medical leave from work.

It wasn't a satisfying explanation. I felt better while in the hospital, but that was largely due to the prednisone, a garden-variety steroid, and as that boost of artificial energy worked its way out of my system, I deteriorated again. For days I lay in bed, resting but only getting weaker, feeling a creeping unease. At the same time, I began hearing scurrying sounds in the kitchen just a few feet away. I hadn't cleaned up before my hospitalization, unexpected as it was, and I began imagining a nest of mice had infiltrated the apartment and were multiplying behind the walls and inside the cabinets. I asked my then boyfriend if he heard anything, but he said he didn't. I worried I was losing my grip on reality.

Several more days passed, and I was still in bed, still sick and weak. My skin had turned a pallid gray and the inside of my mouth was covered in painful lesions. "Something's seriously wrong," my boyfriend said. "We need to go to the emergency room."

My bed was lofted above my desk, and the idea of climbing down the ladder felt impossible, like trekking down a mountain. "I can't," I said. "I'm too tired."

"A sign that you have to," he said.

I finally dragged myself down and we went back to the hospital, where tests revealed my blood counts had plummeted. The doctor told me that if my hemoglobin level dropped any further, I would not be allowed to fly and recommended I return home to New York as soon as I could. We went back to the apartment, where my boyfriend immediately began coordinating with my mom to book a flight and I packed my suitcase. Afterward, I climbed into bed, terrified and exhausted, yearning for the oblivion of sleep.

Right about then, the noise began again—only louder, and my boyfriend heard it, too. He hurried into the kitchen and threw open the cupboard below the sink. From where I was, I couldn't see him, but I heard a yelp and felt panic rising. "Are there mice?" I shouted.

"No, just a bug!" he said.

Next came a series of crashes and bangs, doors slamming, pots clanging, and a thwacking sound like a broom hitting the floor. I asked again, knowing and insistent. "Tell me the truth. How many?"

He paused before he answered. "More than I can count."

I suddenly felt invaded, as if my perfectly shabby little Parisian studio, with its big windows looking out onto a courtyard terrace, with its pink clamshell bathtub, had been infiltrated by some kind of pestilence. In my mind, the mice were an omen.

I flew home the next morning. A few weeks later, I was diagnosed with myelodysplastic syndrome, which had progressed into acute myeloid leukemia. At that point, fear became the dominant emotion coursing beneath everything. Fear of needles. Fear of time slipping by. Fear of being a burden. Fear of being alone. Fear that all of my plans and dreams would never come to pass. Fear of grief—not only my own but also of becoming a source of grief to the people I loved. Fear of pain and that pain turning me into someone I didn't recognize, someone I didn't necessarily like. Fear of the next biopsy. Fear of death.

These fears were warranted, of course, and though I didn't like them, they made sense to me. Fear of death is something we all share, whether our own or that of a loved one. But more confusing was what happened after I emerged from four years of treatment. Having survived, I found that I was afraid of living—a fear that's much harder to explain. I was afraid of my own thoughts and my burnout and depression. I worried I'd get into bed and never get out again. Having lost so many friends to illness, having lost that boyfriend to the toll of treatment, I feared opening myself up again to new love. I was afraid of the future, of making plans and rebuilding, only to have those plans undone by some errant leukemia cell or other calamity.

I spent a year that way. I'd wake up with the best of intentions, and I'd end up back under the covers, so snowed in by fear that I didn't know how to function. And when you're in that kind of spiral, another fear creeps in: the fear that you'll never figure it out, that you'll never feel better, that you'll never experience uncomplicated joy again.

After a year of languishing, I did manage to shake myself loose when I embarked on my solo cross-country road trip. I didn't realize it at the time, but I can see now that it was an extended session of self-styled exposure therapy that began with confronting my fear of driving—which had actually prevented me from ever learning. I took lessons from a friend, and after months of practicing on the windy dirt roads of rural Vermont, at age twenty-seven, I got my license. Then I loaded up a borrowed Subaru with some camping gear, a crate full of books, and my dog, and I set off.

Things went sideways before I even left New York City. Only five minutes into my drive, I turned the wrong way up Ninth Avenue. Cars were flying at me, horns blaring. I cranked the wheel, made a desperate U-turn, and thought, "I need to call this off. I'm not ready—not well enough, not a good enough driver. This is a stupid idea." But the alternative, which was going back to my apartment—and the stuck state that I had been in—seemed even scarier. Living in fear had become more terrifying than confronting it. The line that comes to mind is one attributed to Anaïs Nin: "And the day came when the risk to remain tight in a bud was more painful than the risk it took to blossom."

Over the next hundred days, I faced one fear after another. I forced myself to be out in the world, to learn to care for myself, to trace the shape of my limitations and to accommodate them. I met new people and also grew comfortable being alone. I began to befriend my ghosts. Rather than numbing my grief and pain, I sat with it, and I found that I could carry what lingered, from the fallout of lost love to the imprints of illness.

I also interrogated my fears in the pages of my journal. Sometimes you're so afraid, you don't know where the fear is coming from anymore, and that makes it seem unparsable and totally intractable. But in writing your fears down, you give them a container, and you can begin to evaluate them—to see which ones are valid and which ones have no grounding in fact.

I found that the more clearly I could see my fears, the more I understood them, and the more I began to notice a strange irony: *I feared the things I wanted most.* If you've had your sense of stability ripped away, it can feel dangerous to have hope or to take risks. Hope can be dashed; risks can end in failure and disappointment. Fear has an evolutionary purpose, as we know; our anxious minds say, "Protect yourself." But in many cases, my fear was not protecting me from harm, but preventing me from attaining what I wanted most: to be independent, to feel physically strong, to begin writing again, to dream big dreams, to fall in love, to live boldly and daringly.

Once I had that knowledge, I got to choose. I could brace myself against pain or discomfort, or I could be open to it all—though I have to say, being in the world and facing my fears didn't always feel good. It was like building a muscle: often uncomfortable, sometimes painful, always exhausting. But each day, I got stronger, and I began to see the rewards. I realized that the more I ran away from my fear, the bigger and more looming it became. Yet if I confronted the fear, it lost its power. As the fear evaporated, other feelings materialized in its place—feelings like wonder and curiosity. And as the author Elizabeth Gilbert once said to me, "You don't have to be particularly brave. You just have to be a tiny, tiny bit more interested in something than you are frightened of it."

You just have to be one percent more curious than afraid: This idea is powerful and transformative. When you're in a fearful place, the idea of charging forward without a trace of apprehension is intimidating. Such an expectation can immobilize you. And so, rather than moving forward and through, you remain stagnant, ruminating about something that may or may not come to pass.

Which brings me back to the omens. In the decade after my first bone marrow transplant, my fear of mice and my belief that they were harbingers of doom continued and even grew. Mice seemed to show up wherever I went. The entire year before my road trip, when I was so depressed, I had a mouse in my apartment. Directly within view of my bed was a little hole in the baseboard where it began poking its head out, scurrying out, scurrying back in. I was petrified of it, as was Oscar, my bold little terrier mutt (who had once chased down a bear in the woods of Vermont). I tried caulking the hole, and I became maniacally clean, thinking if I could keep my environment sterile enough, there would be nothing to lure it into my apartment. But it simply chewed through the caulk, and it only got bolder and bolder as the weeks passed, spending more time out in the open. I always knew that the mouse had made an appearance when I'd find Oscar trembling in a corner.

One could easily attribute this to living in New York City, where mice and their more terrifying cousins, street rats, are everywhere. I often avoided walking Oscar at night when the trash was out because it was so common to see the bags writhing with them, to see them dart from one to the next with bewildering speed. But when I moved to that remote cabin in the woods of Vermont, the little country mice proved as relentless as their city counterparts. Nuts and grains had to be stored in airtight plastic bins, fruits and veggies in baskets hanging from the ceiling or under mesh cloches. Even a few crumbs left on the counter were likely to invite them in.

Years later I moved to an old farmhouse in the Delaware River Valley—a rural place, but not the middle of the woods. And what do you know? Lovely bucolic hamlets in the rolling expanse of the Delaware Valley also have mice. Each time I saw one, I would call my neighbor Jody. I couldn't figure out how to get rid of them—I couldn't even bear to look at them. That old superstition still held sway.

And then my greatest fear—the one that had grown statistically less likely every year, but that I worried was foretold each time I saw a mouse—came to pass. In late 2021, I learned that after almost a decade-long remission, my leukemia had returned. To relapse after that long is extremely rare, and it meant that my disease was aggressive and stubborn and my prognosis was not good. I thought, *I might die this time,* and of course that felt frightening and heavy. But I had done a lot of work to figure out who I am, what I want, and even how I would do things differently if I got sick again.

And rather than feeling frozen by fear, I engaged with my circumstances creatively. When my vision was temporarily impaired due to a cocktail of medications, instead of writing, I turned to journaling in voice memos and painting watercolors. When my husband, Jon, and I had to be apart for weeks at a time, we stayed connected through the lullabies he composed for me. And when I grew so weak, post-transplant, that I was forced to use a walker to get around, my friend Carmen and I ordered a bag of colorful rhinestones and some glue, and we spent several evenings bedazzling every square inch of its drab frame. After that, instead of pitying looks, Lil' Dazzy and I were met with curiosity and delight and, incredibly, even a passing shout of "Cool walker!"

I survived that second bone marrow transplant, but this time, I will never be considered cured. I will be in cancer treatment indefinitely, and given the aggressiveness of my disease, relapse is a valid fear, something I write about in my journal often. In doing so, I notice my relationship to that fear. I note how it ebbs and flows and when it spreads, like in this entry in the weeks before I learned of my recurrence:

> I'm afraid of relapsing, therefore I'm afraid to make plans, because what if I get sick and have to cancel them? I'm afraid to get married—because what if the relationship doesn't survive the trauma of illness? I'm afraid of having kids, because what if I leave them motherless?

But giving fear free rein makes it hard to live a life. You're afraid of rebuilding, because it will collapse—but then you're just existing in wreckage. A life without shelter, without comfort, without beauty. And the truth is, sometimes fear makes it hard to see the ways in which you *are* okay, or to see when things are safe and good. When I finally returned home a few months after my transplant, I opened my bedroom closet, and I saw something shadowy and rodent shaped on the floor. Immediately I slammed the door and called my neighbor Jody, who came over to investigate. Afterward, he came downstairs and told me I had a serious problem on my hands. I felt seized with panic and asked if I needed to call an exterminator.

"No," he said. "A shrink." It turned out that rather than a mouse, it was a pouch of patchouli.

Soon after that, I began working on my fear of mice in clinician-directed exposure therapy—and if that sounds terrifying, it was. For a month, I watched videos of mice on YouTube, starting with baby mice, then graduating to full adults. It was deeply uncomfortable at first, but with each video, they felt less foreboding, and at some point, I started thinking they were pretty innocuous, even cute. And it worked. As the old saying goes, the only way out is through. I no longer feel like mice are harbingers of doom. I understand that they're a fact of life, be it city or country. And while I would still prefer to have Jody—whom I call "Angel Man" for all the miraculous ways he comes to my aid—deal with the occasional mouse, I no longer feel like I need to immediately sell my home and move. If it came to it, I could deal with it.

And that ultimately is what I found on the other side of my fear: the knowledge that I can handle it, whatever "it" is. There's strength and a sense of possibility in that belief. In the past, I was fascinated by people who seem to be missing the fear gene, by people who free-climb El Capitan or surf hundred-foot waves. But I have come to understand that many of these people do not have any less fear than the rest of us. They simply persist in spite of their fear; they do the things they want anyway. Like Georgia O'Keeffe said, "I've been absolutely terrified every moment of my life—and I've never let it keep me from doing a single thing I wanted to do."

In the following pages, you'll find ten essays and journaling prompts about fear—for tracing its contours and outlining its shape, for naming and taming it, for making peace with it. May they help you be one percent more curious than afraid.

GUILTY UNTIL PROVEN INNOCENT

Liana Finck

When I was about six, my little brother and I were outside playing in the snow when we looked up and saw our parents walking toward us from the house. They looked stern.

"We found something in all of our boots," said my dad. There was a serious pause.

"It was dog food," said my mom. "Was it you?"

It wasn't, and I said so. But the one thing I'm worse at than lying is telling the truth with a straight face. They just assumed it was me.

It kept happening. Every morning that winter, there was dog food in our boots. The false accusation awakened in me a sense of injustice. We lived in the country. About half a mile away, technically across the street, lived a family we were afraid of (they sometimes shouted, and the kids used to sit on the roof). I was sure this family was sneaking into our house every night and filling our boots with dog food. Either that, or it was something supernatural. I envisioned a tall, spooky character in a mask. I dubbed this character "The Dog Food Person."

As winter ground on, The Dog Food Person was undeterred—and I was still the main suspect. My parents tried reasoning with me, then threatening me. When nothing worked, they gave up and stopped mentioning it altogether.

(And now, dear reader, a foreshadowing break: Our dog, Pepper, ate a brand of dry dog food called Purina RX. It came in big blue bags, which we kept—unsealed—on top of the washing machine. Pepper, it should be noted, wasn't the kind of dog who ate everything in her bowl.

She ate when she was hungry, unless it was something irresistible, like chicken. The dog food was often left out in her red plastic bowl overnight. This is an important detail.)

Eventually, I started sneaking into our laundry room every morning to empty the boots. This went on for years, until we moved when I was fourteen. At one point, my parents even confided in our rabbi. I remember being asked to speak to a detective we knew. Mostly, though, they must have been too confused—and maybe even ashamed—to pursue it. Maybe they had some sense that the ending wouldn't be a pretty one. Because when my parents finally told their closest friends the whole story, ten years later, they immediately exclaimed, "Mice!" Mystery solved.

PEPPER

THIS IS YOUR PROMPT:

Do you have a story about vermin? Most people do! Tell it now, while no one is listening.

WHAT ELSE?

Molly Prentiss

It was the first really cold day of the year. We'd had a warm November, and I had relished it, dreading the arrival of this day, which meant many days like it: too cold for long walks and outside playdates for my energetic four-year-old; too cold for all the things that make the Hudson Valley wonderful: farms, trails, hillsides, orchards, lakes, and rivers. I'm not sure if it was the cold or the morning sickness—I'd recently found out I was pregnant again—but I felt a sadness creeping in.

I managed the school drop-off and responded to all pressing emails, but by eleven A.M., the melancholy had overtaken me to the point of exhaustion. I had planned a walk but feared the chill, so decided against it. Instead, I drove home, lay on the couch, looked up at the sorrowful clouds passing over the skylight, and promptly fell asleep.

The nap should have revived me, but instead it made things worse. I woke up drooling and sour-mouthed, angry for no reason I could articulate. I stood up and stomped around the room, taking my mood out on the old floorboards. I'd slept so long and hard that it was already time to pick up my daughter.

On the gray drive, I called my mom, masquerading it as a check-in. But my mom knows me too well. "You're upset," she said. And I was. And I cried. It was the cold, I blubbered. The impending winter, the gloominess, the isolation and time cooped up. I couldn't do it all over again.

"What else?" she asked.

The new baby, I said. How were we going to have another when we could barely manage one? When neither my partner nor I could work full time anymore and never seem to make enough money?

"What else?"

Me, I said—my impractical decisions. How had I ended up here, driving this lonely East Coast highway, when everyone I loved was across the country? Why couldn't I be more like my sister, have my shit figured out?

"You can't be her because you're you," my mom said. I cried a bit more and she let me. Before hanging up, she told me I'd feel better in the morning.

Only moments later, my daughter climbed into the car and burst into tears. The teachers hadn't let her pick an activity; Fiona didn't want to play with her; her pants had a hole. I wanted to sob along with her, but I knew that in that moment, I was the mother on the other end of the line. I tugged my own feelings toward me, as if I were wearing some kind of emotional corset; suddenly I was held tight by my own ability to feel. I could give her this, I thought. I could offer her my strength, but only because I could also offer her my vulnerability.

I nodded and told my daughter that yes, it was a bummer of a day— I'd had one, too. Things will be better in the morning, I said. But until then she could feel free to complain to me, to cry, to melt. My daughter took a few ragged breaths, and her crying fizzled. I reached back, and she grabbed my hand, held it all the way home.

That night, the cold sky broke open and it snowed. The next morning, the world was white and quiet, sparkling from certain angles. I felt rested and good. When my daughter woke up, she bounded out of her room and leapt up to hug me. "It's a nice day!" she cried.

I smiled. It was.

It is. We step out into the snow together and spin around.

THIS IS YOUR PROMPT:

Indulge in your own "What else?" Start with a grievance, a frustration, or a fear. Ask yourself "What else?" after each sentence for as long as it takes to feel a little catharsis.

THE GLORIOUS AWKWARDNESS

Jon Batiste

A couple of years ago, I crept into Jazz at Lincoln Center to practice in one of the empty concert halls on a massive Steinway—something I'd done since I was a student at Juilliard. I was a few weeks away from embarking on my first piano-and-microphone tour, where all the shows would be in the round, and I wanted to get into the zone. That morning I left the house without showering, wearing sweats, with the single-minded purpose of figuring out this new performance configuration, and I ended up playing for several hours in that empty concert hall, losing track of time and space. I was on Mars by the end of it, delirious. I played until I was bleeding sweat—in fact, I had conjured up a good funk, figuratively and literally. I needed some fresh air.

It was night by then, and the British musician James Blake was playing a concert in the same building. It was a solo piano concert, which was atypical for him, so I decided to check it out and see what I could steal. One of the security guards invited me backstage to listen and say hello to James. "Yeah," I said. "I'll say what's up." So I stuck around—still in my stanky sweats—until the show was over.

But to my surprise, when James came backstage, he wasn't alone. He also brought Beyoncé and Jay-Z. They were dressed up, all Lincoln Center vibes: She was in a gown, and he was clean, and they had that royal energy. And here I was, in sweats, stank, and not even a fresh hairline or a pair of crisp kicks!

I had briefly met them before. He reached out to shake my hand and said, "How you been?" and I blurted out, "I think we met before, at the wedding, right?" As soon as the words left my mouth, it occurred to me—you don't *think* you met Jay-Z. It's not like he's somebody you bump into at the supermarket, and you're like, "I think maybe we've met before." But I was so discombobulated, still reeling from my practice sessions, and had momentarily forgotten how to communicate. (In fact, I was seconds away from rapping one of his verses at him.) All I could think was: *Wait—what am I supposed to do now? Who am I? Who are you? Oh, you're that guy I've been listening to for like fifteen years. Oh yeah, that's you! Right?!*

Meanwhile, Jay-Z was looking at me like I had a head injury or something.

At that point, Beyoncé leaned in to say hello and hug me. I was still in my head and so caught off guard that I forgot about my stankness. But as soon as I lifted my arms to hug her back, I could feel the whiff of heat emanating from my sweatshirt, and I was like, *Oh no. I done fumigated the Queen.*

She didn't mention it, of course—just pleasantries like "Good to see you again." And then there was a pause. The kind of pause that happens when Uncle Ned drops the Thanksgiving turkey. That awkward handshake hello. That hug where we both knew what happened and didn't want to say anything. It was ground zero of Glorious Awkwardness, but it didn't end there.

Alas, although our greeting was not fully realized, it was time to move on to the next phase of social interaction. James broke the ice and, addressing the group, said, "Shall we go to the dressing room and catch up?" I started walking with them—still in my head—but after a few steps, I thought, "I don't really know these people. Also: I done fumigated the Queen."

So instead of continuing on, I just peeled off in embarrassment, heading toward a barricade fence for crowd control. It was only when I'd thrown one leg over that I realized I'd neglected to say goodbye. When I turned back—one leg still over the barricade—they were all staring at me like, "Huh?"

I don't even think I waved, just mumbled, "All right," and kept on going.

THIS IS YOUR PROMPT:

Reflect on a particular moment in your past when you felt most in touch with your "Glorious Awkwardness." It could be a cringeworthy moment you've replayed a thousand times in your mind. Or something essential about who you are, something unchangeable. Go back there. What did you learn from it? Can you laugh about it? And if not, why?

THE WISDOM OF NO ESCAPE

Laura McKowen

Earlier this spring, my four-year relationship ended. We were engaged and planned to get married this fall. This was the first significant relationship I've had since my marriage, which ended over ten years ago. Back then, I was so deep in my addiction and cut off from my heart that I felt nothing but relief when my ex-husband and I finally split. I kept waiting for the grief to hit me like people said it would, but it never did. I'd long been praised for my positivity and strength and courage, and I thought this was more proof of my resilience.

This time, I've fallen apart completely. For months I've struggled to work. I've had panic attacks, waves of pain so strong I've had to lie down on the kitchen floor or pull over on the highway. There have been countless sleepless nights and many days I've been unable to get out of bed. I've been stunned at how much I've cried, and how quickly it comes on. I've been enraged, jealous, confused, sad, and indignant all in the same hour.

What I haven't done, though, is drink. I actually haven't had a drink in almost ten years, so this isn't new, but it's still something. More interestingly, I haven't wanted to drink. This is its own miracle, but even more incredible to me is I'm not doing anything else destructive, either. What I learned pretty quickly in sobriety was that alcohol was just a symptom. Once it was removed, I found other ways to escape: work, food, productivity, achieving, sex, and the big one for me, love, or the pursuit of it. The problem, it turned out, was not alcohol—it was that I couldn't be present for my pain. And I literally mean it when I say I couldn't. I had no skills or tools to stay with myself, and it's taken ten years to build that inner safety.

As I've been moving through these months, I've often thought of renowned Buddhist teacher Pema Chödrön, and what she had to say about "the wisdom of no escape," which she says is "an alternatingly painful and delightful 'no exit' situation." According to Buddhist principles, in seeing ourselves, our emotions and thoughts, exactly as they are right now, and in not trying to make them go away or improve or change them, we have the opportunity to befriend ourselves and cease suffering. This no-escape witnessing, when we can do it with "precision and gentleness" (the gentleness is key), holds our innate wisdom.

I haven't found this to be easy—quite the opposite—but I've found it to be true and so heartening. As often as I've joked about wishing I had an escape hatch of some kind left, I know the exquisite pain I feel and can hold myself through is proof of my aliveness. This is actual resilience, strength, and courage.

THIS IS YOUR PROMPT:

Without judgment—because we all do this—write about the ways you escape your pain. What do you think might be on the other side of these escapes? What are you trying not to feel or know? What might be possible if you allowed yourself to be present with those feelings and thoughts?

IF YOU REALLY KNEW ME

Noor Tagouri

I have known I wanted to tell stories since the age of three, and for years now, I've toured the world speaking about breaking barriers through storytelling. One way I do this is with an exercise called "If you really knew me."

I first did this activity in South Dakota at a college event, where I was told—upon my arrival—that I'd been booked as a speaker because there was a "white supremacy problem on campus," and the students were hoping my speech could "help fix it." [*nervous laugh*] When I walked into the room of six hundred people, I could feel the energy of mistrust and fear—and I was also projecting my own. I didn't know how I would connect with them. But I later realized that most of the audience was feeling the same thing, for other reasons.

They said things like:

"If you really knew me, you'd know I still collect stuffed animals to feel less alone."

"If you really knew me, you'd know I was sexually assaulted at fifteen and told to shut up about it when I spoke up."

"If you really knew me, you'd know I never feel good enough and I don't deserve the position I have at work."

When I do this exercise with a room full of people, inevitably it leads to vulnerability, then to strength through connection. The story of "if you really knew me" has become the story of every paused breath in an interview. Every time people have poured their hearts out to me in person or in a letter from thousands of miles away. It's the story of all of us.

It's the reminder and the constant. The foundation of it all. It's where I have found myself over and over again and have found light in others when it barely flickered.

When you are known and lean into yourself, people have no power over you. And chances are, they will find comfort—because more often than you realize, they're going through things, too.

THIS IS YOUR PROMPT:

Complete the sentence: "If you really knew me . . ." You can write one or many of these statements. Then sit with them. Ask yourself: What would your life be like if people knew these things about you? How would your circle of friends change? What about your job?

WEEDING

Hollynn Huitt

The day before we left on a two-week trip, I stood looking at my garden, feeling regretful. It had never looked better. The flowers seemed to all be blooming at once, the black caps ripe, the tomatoes green but perfectly round. I preemptively mourned for the state it was sure to be in upon my return.

When we got back—as soon as we drove up, in fact—my fears were confirmed. The garden looked as though we had been away for years. The feet of the blueberry bushes were choked with tall grasses, bindweed had conquered the currant bush, and some yellow flowering weed had grown as tall as the asparagus, which is to say over my head. All our hard work had been undone in a matter of weeks. Where would we find the time to fix this? There was only enough time to keep things running in our lives, never enough to correct for a problem as big, as exhausting, as this.

My instinct was to avoid the garden, but my young sons, undeterred by the weeds, hopped out of the car, pulled me toward the gate, and got to work foraging: picking midnight blueberries and scarlet cherry tomatoes and spiny cucumbers, wiping them across their palms before eating them through the middle. As they ate, I decided to begin weeding, though I was certain that what little I could do in the next few minutes would be negligible. I pulled the first weed and it came up effortlessly, with zero resistance. I laughed, a single surprised "ha." What luck, to have chosen the easiest one on my first go! But the next weed was the same, then the next.

Within minutes I had a pile worthy of a wheelbarrow. I sat back on my heels, looked down the length of our garden, and felt a kind of vertigo. This task, which I had dreaded before it even happened, which had disheartened me weeks before, had been nearly effortless. There were lots of reasons why, from diligently weeding the garden for years to the soil on that day—soft from a recent rain, crumbling from the morning's sun—being amenable to weeding. Still, the feeling remained: Some of the hard things I had been worrying about might just turn out all right. Instead of hunkering down and bracing for impact, I could, just maybe, hope for the best.

THIS IS YOUR PROMPT:

Write about a time you dreaded something, but it turned out to be okay—maybe even easy or pleasant. Try to isolate the moment of realization. How did it feel?

WHENEVER I FEEL AFRAID

Sarah Levy

I have always been afraid to fail. At a school choir performance when I was six, I stood up on a piano bench and launched into a solo rendition of "I Whistle a Happy Tune" from the 1951 Rodgers and Hammerstein musical *The King and I*. All eyes were on me, and I was nervous. In a home video, my voice shakes as I start to sing, but the lyrics carry me forward.

> *Whenever I feel afraid / I hold my head erect / And whistle a happy tune / so no one will suspect / I'm afraid*

Two decades later, I had perfected the art of faking it. I was in my early twenties and frequently found myself waking up on sticky couches, dazed and hungover in the aftermath of blackouts. No one suspected I had a problem with alcohol; I was young, accomplished, and partied socially, never alone or first thing in the morning. Despite my external facade, a voice deep within had started whispering the same refrain: *You need to stop drinking.*

I tried and failed to quit. A two-week stint at twenty-three, a dry month at twenty-five. These starts and stops were frustrating but essential for ultimately surrendering to sobriety at twenty-eight.

In my early months of recovery, I grieved my old life and the party girl persona that allowed me to mask insecurities. At the same time, I started to cherish the seeds of sobriety I was planting. At three months sober, when I ordered a virgin Bloody Mary at brunch in New York

City, the waitress accidentally served me the alcoholic variety. I felt the vodka burn as I took my first sip, but it was too late to spit it out. Out on the sidewalk, January wind whipping across my cheeks, I called my dad in tears. Did I have to start over? My dad reassured me that the sip didn't count as a slip. I hadn't intended to drink, therefore my sobriety was intact. His response was comforting; I couldn't bear the thought of failing at this again.

I started writing about my road to recovery, and a few years later, my memoir, *Drinking Games,* was published. In going public with my sobriety, I discovered a beautiful community of people who related to my struggles. I no longer worried about drinking; I didn't miss the way alcohol left me feeling shriveled like a prune. Instead, I feared that my sobriety would get stale as the sheen of early recovery started to wear off. I worried about setting a good example or failing my readers.

My instinct was to fake my way through and whistle a happy tune so no one would suspect I was afraid. But over time, I began to reframe my fears of failure as powerful pieces of information. We are afraid to fail at the things we care about. My fears of failure are a beautiful reminder of everything recovery has given me—everything I fought so hard to gain and don't want to lose.

THIS IS YOUR PROMPT:

Write about your most looming fear of failure—where it shows up and when. Now call to mind the people, experiences, and things in your life that you care about. How does your fear of failure overlap with what matters to you most?

THE MAYOR'S UNDERPANTS

Lindy West

Every morning I wake up at six and turn on the television set. It only gets three channels: the weather (sunny and clear all day), the fortune-teller (bad luck—the spirits are annoyed), and a third channel that only shows cooking tutorials and farming tips. I don't mind—I have too much work to do anyway. I go out into the blustery autumn air and pet my dog, Snooch, who confirms that he loves me (for now) and then, inexplicably, runs headlong into the wall of the barn. I wish it was raining. I own only one sprinkler, so I have to water most of my crops by hand—my fat pumpkins, my twining hops, my cheerful corn—which takes hours. *Oh no,* I realize. *I've forgotten the chickens.* I run to the chicken coop and let the chickens out so they can peck in the grass. They're angry with me, but when I look inside I find they've laid some eggs anyway. I place their eggs one by one into my row of throbbing mayonnaise machines and head into town to give my boyfriend a pomegranate for his birthday. If I give him enough pomegranates, eventually he will marry me. When I return home, my machines have produced three jars of fresh mayonnaise, one of which I can give to my neighbor Marnie in hopes that she will let me snoop through her private bedroom, where I suspect I'll find the mayor's missing underpants. I place the two extra jars of mayonnaise in my shipping container, which will net me $228 overnight, and make sure I'm asleep by two A.M. The next morning I wake up and do it all over again.

My book is due in three days.

My real book is due in three days—my first book in four years, the linchpin of any future financial solvency—yet I'm spending what some (me) might call a medically disordered amount of time running a fake farm in a video game called *Stardew Valley*. I find video games cathartic in times of stress because they provide a concrete list of achievable tasks (bring the wizard a coconut) in exchange for a tangible reward (a large-mouth bass), unlike real life, which provides a nebulous haze of crushing responsibilities (write a book, do your taxes) in exchange for terror and pain (get criticized in the newspaper, send the government twenty thousand dollars). A guided meditation through someone else's life, a facilitated disassociation to another world. Unfortunately, "stress relief" has diminishing returns (unlike my mayonnaise) if you aren't also accomplishing the stressful thing from which you need relief! I simply must get my writing machine throbbing again or I will simply die.

I text a friend who also plays *Stardew Valley* yet somehow maintains a successful business. "The Stardew gameplay loop is ruining my life," I say. "I tell myself: Just one more day, just one more day, but then I go to sleep, I wake up, oh, my cheese is done, oh, Demetrius needs a puffer fish for his research, and I'm in it again!"

"Gameplay loop" is jargon for the set of repeating activities that make up a video game, usually with escalating incentives to keep players hooked. It's also known as a "compulsion loop." It's what makes games fun, and it's what makes weak-minded procrastinators have to pay back their book advances.

"Okay, picture this," my friend says. "Gameplay loop—but it's your real life. You wake up, you feed the chicken (*you*)."

I laugh. "Yes, I harvest my *ideas* and I plant *words* in my manuscript."

"Truly!" she says. "You pet every pig in the barn (*your mental health*)."

To my surprise, the silly reframe works. The video game metaphor is set dressing, but I find myself fortified by my friend's easy conviction that I am worth prioritizing above "feed imaginary chickens." It's a tether, jerking me back into the real world. I have a real task to accomplish, and a real reward at the end. I put the game away, for now, and think about how many mayonnaises will be waiting for me when I get back. Hell yes. I'm gonna be *rich*.

THIS IS YOUR PROMPT:

Is there anything big in your life, professionally or personally, that you're avoiding in favor of an alluring distraction? Are you hiding from big projects or big feelings by letting yourself be consumed by a "compulsion loop," literal or metaphorical? What would the ideal gameplay loop of your life look like?

SING OUT, LOUISE

Nafissa Thompson-Spires

I grew up in a fundamentalist religious tradition that urged women toward modest behavior, away from attention seeking, obvious self-expression, makeup, and strangely, wearing pants. At the same time, my cultlike church also hosted regular fashion shows and child stage performances in which my mother coached me to perform gospel's greatest hits, such as "Go Tell It on the Mountain," starting at age two. She has since apologized: "I didn't know what a shy child you really were. You looked terrified onstage with the microphone in your hand."

By grade school, however, I loved the theater and classic Hollywood cinema, especially musicals. Around age eight, I sat awestruck through our community theater's production of Shakespeare's *The Taming of the Shrew*, and though I knew I did not want to become a termagant—"a harsh-tempered woman," a word I knew because I loved playing in the thesaurus and throwing new words around every chance I got—I did not want to be made into a Nafissa conformable, either. At nine, I starred in our class production of *Twinkle*, a play within a play, and soon, no one could stop me from mucking up the hallways with my little numbers and bits. I was especially fond of pairing my little joke-book stand-up routine with Joey Gladstone of *Full House* fame's "cut it out" finger gestures and Mr. Woodchuck impressions. Clowning escalated to accosting my peers with drawn-out performances of Veruca Salt's Oompa Loompa song. My Southern California Christian private school was close to Los Angeles, and many of my classmates were working actors, but I was not allowed to go on auditions until I was eighteen, so I devoured every film on Turner Classic Movies on weekend afternoons, dreaming of the day when I would become a star. I, unlike that ungrateful young Gypsy Rose Lee, was happy to "sing out, Louise."

My showiness came to a head in eleventh grade, during the drama club's production of *Anne of Green Gables*. I played Josie Pye. I had a feeling the drama teacher was growing annoyed with me when she offered a stern "No" to my request that all of Josie's wardrobe be monogrammed with a little cursive *J*, like Laverne's from *Laverne & Shirley*. Her annoyance was confirmed when, after I improved a line to add a little dazzle, she took me aside and screamed in front of the entire audience, "Nafissa, stop upstaging Anne!"

I learned that night that there is indeed a time for modesty and the puritanical plainness driven into me, and there's a time for jazz hands and the thesaurus, too. The best artists know the alchemy of discernment.

THIS IS YOUR PROMPT:

What would your sentences look like if you tried on a persona for a moment? Throw in some jazz hands or a thesaurus. Let your pen sing like Julie Andrews from a mountaintop, or strut across the page like a drag queen on a ballroom floor. Afterward, ask yourself, How did it feel? Can you ever imagine yourself using this language, channeling this freedom, again? And what might happen if you did?

REWIRING

Margo Steines

When my child was newborn, I had what I now understand to be severe postpartum anxiety. Her birth was not easy—few of them are—and I emerged from it feeling shaken, ill at ease in my body and confused by my mind. I found myself consumed with intrusive thoughts of danger and harm: Would someone stab me while I was walking with her and leave her helpless body lying in the road? Would a painting fall off the wall and hit her while she played on the floor? Would I fall asleep and roll over on her? Along with this chorus of possibilities, I felt a deep worthlessness. I was a new mom with a history of depression, living far away from family, during a pandemic, in a triple-digit climate, so it was easy to dismiss everything I was feeling as the natural and appropriate reaction to conditions. It was easy to dismiss myself.

Becoming a parent made me realize that while I had moved on from my younger life, which was marked by violence and addiction, I never actually healed the trauma of it. I just stepped over it like a leaking bag of trash on the sidewalk, as if it no longer had anything to do with me. But once I was holding the tiny person I had spent ten years hoping and wishing and atheist-praying for, the stakes were different. I couldn't burn down or exit my life, because she needed me. She will always need me.

In therapy I learned that while I had managed to clear my mind of the chaos that used to drive it, I never healed my body. My nervous system was wrecked by the compounded effects of years of various forms of violence and chaos. I haven't taken a drug in seventeen years, and I haven't sustained any sort of violence in more than half a decade, but my autonomic nervous system has been stuck in a whining idle for a good twenty years, and that does something to a person.

I learned that with somatic therapy it is possible to retrace my steps, to use bodywork to rewire my mind. I learned to press the flats of my knuckles into a hard cool wall when I feel the dull buzz of panic rising in my chest. I learned to place my palm over my heart, to feel the floor against my feet, to experience myself safely existing. I learned to breathe the way my child does when she is regulating her nervous system, a skill that came wired into her: two fast inhales and a slow exhale, the physiological sigh. I learned more from her than I ever expected, like how to simply exist as a human being—a skill I am still working on.

THIS IS YOUR PROMPT:

Write about a time you realized you were struggling. What prompted the uncovering? What resources did you turn to in the wake of it? What is your relationship with that particular struggle like today?

CHAPTER 4

ON SEEING

I've learned over the last decade that creative work comes in four seasons. There is the season of ideating and researching, figuring out the form something should take, dreaming about what it could become. There's the season of actually making the thing—the Anne Lamott butt-in-chair phase. (To quote her: "How to write: Butt in chair.") There is the season of putting the work into the world, letting it fly so it can go out and find the person who needs it most, at the moment they need it most. Then there is the fallow season, when you're in between projects, when you're not sure what you'll create next, if anything, where you must give yourself grace as you become a different person with different questions, ideas, and concerns.

As I write this, I'm squarely in the butt-in-chair phase, which is my favorite creative season. I'm currently at a painting residency, making large-scale watercolors for my first art exhibit. I'm lost in the world of the work. I think about the paintings all day and dream about them at night. It feels like I'm living in a parallel universe. When I'm in this season, time starts to warp. A few days ago, I took my dogs to the vet, and when I was filling out the date on the intake forms, I wrote the wrong year—not once, but twice, and with great conviction.

I used to fall into the trap of spending more time talking about the projects I wanted to do rather than actually doing them. Prior to getting sick, I confused busyness for meaningful productivity. I was always running around, attending to a million extracurricular activities and social events. But when I entered cancer treatment, I suddenly had only a few hours of usable energy each day, so I had to get really clear on how and with whom I wanted to spend my time. At the same time, I found that the forced stillness of being stuck in bed was strangely fruitful. It seemed at first like I was doing nothing, but I soon realized that there was so much happening. In that quiet, there was depth, and from that depth came inklings of inspiration. Now I intentionally carve out time and space for that. I clear my calendar so that I can be fully immersed in the work—even if the work sometimes doesn't look like work, even if it's reading, or journaling, or taking notes on index cards, or going down a rabbit trail of research about East African fertility masks, or lying down for a nap.

Rest, I have learned, is an important part of the creative process. The other day, I was painting, and I got to a point where all I could see were mistakes: time to step away. I left my studio and brought my dogs down to my favorite swimming hole in a nearby tributary of the Delaware River, and for half an hour, I watched them play. Behind them, the bank was dotted with dandelions and some wild daffodils, and I let my tired mind rest, and just took in the sights and the sounds and the colors: so much yellow. Suddenly, I felt awake—alive—again. "When I see this way, I see truly," Annie Dillard writes in *Pilgrim at Tinker Creek*. "As Thoreau says, I return to my senses."

My first real lesson in seeing took place when I was twenty-two. Before I entered the hospital for my first monthlong stay, I didn't appreciate how the smallest detail, like the vibrant yellow of a dandelion or the delightful snout of a daffodil, could provide such nourishment. I hadn't given any thought to the fact that once I was locked in a hospital room for weeks on end, I wouldn't be able to feel the breeze, the sun, the rain—that I wouldn't even be able to open the window.

When I was finally discharged, the sensory experience was almost overwhelming. All my life, I had overlooked so much. The sky, breeze, trees, even the brilliant but ephemeral beauty of flowers were a given— something everyday. I saw them, but I didn't see them. As Georgia O'Keeffe wrote, "Still—in a way—nobody sees a flower—really—it is so small—we haven't time—and to see takes time, like to have a friend takes time."

To see takes time and practice. I think now of one of my greatest teachers in seeing: sweet Loulou, the shaggy red hound dog mutt that my family rescued from Tennessee. I found her on an animal shelter website a few years ago, and I sent the listing to my brother, Adam, hoping he would give her a home. And he did, and he fell in love with her and began spending all his time taking her to different dog parks in New York City, training her to sit and stay, and she seemed to be thriving. But a few months in, she fell suddenly ill. When he took her to the vet, they said she had blastomycosis, a deadly fungal infection that is common in the river valleys of Tennessee.

It was touch and go for weeks, but eventually Loulou pulled through, though she lost her sight. Afterward my brother nursed her diligently, but in her newly blind state in a city like New York, she was terrified. Every skateboard that trundled by on the sidewalk sent her into a cowering panic. At every car horn, she clung to him like a life raft. As the days passed, the stress took a toll. She wasn't eating. She wasn't sleeping. She needed to leave the city. So Loulou came to live with me in my bucolic corner of rural New Jersey.

At first it seemed like a disaster. Loulou was eating and sleeping and moving around again, but she was also running into everything—every wall, every doorway, every tree in our backyard. I worried that she would injure herself. I talked to my neighbor Chuck, who loves dogs and also dabbles in inventing, about how I might help her, and he began dreaming up a device for her collar that would beep anytime she neared an object.

But before he had the chance to get tinkering, a small miracle began unfolding. Loulou started mapping our house and garden in her mind's eye until she knew every sharp corner, until she could gallop through the living room, tilting her torso to avoid the piano bench, the ottoman, the potted plant perched on a wobbly old pedestal. Not only that, she memorized the landscape of Chuck's woods, where I took her for a walk each morning. Soon she was navigating the trees and the ponds. She knew when we reached the hayfield, huge and open, freshly mowed. There she would run as freely as she wanted, without caution or restraint.

I have learned so much about seeing from Loulou and from the other creatures around me. With each dog I've added to my pack, I

see the landscape anew. When walking with Sunshine, my chihuahua-
dachshund mutt, the logs, which she has to leap over, come into view,
and the twirl of a falling leaf, too, as she rears on her hind legs and
dances to catch it. Same with snowflakes, same with rain. With my
black lab, River, it's the dense reedy grasses at the hayfield's edge, and the
pond they fringe, which I didn't even realize was there until River barged
through the reeds, plunged into the water, and emerged dripping.

Simone Weil said that "attention is the rarest and purest form of generosity." It's also a kind of presence. I've heard it said that depression is
an overfixation on the past and anxiety is an overfixation on the future.
If that's the case, seeing is a bulwark against both, as it's a fixation on the
now. I try to be present with whatever is around me and let that lift me,
which wards off the temptation to time travel, either backward or forward. Given my health status and my likelihood of relapse, I have more
reason than ever to fly forward to a terrifying eventuality, to engage in
aggressive futurism. But even before I was sick, that was true. I look
back at my journal entries from college and they're all aspirational. Five-
year plans. Ten-year plans. What will I be?

I look back on those journal entries, and they reveal something about
me—about my relentless daydreaming, about my plans for who I
wanted to become. But I wish I could read back and recall what was
actually happening—what I was feeling in the moment, what parties I
went to, how my professor responded when I shared about my first big
heartbreak during office hours, or the funny way she tilted her head
when she said the word "patriarchy," or what the foliage on campus
looked like on a fresh spring day.

We remember the day we got into a car crash, but we don't remember
the many pleasant drives we took and all the times we arrived safely at
our destination. "We live half our waking lives and all of our sleeping
lives in some private, useless, and insensible waters we never mention or
recall," says Annie Dillard in her essay "Total Eclipse." "Useless, I say.
Valueless, I might add—until someone hauls their wealth up to the surface and into the wide-awake city, in a form that people can use."

Recently for me, that "someone" has been a new creative practice:
painting. It has been a great and generous teacher in paying attention. It
has allowed me to see shapes and colors in new ways. I find myself al-

most stricken by the sight of a flower on a vine—by its pom-pom shape, by its magenta hue more saturated than seems physically possible. I stop to snap a photo of it, hoping that later I can re-create in pigment its dynamism, its vibrancy.

Over the years, there have been many times when I've been struck still by the grandeur of nature, be it looking into the gaping maw of the Grand Canyon, beholding the sheer force of Niagara Falls, or experiencing the oceanic vastness of the Sahara. It's the sublime: I am made small in the most wonderful way. But now I can also experience that dizzying thrill when I stop and study the magenta-hued pom-pom, or the complex constellations in a sprig of Queen Anne's lace. I am more awake and alive. Less world-weary, more filled with wonder.

In the pages that follow, you'll find ten essays and prompts on seeing—on paying attention, on presence, on wonder. May they lead you to seek, to find, and to truly behold whatever it is you're looking for.

THE SUNSET LOG

Jia Tolentino

In 2019, I was on the subway, traveling from Brooklyn to Manhattan, when I opened my Google calendar on my phone and realized that I didn't have a day free of work obligations for the following three months straight. I started spiraling, wondering how exactly I'd made my life so overdetermined yet under-considered, how I'd managed to use my considerable freedom so poorly, how I'd tried so hard to make use of myself as a human that I'd left myself with a minimum of time to feel human in any meaningful way. I was about to publish a book, which I'd started writing in part because I'd spent the previous half decade instantly relocating my thoughts from my brain into monetizable public blog posts, and I'd thought that a book would give me the chance to write in private, for myself, just to see where things went. I'd done this, and loved it, and then been confronted with an alternate story: The book was a public commodity, and my life a marketing tactic, and these things that had seemed so clearly like ends in themselves had been reconfigured as instruments and means. When I got off the train, the sun was setting, a neon pomegranate flush behind the skyscrapers. I decided, as the first step in a recuperative process of doing more things that would bring zero measurable gain to anyone, to start keeping a log of sunsets on my phone.

The exercise was nice. It felt deliberately aimless, rather than accidentally pointless, as so many things had begun to seem. It was a structure to encourage myself to simply stop moving for long enough to take in the sky. On September 14, the sunset was blue gray like an oxford shirt, striped with slate clouds lit up from under with glowing burgundy. A week later, the sunset was a radiant peach, a dark cloud crossing the vista like a battleship. In December, several time zones west, there was a band of parakeet gray above the ocean, topped with lemon meringue and hazy mauve. I recorded a sunset in Iowa in February of 2020, at 5:24 P.M., that looked like a shaved-ice gradient of apricot and banana and grape.

I stopped recording sunsets a few weeks later, in early March, once it no longer felt appropriate to linger for long moments outside. Then we entered isolation broadly, and I waded deeper into this reckoning with my relationship to work, and to writing. I had no interesting thoughts about anything, and that felt okay, and then amazing. I couldn't see the sunset from my window, but I started taking notes on the trees and the weather. I wrote about how dusk over snow made everything glow like black light, about the cottonwood blossoms that swirled in the wind, about the day the sky turned gray green like a cat's eye and I hurried the dog inside before it started to hail. This was beauty, sensation, knowledge, simple translation, that all existed for its own sake. Since that year I've gotten bad, once more, at remembering that writing can just be like that. It might be time to start keeping a log of sunsets again.

THIS IS YOUR PROMPT:

Go outside for fifteen minutes, at sunset if possible, and pay attention to nothing but your immediate surroundings. Write down what you see and what it makes you think of. Try your best to avoid extrapolating usable meaning for once. Just be an eye.

THE CLARITY OF DARKNESS

Michael Koryta

I was working on a book about caving when I had the idea of doing some firsthand research on the experience of total darkness to enhance the sensory detail I could provide for the reader. My plan was to see how well I could track time in the sensory deprivation chamber that is full darkness.

I set a goal of twenty minutes, with my only rule being that I would not count. The obvious things happened—a heightening of other senses, for example, hearing in particular. I was surprised by how disturbing the blackness was even though I knew that the light could be restored at any moment. I closed my eyes and focused on my breathing, and a remarkable thing happened: When my eyelids shut, the darkness seemed to lighten.

As my thoughts wandered, I began to see clear images. It was akin to dreaming, although I was in a hyper-alert state. Each recollection or idle thought seemed to call forth an acute visual memory in a way I couldn't have achieved with my eyes open, in the light, hard at work on the task of remembering.

At some point, sure that I'd achieved my twenty-minute goal, I turned on the light and checked the time. Seven minutes had passed. I decided to try again. This time, nearly forty minutes passed. I had achieved little toward my original goals of enhancing the sensory detail I could provide the reader about cave exploration in full dark. What I had achieved, though, felt far more revelatory: My visual memory had been heightened via the absence of the visual field.

It's a technique I've fallen back on for writing countless times since, and one I now enjoy simply for the experience. I sit like a spectator of my own subconscious, curious to see what it will deliver. I know that if I "direct" my breath toward my teeth, I feel my belly expand with the breath. Direct it toward the ears, and I feel my chest expand. Direct it toward the eyes, and my upper lungs seem to fill. It's all the same inhalation, in through the nose, out through the nose, and yet I'm fascinated by the way it seems as if I can "aim" the breath. This slows me down, which allows the mind to wander, and the visuals come with the wandering. I don't try to guide the visuals, only note them—and appreciate them.

THIS IS YOUR PROMPT:

Take a seat in a dark room. Keep a relaxed but upright posture. Close your eyes. Breathe in whatever fashion you wish, directed or not, and let the mind wander. Set a timer—or don't. At the end of the session, write your recollection of the visual memories that passed through your mind's eye. Note the surprises—faces you haven't seen in years, places long forgotten—and appreciate what the darkness made clear.

A BRIDGE THROUGH TIME

Gloria Steinem

Once, when I was returning from travels within this country, I was driving into New York's Midtown tunnel, on which some daring graffiti artist had written in white paint: WHEELS OVER INDIAN TRAILS. Those words cast my mind beyond the limits of the present, and I silently thanked the lawless hands that had painted them there. For years after they had worn away, I saw them in my mind's eye.

This has given me a feeling for the history that is always beneath our feet, a vertical history of the many generations of people who have walked, worked, and laughed before us in these very same places.

Ever since then, especially when I am on natural ground where land, rocks, and paths must have known the touch of many generations, I think about this physical connection to people of the past who are no more. I find it much more intimate and moving than the words of historians and scholars who take us back with facts and names. There is something about knowing you touched the same rock and stood on the same land that is more personal than any history.

For instance, I've lived for many years on the same two floors of a brownstone in New York City. It feels more intimate to go to nearby Central Park and touch the huge outcroppings of igneous rock that people must have touched since the beginning of time.

When I speak on a college campus, I ask students to stand on the ground that was touched by generations before this subcontinent was called America. This creates not just an intellectual connection, but a visceral and all-five-senses one. It can bring a deep understanding that requires no ability to read or speak the same language.

Try it at home. Try it as you travel. Create a bridge through time.

THIS IS YOUR PROMPT:

Wherever you are in the world, your surroundings are shaped by the decisions of generations who lived before you. Similarly, our decisions today will create ripple effects for generations into the future. Write— whether real or imaginary—about what once was on the land where you live or work or study today. It might be a description of a flowing stream that is no more, or of the tenants of your home many generations ago. How did these past moments shape your present? How will you shape the future?

BEAUTY HUNTING

Raven Roxanne

A few years ago, someone I loved was struggling with addiction, and I found myself reckoning with my own deeply ingrained pattern of co-dependency. It was a turning point in my life. People say that beauty can come from the darkest places, but when you're in a dark place, making something beautiful can feel impossible. How do you even start?

I began with a simple practice of going into my studio, thinking about how I felt, and playing. I started with color, choosing ones that matched my emotional palette for the day. As I put paint to the surface, loosely weaving the colors together, I found myself somewhat unconsciously constructing a nest. Yes, I know—with a name like Raven, it seems too obvious. Yet the symbol of a nest has grown to mean so much to me through this process. It's such a perfect representation of life— messy but beautiful. One painting turned into a series, then the series turned into a storybook for children.

Since then, other objects have taken on meaning and helped me in difficult moments. One morning I was out for a walk with my scruffy rescue pup, Willie, and I was feeling anxious. As I wandered, I was actively asking myself, *Am I in a funk?* I kept on, avoiding the talking trap of the gray-haired man who sits on his porch smoking cigarettes. I came to the white house with big white columns, the one with the overgrown front garden. I stopped to stare at the lily pond, flowers blooming from an old moss-covered fountain. I wanted to peek through the foliage; I wanted to magnify it, to spread it with two fingers like a static image on a screen, to get a glimpse inside the flowers.

At that moment, a man came down the stairs, and I burst out eagerly, "Excuse me, sir! Can I take a closer look at your fountain and flowers?" I could tell he wanted to say no, but he reluctantly agreed. I opened the hip-high iron gate, and Willie and I stepped into the garden. The lily, which burst from the thick water between leaves the size of watermelons, was so heavy it was leaning over. I bent down to take a closer look and I noticed the petals were like tissue paper, soft and pink, the light behind them revealing how delicate they were. The wiry yellow stamens looked like tentacles surrounding the stigma, like an inverted cone, so strangely flat. *This shape probably inspired some sci-fi character,* I thought to myself. I was taking it all in, getting lost in the flower, getting lost in thought, getting lost in myself.

It was then I noticed the feeling in my chest—the tightness, the feeling of being trapped, of maybe being depressed—had eased. It felt like I'd opened up.

THIS IS YOUR PROMPT:

Think about the last time you looked at something and noticed a change within—studying a painting, an animal, a flower, a piece of fruit, what you saw through a window. Write about what you saw and what you felt shift.

POETRY BY ERASURE

Natalie Warther

I began playing with erasure poetry in the early months of quarantine. When I felt overwhelmed by the world around me, it was much less daunting to manipulate a preexisting thing than to create something from scratch.

And that's all erasure poetry is: a manipulation, creation through elimination, an intense form of revision. It's a whittling down until the original text is unrecognizable, until it no longer belongs to its original creator—until the thing that needs to be said through you is left there on the page.

The great poet and writer Mary Ruefle describes her experience creating erasures: "All the words rise up and they hover a quarter inch above the page. I don't actually read the page. I read the words, which is different."

In an original text, words strung together into sentences and paragraphs possess coherent and specific meaning. But when the words are isolated, rearranged, and placed in conversation with blank space, they show their true personalities. They detach themselves from narrative purpose. They become sonic, and rhythmic, and maybe, a little, they hover.

To me, the job is freeing in its simplicity: eliminate words until a new path is cleared. It's meditative, it's playful. It's a space where we can be writers without ever writing a word.

THIS IS YOUR PROMPT:

Select a text to erase—an old book, a print newspaper, or some article online. Study the page, and see what rises up. Maybe use a notebook to jot down fragments, interesting words, and sonic patterns. How does using whiteout, blackout, or cross-hatching change the final composition? Which appeals to you?

Begin to write your poem by erasure.

SEEING AND KNOWING

Debbie Millman

I often wonder about how we know what we know. This curiosity has led me to the work of people like John Stilgoe, a professor in the Harvard Graduate School of Design and the author of several books, including *Outside Lies Magic: Regaining History and Awareness in Everyday Places.* Stilgoe believes the power of acute observation is one of nature's most useful learning tools. He teaches his students to consider "another way of knowing" beyond words and numbers; he believes that people are so focused on a goal or zeroing in on what appears to be obvious that they often miss what is right in front of them. It's not that they are unable to see the forest for the trees; they are unable to see the trees for the forest. Professor Stilgoe attributes this to the "constant blur of modern life."

It's no wonder: We live in a world of sensory overload, bombarded with more images than we could ever fully process. As a result, we *choose* to see the things we know and can relate to. Our ability to break through existing patterns of recognition to see new things is thwarted by our deep, instinctive craving for certainty. We feel safer and more secure when we are surrounded by what we believe to be objectively tangible and clear, to see things that can be reliably correlated with observable reality.

But what about the things we believe are objective and true but *can't* be proven? These are *subjective,* which creates a bit of a conundrum. Subjectivity is undependable and unpredictable. Still, I believe that welcoming subjectivity into our lives opens the doors to seeing the unseen.

Subjectivity offers us a way of seeing from different angles and myriad perspectives. It fuels an examination of a nascent point of view and helps bring clarity to the amorphous, fuzzy concepts and questions we grapple with. It is only when we experiment and play with these enigmatic thoughts that we can begin to create space to see and understand and welcome the unknown.

The poet Rainer Maria Rilke says: "Have patience with everything unresolved in your heart, and try to love the questions themselves, as if they were locked rooms or books written in a very foreign language. Don't search for the answers, which could not be given to you now, because you would not be able to live them . . . Live the questions now. Perhaps then, someday far in the future, you will gradually, without even noticing it, live your way into the answer."

I can think of no better call to action or guide for seeing and knowing and surrendering to unknown unknowns.

THIS IS YOUR PROMPT:

Write about yourself as if you are writing about a stranger. Describe whom you see, both the tangibles and intangibles. Include as many details as you can. Be kind and generous. What is this stranger like? What do they enjoy? What are their strengths and weaknesses? What makes them laugh and cry? What makes them happiest? What are their hopes and dreams? Let your imagination run wild.

When you are finished, if you'd like, tape a copy of your journal entry to your bathroom mirror. Read it often, and look deep into the mirror and try to see yourself.

HIDING IN PLAIN SIGHT

Jill Kearney

I am the daughter of a sculptor who frequented the dump in Province-town, Massachusetts. My father's career was made possible by the things he discovered buried under heaps of rotting bananas and broken beach umbrellas. I accompanied him on these forays, and I loved it there. I was a beachcomber and constructed museums on the sand flats at low tide out of broken shells, shoe leather, and the most lovely thing of all: fragments of eighteenth-century Irish clay pipes that still washed in with the tide.

Treasure hunting is a creative and hopeful act, a commitment to finding beauty in what is ordinary, discarded, or hiding in plain sight. And for me, the finding is only the beginning. After that comes the process of inventing something out of what I have found. These objects speak to me while I'm driving, or in the shower, and tell me what is next. It isn't the thing itself that matters, but the meaning I coax out of it, or where it leads me, or the new use I find.

This act of finding the extraordinary in the ordinary reminds me of the photographer Sally Mann, who pointed her camera at the thing that was inches from her: the quotidian life of parenting, stripped of its romance but bursting with mystery, sadness, strangeness, impermanence, and beauty. How many photographers before her failed to notice what was right under their noses? She was a close observer of the minute details of her own lived experience, which is, in essence, what art and treasure are made of.

THIS IS YOUR PROMPT:

Reflect on an experience of finding something of great value that was hiding in plain sight. How did it speak to you? What use did you find for it? What meaning does it hold?

CLOSED-EYE GIRAFFE

Marie McGrory

Back in 2012, I was catching up with my good friend Sofia at a coffee shop. I had my notebook with me, as all good journalists do, and at one point we started doodling together using a closed-eye drawing technique I'd learned in high school called blind contour. We warmed up with the easy objects—first she drew a boat, then I drew a water bottle—before we upped the ante. "All right," I said, "now draw a giraffe." And to my delight, she proceeded to draw the most incredible giraffe—with her eyes closed!

I was so impressed that I started pulling out my notebook and showing Sofia's giraffe to friends and colleagues. Everyone who saw it was also impressed and wanted to try their own. The closed-eye giraffe brought so many smiles that I never stopped. I asked strangers on the train and baristas at coffee shops. Dozens of notebooks later, I finally made an Instagram account to archive them—and so @ClosedEyeGiraffe was born. I've gotten submissions from all over the world, in every medium.

In my eight years of collecting closed-eye giraffes, I've heard many amusing and thoughtful questions about these creatures as people try to remember details to add to their drawings. What are those horns on their head called? What shape are their spots? Do they make noises? They have tails . . . right? It's an activity that is so easy and accessible, that brings so much joy.

Now it's your turn to try.

THIS IS YOUR PROMPT:

Close your eyes and draw a giraffe. Your drawing can be of the giraffe's bust or its full body. It can be in a setting or alone on the page. If you're feeling bold, you can attempt a tower of giraffes.

When you finish, open your eyes and write about your giraffe. What questions and ideas came up? How does your drawing compare to the image you had in your head? What did this exercise reveal—maybe something about your creative practice? Or something about control—and what it's like to cede it? About trust?

DANDELIONS

Azita Ardakani

By the time I was sixteen, I had moved over fifteen times. It was such a blur that I just lost count. Some of the moves were dramatic, like from war-torn Iran to Canada. Others were more easeful, just three blocks away. Every time I moved, I had to rearrange my inner furniture to make sense of my new surroundings. I put grief further in the back corner, then eventually moved it up to the attic. I plastered the walls with a thin facade of courage and hope for everyone to see.

But one day, stepping off the bus, I realized it was the wrong stop. I had forgotten where I lived; I didn't know how to make my way home. Immediately I fell to the hot sidewalk and began to weep. I was placeless, entirely unoriented, wondering if the concrete could hold my weight, or if I'd descend into some abyss.

Right then, my eye caught a dandelion cluster. Impossibly yellow petals contrasting their proclamation of life against the sky's blue. The promise of transformation right next to it—another dandelion, this one a feathery white orb of seeds. They, too, were barely hanging on. They, too, were a whisper away from a journey into the total unknown.

Maybe it was my desperation, maybe it was Mother Nature's spirit herself, but I felt their wisdom, as certain and rooted as an elder. Against all odds, they'd found a place to grow. Their stems upright, their seeds designed for easeful dispersal, a kind of trust in the movement of life. As if hearing the question I didn't even know I was asking, a gust of wind arrived, and with it the tiny radiating discs with their impossibly thin threads parachuted away, swaying, dancing, out of sight. I stood upright, like the stem below, I lifted my head, and I was home.

Years later, I was looking at my handful of childhood photos, and I noticed one from when I was a baby and one from when I was about six. In both, I clutched a single dandelion. It turned out they were drifting with me all along.

THIS IS YOUR PROMPT:

Write about a time when you had a pressing question and nature provided the answer.

DUTCH TULIPS & A DODO BIRD

John Green

I've never actually seen much of what I've seen. I've never seen row upon row of flowering Dutch tulips—but I've seen them on Instagram. I've never seen the surface of Mars—but I've seen it through high-definition photographs. I've never seen the long-extinct dodo bird—but I've seen it through illustrations. I've been fascinated by what we'll never see since the artist David Brooks told me the story of William Beebe, an eccentric scientist of the early twentieth century who hired artists—including Ruth Rose, who went on to write the screenplay for the 1933 movie *King Kong*—to illustrate the wonders of the natural world. Beebe often descended into the deep ocean in a small submarine that was connected to a boat on the ocean's surface. From thousands of feet below the sea, Beebe described the fantastic creatures he saw to the artists via a wired telephone. The artists then drew the creatures—animals that they would never see—based on Beebe's descriptions. The resulting illustrations include strange and lovely squids and viperfish.

A friend of mine who died a few years ago once told me that if you look at a tree, really look at it, you do not get tired of looking at it. There is plenty of tree to take in, from the mountainous bark to the fingering leaves to the branches that themselves branch out into yet more branches, and more. And then, my friend noted, there is the tree you can't see— the vast root system below, branches branching out wider than the tree's canopy, a kind of invisible symmetry. You know the root system is there, but you cannot see it. My friend told me: Think of these roots, and think of the tree, overwhelming in its complexity and wonder and persistence. And then consider: There are more trees. There are billions more. Despite our best efforts, there are more trees than people by a very wide margin, and we are utterly and entirely dependent upon them. We live in their shade, breathing their oxygen, and yet while they live, we can never see the vast root structures that hold them aloft.

For almost all of human history, we also could not see the inside of a living body. I often think about this eighteenth-century German doctor, described in Barbara Duden's brilliant book *The Woman Beneath the Skin*. This doctor, Johann Storch, had no way of seeing inside his patients. He could not use X-rays or MRI or CT scans or colonoscopies, of course, but he also couldn't listen to the body through a stethoscope (they weren't invented until 1816) or even glimpse the workings of the throat using a laryngoscope (they weren't invented until the 1850s). And so the inner body was an absolute mystery to him—something he could see illustrated in medical journals but could never see himself in a living patient. But then again, it occurs to me that I've also never seen most of the interior of my own human body. I can tell you approximately what my heart looks like, but I haven't seen it—and frankly hope I never will.

THIS IS YOUR PROMPT:

Think of something you've never seen but nonetheless know something about. Maybe you've read descriptions, or seen pictures, or imagined what it must be like. Write about what you've never seen until you feel like you can, at least in some way, see it.

CHAPTER 5

ON LOVE

When I first entered the kingdom of the sick, I wasn't interested in befriending my fellow denizens. Only twenty-two, with limited understanding of grave illness—or loss—I found the idea of a cancer support group for young adults wholly depressing, and I didn't want to get too comfortable with the identity of the cancer patient. Unsurprisingly, a year into treatment, I was as isolated and lonely as I'd ever been in my life.

Right around this time, the young adult novel *The Fault in Our Stars* by John Green exploded in the popular imagination. I devoured it, and I found it so important—for two reasons. First, the narrative didn't follow the same tired illness tropes. The characters were not pity-worthy cancer patients but normal teenagers complaining about their parents, obsessing over crushes, and fretting about everything from the big, existential questions to if and when they'd lose their virginity. There was sorrow, but there was also joy and humor and love. So much love. The second reason it was important to me was seeing the quality of the characters' friendships—how deeply they connected, how they showed up for one another in the hardest moments.

Up until then, I had prioritized quantity over quality when it came to friendship. Attending six schools on three continents before the age of twelve meant that I was skilled at quickly forming friendships, but not necessarily at sustaining them. While moving around, I maintained pen-pal correspondences with my best friend Molly in upstate New York, and my best friend Ranya in Tunisia, and my best friend Eléonore in Switzerland. But without a clear idea of when (or even if) we'd see each other again, and with all the address changes, our letters would peter out. The message I took from it was that relationships have a shelf life.

At college, I was a social butterfly, flitting from group to group, making fast, but not necessarily deep, friends. Many of those friends disappeared when I got sick, and I felt hurt, angry, and betrayed. With time, I came to realize it wasn't some huge failing on their part—of course the people I played beer pong with were not at my bedside when my hair was falling out! To sustain a relationship through that kind of crisis requires stronger bonds. I had to know people deeply and to let them know me deeply, much like the characters in *The Fault in Our Stars*.

If I hadn't read that book, I don't know if I would have ever actively cultivated friendships within the kingdom of the sick. I'm pretty sure I would never have forged a bond with Anjali, whom I met in a hospital waiting room. Anjali was pretty, petite, with tawny skin and a beaked nose like mine. She was wearing a knit ski cap over her bald head and a face mask across hollowed cheeks. Did she know that she scared me when she marched over and fell into the chair next to mine? Though shorter than me, though frail from months of bed rest, she exuded fierceness.

"I know who you are," she said with a trace of an Indian accent. "You write that fucking column." On this particular day she happened to be in a good mood, and what she meant was: *Hello, it's nice to meet you.* I simply wasn't good at reading between her lines yet.

Over time, we traded stories and learned we had many in common— stories of immigration, of being the only kid on the first day of school who didn't speak English, of feeling like a misfit wherever we went. I learned that her parents were dead, and she was estranged from her brother, who'd never returned her call about being her bone marrow donor. I came to understand that was why she wore so much armor. She felt she had to protect herself to survive.

Anjali and I also shared the same diagnosis. We did the same chemotherapy regimens at Mount Sinai Hospital, administered by the same doctors. We both transferred to Memorial Sloan Kettering Cancer Center to undergo bone marrow transplants around the same time. A hundred days post-transplant, we both received our biopsy results. Mine came back clean, no sign of leukemia. Hers showed she had already relapsed, and further treatment was not an option.

By then, I was twenty-four. I had never been a caregiver, much less accompanied someone as they neared the end. But I understood the pain of having people not show up—and here was an opportunity for me to show up. For the next few months, I brought Anjali food, accompanied her to doctors' appointments, and brought her home with me on holidays. Then, when she got too sick and weak to live at home alone, I called an ambulance to take her to Bellevue Hospital's hospice ward.

When the ambulance arrived, Anjali looked at me and howled. She called me a traitor, she said I was a terrible friend, she said she hated me. But I didn't take it personally. I knew how fear and pain can make you angry. I myself had lashed out at loved ones in ways that I didn't know I was capable of before illness. I understood that her rage was not toward me, but toward a world in which she had never fully belonged, a world from which she'd soon be gone.

I rode with her in the back of that ambulance, and for the next week, I held a round-the-clock vigil by her bedside. The day before she died, Melissa and Max, whom I'd also befriended in treatment, and another friend named MJ, who was a cancer survivor (and who may or may not have volunteered as our weed supplier in those pre–medical marijuana days), joined me there. A talented musician, MJ brought a guitar, a shruti box, and a harmonica, and played a few songs, including "Love More" by Sharon Van Etten. We all sang along: "She made me love, she made me love, she made me love more." Anjali was so close to the veil that her hearing was failing. I didn't know if she could actually hear the music, or if she was only seeing us experience it, but she was so happy.

I remember a nurse watching us from the hallway. Later, she told me that in all her years of working in hospice, she had never seen that before—other young people with bald heads and waifish bodies ushering a fellow patient through their final days. I understood why she was taken by the sight. To watch anyone die is scary, and it's even scarier to watch someone die from the same disease that might kill you. No one would have blamed us for avoiding it, but we were all stricken by the fact that Anjali had no family. Her great fear, given that she was an orphan, was that she would die alone, and it seemed unconscionable to us to let that happen.

It remains one of the most harrowingly beautiful and meaningful experiences of my life. I felt like I got to meet Anjali the child in those last days—the Anjali who had not yet been hurt, betrayed, or abandoned by the world. Anjali's life had taught her to expect the worst of others, to assume it was only a matter of time before everyone would disappoint or leave her, but there at the end, it seemed she finally trusted that someone would stay, maybe for the first time in her life. She softened; she became calm. Every time her eyelids fluttered open, she would reach for my hand. She was so skinny, and her big, dark brown eyes seemed even bigger by contrast. Tender, open, unarmored, she seemed— paradoxically—healed. She died on Valentine's Day. The last word she said to me was "love."

I realize that what I have written so far may not conform to your expectations for a chapter called "On Love." But what I want to speak to transcends the happily-ever-after fairy-tale notions of romantic love. What I want to invoke is the radical power of seeing, understanding, and showing up for another human. As Alain de Botton writes in *A Therapeutic Journey*, "The word is so fatefully associated with romance and sentimentality that we overlook its critical role in helping us to keep faith with life at times of overwhelming psychological confusion and sorrow."

By the time I finished treatment, I had learned this lesson. Illness had taught me how much we need one another. How we come into this world needing so much care, how we die needing so much care, how we get that from the people we love and who love us: our family—blood or chosen—our partners, our friends, our communities. But over nearly four years, illness had also taken a toll. I had lost my romantic relationship, my sense of self, and my trust in the future. I had lost friends like Anjali and Melissa, and soon Max, too, would be gone. I was deep in grief, and I felt an almost primal impulse to shut down, to retreat like a wounded animal. I thought, *If I never get close to anyone again, I will never be hurt again.*

Somehow, despite the sorrow and confusion, part of me knew I needed to try to get to the other side of my fear and grief. I was beginning to see that to live within those protective confines was to live a safe life, which is to say a small and diminished life. I didn't want that for myself, so that's why I embarked on my cross-country road trip, seeking out people who could show me how to navigate my grief and uncertainty.

Again and again, they taught me about the necessity of love. In Seattle, I met up with Isaac. His marriage had just fallen apart, and he was bereft but also determined not to armor his heart. "Living with that openness means feeling pain," he said. "The alternative is feeling nothing at all." In California, I met Katherine, who had endured every parent's nightmare—the loss of a child to suicide. Yet rather than letting the grief overwhelm her and shut her down, she had chosen to be guided by love. "That's all you can do in the face of these things," she told me one night. "Love the people around you. Love the life you have. I can't think of a more powerful response to life's sorrows than loving."

Over the next several years, I became a student of love. I actively sought out people who loved beautifully and deeply, whether it was self-love, familial love, romantic love, or platonic love. And in studying people who loved well, I saw that they all had vibrant, tight-knit, supportive communities. I became fascinated by how people form these communities, and how radically transformative they could be, especially when they occurred in unlikely places. Take my friend Quintin Jones, for example. Quin had written after reading an essay of mine to say that my story had "touched a death row inmate heart." For more than two decades, Quin had spent twenty-three hours a day in solitary confinement, yet he had cultivated an international, multigenerational community of more than two dozen pen friends. In letters written in looping cursive, he gave them his attention, his care, his thoughtfulness. They gave him a sense of purpose, a glimpse of the outside world, and a kind of unconditional love that he'd never known.

Another unlikely place was a hospice in a prison called the California Medical Facility, which I wrote about for *The New York Times Magazine*. In this facility, the hospice workers are the inmates themselves. They take on the practical work of caregiving, brushing the patients' teeth, massaging their sore limbs, stripping soiled sheets, and assisting the medical staff. But they also are a stand-in for loved ones, for family. In the final hours of a patient's life, they hold a bedside vigil. They take pride in the fact that no prisoner dies alone. And as it turns out, caregiving transforms them. National recidivism rates show that 25 percent of federal inmates will return to prison within eight years, but for the hospice workers, it's just above 1 percent. More than a story about prison or about hospice, it was a story about community, about how we care for one another, and how that changes us—how it saves us.

That may sound overstated—that something like love can be the difference between life and death. But studies show that social isolation is associated with a greater risk of cardiovascular disease, dementia, stroke, depression, anxiety, and premature death, and that being socially disconnected can have the same impact as smoking fifteen cigarettes a day. As far back as 2017, the U.S. Surgeon General, Vivek Murthy, began calling attention to loneliness as a public health concern, arguing that we can live healthier, more fulfilled lives by strengthening our relationships. "Answer that phone call from a friend," he wrote in a 2023 report. "Make time to share a meal. Listen without the distraction of your phone. Perform an act of service."

It's interesting to note that each of Dr. Murthy's proposed actions is, at its core, an act of generosity: Be fully present, listen, give of yourself to another human. It lines up with my experience, and also the technologist Andrew Zolli's research on resilience and community. Zolli writes that psychologically hardy people have strong communities, and he gives two main rules for building them: The first is that you build community before you need it. The second is that you start with an act of generosity.

Of course, this can't be done with an overtly transactional mentality. Giving to others just to make them obligated to you is something they can sense—and it feels terrible. Instead, what I'm talking about is connecting with another human as an end in itself. It's knowing someone simply to know them. It's love for the sake of love.

In the pages that follow, you'll find ten essays and prompts on different types of love—like self-love, universal love, and love as service. May they help you find new depths of love, and new heights, too.

LETTERS FROM LOVE

Elizabeth Gilbert

In 1990, the meditation teacher and author Sharon Salzberg met the Dalai Lama for the first time—in a gathering that included many other prominent philosophers, psychologists, and spiritual leaders. When Salzberg had the opportunity to ask the Dalai Lama a question, she invited him to shed some wisdom and hope upon the terrible problem of self-hatred. The Dalai Lama did not understand the question. This was not because his English was poor; it was because he literally did not understand the question. He kept having to consult with his interpreter to make sure he had heard her right. He kept asking Salzberg for further clarification: *Who is the person that you hate? Who is the enemy? Who is it that are you in conflict against?* And she kept reiterating: *Myself.* All the other Westerners in the room nodded in agreement—for they, too, struggled against demons of self-hatred.

When the Dalai Lama finally grasped what these Westerners were getting at here (that they were all at war against themselves, and that they all assumed this was a completely normal state of being), he was dismayed. He said, "I thought I had a very good acquaintance with the mind, but now I feel quite ignorant. I find this very, very strange."

Most of us don't find it strange to hate ourselves. For many of us, it's the default setting of our consciousness. We are wracked by shame, tormented by all the ways in which we have failed, and far more likely to bully ourselves than we would ever bully another human being. We are merciless toward ourselves. And we never, never let ourselves off the hook. Worst of all, we think this is normal. It isn't. Just because mercilessness is what we have been taught does not make it right, sane, or normal.

I'm not smart enough to know exactly why Western civilization has created millions of souls who truly believe they are miserable wretches, but I suspect it might have something to do with centuries of religious teachings that specifically instruct us to believe that we're miserable wretches. It might also have something to do with the inherent cruelty of a capitalistic system that reduces everyone's value to what they can produce, what they possess, and how much status they hold. This is fundamentally inhumane, and it makes people sick with shame and lack.

Many of us are sick like this. Many of the most compassionate and accomplished people I know still struggle with the belief that they are fundamentally bad and wrong. They certainly have trouble believing that they are intrinsically worthy of being loved. I have struggled with this, too—to the point that it has become my life's work to dismantle the lie.

My best tool against my distorted habit of self-hatred is to write my-self daily letters from love. I have done this for nearly twenty-five years. This practice has carried me through a quarter of a century of challenges—through two marriages and two divorces, through losing the love of my life to cancer, to facing my own addictions and shortcomings. I have certainly had plenty of opportunities to pick up burdens of despair and shame. Through it all, I have managed to find (if only I listen openly and carefully enough) a compassionate voice within that I can tap into when I need to hear words of love, compassion, and reassurance.

I believe there is a voice of love that is constantly available to all of us—and that it dwells within. I believe that love is our default setting. I believe that simple affection and a stance of unguarded self-friendliness is the natural state of a human being toward herself: Why would it be otherwise? We are the one person we will spend our entire lives with! Why would we be wired to hate the one we are always with, the one we are? It doesn't even make sense, as the Dalai Lama pointed out.

I invite you today to come back to your true nature of self-friendliness by writing yourself a letter from love. This is not fancy writing, so don't overthink it. Just write what you have always wished that somebody else would say to you. Give yourself reassurance, forgiveness, affection. You already know how to do this, because you have spoken to other people with loving kindness in your life: It is no different when addressing the self. Write the words that you would say to a beloved friend who was having a tough time—or even a stranger. Write the words that you have offered to other people you loved who were suffering. Why would you not be entitled to the same grace and kindness? Are you different from everyone else? Are we all not equally in need of mercy and gentleness? We all want to practice universal human compassion, right? But universal human compassion that does not include you is not, by definition, universal. So put down the knife you've been holding to your throat, and pick up a pen.

THIS IS YOUR PROMPT:

Write a letter from love. Begin your letter with this question: "Dear Love, What would you have me know today?"

And then let love itself write a letter to you. Trust that you are worthy of this compassion and affection. And trust—please trust, my friend— that every word of your letter is true.

DARLING, I AM HERE FOR YOU

Elizabeth Lesser

People need people. That's always been true. We also exasperate one another, an evergreen truth. We need one another, but so often we struggle to show up in a meaningful way. That's never more obvious than when someone we love is suffering—whether they have a serious illness, or a headache, or a heartache. When I was my sister Maggie's bone marrow donor, the easy part was having my stem cells harvested (a lovely word they use to describe a not-so-lovely procedure). The harder part was knowing how to help Maggie during some of the most extreme suffering I'd ever witnessed. We've all been there—trying to support the ones we love when they are hurting. And we have all been the ones hurting. And still we flounder in our helping.

I had a front-row seat in the theater of how-not-to-help when I was Maggie's caretaker after the transplant. When well-meaning friends expounded on the healing power of juice fasts, or the amazing clinic in Germany where so-and-so's cousin was cured, or how negative thinking might have caused the cancer, I'd watch Maggie's face twist into a look of weary—and sometimes wrathful—disbelief. Some people were over-helpers, filling the awkward spaces with too much advice, too much talking. I've done that; maybe you have, too. And some friends, in their confusion or fear, didn't help enough. I've done that, too—not make contact because I didn't want to say the wrong thing or intrude on someone's privacy. But avoiding the one who is hurting also goes into the how-not-to-help category.

So how to help our beloveds in their illnesses, their struggles—or merely in these troubled times? My favorite advice comes from Thich Nhat Hanh, the Vietnamese Zen monk, poet, and peace activist who died in 2022. All over the world, thousands of people would gather to listen to Thich Nhat Hanh, perhaps expecting complicated theories that would unlock the secrets of life. But it was his very being that was the teaching. He was the most peaceful person I have ever been around. In an interview, Oprah asked him the best way to help another person, and he said, "The most precious gift you can give to the one you love is your true presence. So my mantra is very simple: *Darling, I am here for you.*"

It turns out that while health articles, a meal chain, and even your bone marrow will go a long way in helping, it is the marrow of our very selves—our unadorned presence—that we need most. When I think back to those dark winter days after Maggie came home from the hospital, what I know she appreciated the most were the hours we spent stretched out on the long window seat in her kitchen—she on one side, me on the other, our feet touching, and the silence, the deep healing silence. And me repeating just under my breath, *Darling, I am here for you.*

THIS IS YOUR PROMPT:

Write about the gift of presence. About a time when someone was there for you. Or when you were able to be there for someone. Or when you wanted to but just didn't know how, or you tried and it was not well received, or it flopped or backfired.

How did it change you? What did you learn?

BLESSINGS

Mavis Staples

Many times in my life I've come across someone who won't smile, who won't speak to me. I'll get on an elevator and say good morning, and that person won't say anything in return. My sister Yvonne—she's different from me. When people are rude or unfriendly, Yvonne'll tell them, "Whatever is on your mind, don't take it out on me." But I'm wired differently. I keep a smile on my face, and I say to myself, *All right. I'll say a little prayer for you.*

And I'll say a prayer that whatever they're struggling with, they'll get through. That whatever is heavy, whatever is burdening them, they'll find a way to lighten that load. That they'll realize, even in the middle of great struggle, there are things to be thankful for.

This is especially true in hard times. When things are difficult, when troubles seem overwhelming, it's helpful to look back and consider all you've gotten through and how far you've come. It's important to remember your blessings, starting with the fact that you woke up this morning. The sun rose again, and you did, too—and here you are, breathing, above the concrete.

Simply acknowledging that fact as a blessing—that can make you feel better. That's what I'm hoping for when people come to hear me sing. When they leave a concert, I want people to feel better, to feel good—because I feel good. I'm singing for myself, too.

THIS IS YOUR PROMPT:

Write about your blessings. About what it was like to wake up today, about the people you love, about the songs that have lifted your spirits. Write about the wind in the trees, or rebirth in spring, or of freedom. Write about whatever gives you life.

DOING HER VERY BEST

Lena Dunham

I think a lot about Brittany Murphy. I probably think about Brittany Murphy more than you think about Brittany Murphy, probably more than anyone who didn't know Brittany Murphy thinks about Brittany Murphy. Her death at age thirty-two in 2009, from pneumonia, anemia, and a cocktail of prescription and over-the-counter drugs, hit me harder than the deaths of rock legends or state leaders or even certain relatives. I followed the details obsessively, trying to piece together a story that made sense and didn't fully upend the image of Brittany Murphy I had cherished and mourned during her lifetime.

It started with *Clueless*. That film was a turning point for me (not alone here), and I decided, quickly and with soul-affirming clarity, that I was a Tai. Her awkward heaving bosom, her slight Jersey accent obscuring her sharp intelligence, her bumbling cheer in the face of the sleekest girls of Beverly Hills—this was the best version of teenage-hood I could hope for, and anyway, she had all the killer lines ("You're a virgin who can't drive").

Then there was Daisy, the emotionally stunted rotisserie chicken lover in *Girl, Interrupted,* pulsing with fragile rage. Angelina may have won the Oscar, but Brittany made me realize we were all just a step from breakdown. She opened me up to the concept of living without judgment because nobody is immune from paralyzing pain.

And then, just like that, she transformed, dropping an alarming amount of weight and blonding herself beyond recognition. There was an odd sense of betrayal—I was a chubby high school senior, a Tai—and I watched alone in my bedroom as she and her brand-new boyfriend,

Ashton Kutcher, hosted the MTV New Year's Eve show. Interviews of the two showed her joyfully giggling as he fielded serious questions about their upcoming film, *Just Married,* with "Cuz she's so freakin' hot." He was mostly interrupting her. She was mostly loving it.

I can imagine now what that must have felt like—the former chubby girl and the cartoon boyfriend hottie, the traces of her former self replaced with jagged edges and puffed lips and the knowledge that she was desired by someone who was desired by everyone. When their relationship ended, I crafted a narrative to try and understand: He was just a buffoon and she was too emotional, too in tune, too much for someone with his limited ability to understand the essential frailty of the human state. There were more romances, both rumored (Eminem, who I'd hazard to guess is a complex guy to date) and confirmed (two broken engagements with behind-the-scenes guys). She would hurt but she'd be better for it, just like every woman who has ever seen a man shrink away in horror upon finally witnessing their totality.

At this point, her career careened between thrillers where her delicacy and shaky beauty were on display and rom-coms where she operated someplace between Lucille Ball and Nicollette Sheridan. Having two modes, diametrically opposed and feeding each other, is not unfamiliar to me: the broken girl and the adorably clumsy one, the crazy one and the *crazy* one. The schism is a gift and a curse, a skill of illusion that ultimately creates a deep sense of isolation.

In 2007, she married Simon Monjack, a portly Brit who was widely considered to be a con man. He moved into the Hollywood Hills home that she shared with her mother. She continued to appear on red carpets, glassy-eyed and clinging to her husband. Her lips were bigger still. Her films went straight to video.

In December of 2009, she collapsed in her bathroom and died just a few hours later. Simon Monjack and her mother did the talk show circuit, and on *Larry King* he casually called his mother-in-law "baby." They insisted that Brittany took opiates only during "that time of the month" and that she was petrified of other drugs due to a heart murmur. She ate like a pig. She'd been happy. Six months later, Simon Monjack was found dead in their shared bed, also from pneumonia and anemia. The horrifying poetry of it was noted by tabloid outlets, then forgotten.

When I came to Hollywood in 2010 I was as sure of myself as anyone had ever been. I knew how I liked my hair (unbrushed), my jeans (skin-tight), and my men (anyone willing to kiss me). I was a bubbling fountain of ideas and I posed pigeon-toed for whoever asked me. I felt lucky to be chosen, but then, upon realizing the stakes, terrified to fail. A certain terror replaced a long-held curiosity, a lazy joy. I met a guy with a tiny apartment we barely left. I experimented with counting almonds instead of eating regular meals. I ultimately couldn't do it, but the only thing protecting me was the control I had over my work and the love of some very thoughtful people. I could have become stick-like, clutching someone who made big promises. I could have leaned on a lost, daffy persona. My public mistakes have all been played out in the realm of language, slips of the tongue and intellectual fumbles, casual fuckups in a world where keeping your shit in check equals staying alive. But they could just as easily have been Ashtons and Eminems and talent managers who bought me fat diamonds. I could have convinced the doctor I needed more drugs, and more still. I have before.

I wish I could talk to Brittany Murphy. I wish I could tell her I understand—that she wasn't giving up toward the end but rather trying so hard. Maybe she thought eschewing food would give her back her sense of control, wrestle it away from her mother or her husband or the people who had decided who she was and what she could be. Maybe she thought the prescription drugs would quiet her fear and give her some sense of joy, of peace, of possibility. Maybe she thought the cold medicine would get her on her feet again, back to set, where she belonged, performing like she had since childhood. Maybe, just maybe, it would all coalesce, she'd remember why she came to Hollywood in the first place, and she'd be back in the warm patch of sun that shines on the people doing their very best.

THIS IS YOUR PROMPT:

Write about a public figure you've long been fascinated with from afar. What first drew you to them, and why? How has the fascination evolved? What does it tell you about yourself?

THE SHAPE OF GOODBYE

LaTonya Yvette

My mother was terrible at goodbyes. Her nickname was Waterhead, since she cried at nearly every goodbye, the kind of cry that turned her banana-colored skin red, made a thick, green vein pop from her forehead, and exposed her tendency to blubber in a heartfelt and laughable way. She had to say more goodbyes than I could count, because of a litany of complex histories. I, too, am terrible at goodbyes. If I do better than my mother, it's because she faced and bore the unimaginable, making the way a little easier for me.

For my friends and family who know me well, I don't speak words when I say goodbye, I look at them and my eyes say, *Okay, I am going to run and make this the least kind of painful.* Goodbyes, I suppose, get easier within generations, because those who came before me cleared the path one by one. Lately, I have been thinking about them within the context of our lives, and the interrelation between our traumas, the people and things we must say farewell to. Like my father, who journeyed from Colón, Panama, to New York City in the 1970s. He immigrated with his mother, right behind his father, and said goodbye to customs, language, and familiarity. I wonder how these, along with all my mother's goodbyes, have been passed down to me.

My dad has been gone for fourteen years this September. Every September, before I realize the time of year, I spend two full weeks feeling foreign, wondering why the bottom of my feet seem to have given out as I trudge along the concrete of New York City, which once upon a time became his adopted sanctuary. Fourteen years of mourning a non-goodbye goodbye and sifting through what remains of him and his choices, somewhere inside of me.

While meditating this morning, I prayed for the long string of goodbyes I've asked my body to absorb: the ones that weren't quick; the ones where words weren't compulsory, or needed more language, more clarity, more feeling; the ones that should have happened but didn't; the ones that did but the heaviness multiplied in their lacking. Yes, fourteen years since my dad died. Seven years since I began therapy. And thirty-seven days since I arrived at the conclusion that all those old goodbyes can sprinkle their dust on the new ones. It circles back to the same damn thing: Goodbyes are difficult.

When Serena Williams announced she was retiring from tennis, she let us down in the easiest way possible: a *Vogue* magazine cover photo of her beautiful figure on a beach, in a sky-blue Balenciaga gown. At first, all you notice is Serena's frame, the setting, and what feels eerily similar to reaching the pearly gates of Heaven. She is freedom and strength personified. As your eye strolls over to the right, you find Olympia, her five-year-old daughter, and her husband, Alexis Ohanian. Suddenly, the goodbye feels different. It's the metamorphosis of a complex goodbye: reluctance and heartbreak, but also joy.

Goodbyes are evolution and transition, Serena said—words that I, too, have said. What remains true for all of us is the importance of how we say goodbye. The words we use to say goodbye. How we take care of others when we do.

Maybe most important, how goodbyes make room for something new.

THIS IS YOUR PROMPT:

Write a goodbye you wish you'd said, or need to say.

LISTENING

Esther Perel

From the very beginning, Western parents tell children to "use your words." The current norm emphasizes direct communication and the ability to clearly articulate one's needs as an essential step to building confidence and self-esteem. We make a point of encouraging one another to be assertive—Speak up! Communicate! Advocate for yourself! Yell it from the mountain tops!—but we don't quite prioritize listening in the same way.

Listening attentively lives at the ebb and flow of the boundary, the together and separate. It's a delicate balance of receiving and reciprocating—taking in information and giving attention and care. In a conversation, you will often find that how you speak shapes the response you will get. It is also true that the way we listen shapes the way the other person will speak.

Consider the old saying: If a tree falls in a forest, and no one is around to hear it, does it make a sound? It's a mindbender that leads us down multiple philosophical paths involving object permanence and the human impulse to center our own experiences. If I don't perceive it, does it cease to exist? Of course not. Unlike most riddles, this one has an easy and obvious resolution. So why has it endured for so long? Why do we continue to pose this question?

It's because this little nature-inspired conundrum isn't about the answer. Inside of this question, there's a poignant commentary about relationships and the reciprocity required to be in one. The tree doesn't just make a sound; it shakes the earth. And how we respond to those vibrations shapes the experience for tree and man. Was it cut down? Was it healthy? Was it dying? Did it crush anything below? Do we need to clear the debris to make way for new growth, or does it need to be left alone? And what does any of this have to do with listening skills in relationships?

No matter the type of relationship—romantic, platonic, familial, or collegial—actively showing that we are listening to the other person validates their experience and their vulnerability. It's not enough to say, "I'm hearing you." Whether we are sharing a story, a grievance, a painful memory, a need, or even a desire, nothing makes us feel more deeply connected than when we are engaged in a healthy balance of thoughtful speaking and hardcore listening. We often focus on the relationship between "I" and "it." Listening emphasizes the relationship between "I" and "thou." One is inanimate. The other is alive and invites two subjectivities into a dialogue.

THIS IS YOUR PROMPT:

Write about the last time you felt someone was truly listening to you. What was it like—emotionally, physically, and energetically—to be heard?

I DWELL IN POSSIBILITY

Rhonda Willers

Many years ago I asked a five-year-old boy the very mundane question, "What's your favorite color?"

I'm an artist, and it's one of my go-to icebreakers with children. It always gets the conversation going, and we explode into all kinds of art talk from there. But this young boy's profoundly wise answer stuck with me. "I love all the colors," he said. "Even the ones I don't know about yet."

The idea of loving unknown possibilities fills me with the biggest joy. It reminds me of when I first met my nephew, just hours after he was born, and then again when I gave birth to my own children. An instantaneous, deep love radiated through me. I remember thinking, *I love you, and I don't even know you.* I often experience this kind of instantaneous excitement, joy, even love while working in my art studio. The moment of creation is so delightful, I find myself laughing in pure bliss.

Emily Dickinson wrote, "I dwell in Possibility." When we think about our futures, what might be our unknown possibilities for joy? I know for certain I will meet more people I instantly love. I will be so enthralled by a future creative idea that I'll need to drop everything and begin immediately. I will see the magic in a foggy morning and love that moment even though it has yet to come into being.

THIS IS YOUR PROMPT:

Consider all the unknown possibilities for joy. What will thrill you? What might you love that you don't even know about yet? What are you certain there is more of?

THE HUMAN MYCELIUM

Fernando Murillo

On November 10, 2020, Gavin Newsom, the governor of California, granted me clemency. Ten days later, I walked out of prison as a forty-one-year-old man after entering on a life sentence as a sixteen-year-old child. In those twenty-four years of incarceration, I really didn't get to see trees up close.

Since my release, I have been enjoying hikes, enjoying my time with trees. California has some big, beautiful ones—redwoods, eucalyptus, oak, just to name a few. I tend to stare at them. I am amazed by all the life these beautiful trees support, for bugs, birds, rodents, as well as people, humanity. But what I am truly amazed by is what we cannot see: the mycelium, that underground fungal network that sustains and enhances life. Trees do not live and function on their own. They thrive and flourish through that unseen network beneath our feet.

As I stare at trees, I think about how, when I was locked in the concrete bunkers of Pelican Bay, I would close my eyes and reconnect with memories of friends and family. In my mind, I reconnected with humanity to keep myself alive.

Nature is so beautiful. I think of Tilden Park in Berkeley and all of its trees, the way they sound when the wind blows through them. Our natural human disposition is to be social. We need one another. These beautiful trees that I have had the privilege of seeing, touching, smelling, listening to—they're teaching me an invaluable lesson: We are so much more than one individual, functioning person. We are mycelium, a network that creates and sustains life and growth. We are not alone; no, we are very much connected.

Now that I am a free man, I have been paying so much attention to our mother (Earth); she has so much to teach me about my place here, and how I can make a difference. I hope with these shared experiences, we can continue to be that human mycelium, gravitating toward growth, hope, and meaningful relationships.

THIS IS YOUR PROMPT:

What is the unseen network that helps you thrive and flourish? Who makes up your human mycelium?

THE GIFT GIVER

Beth Kephart

My mother believed in birthdays. One cake, two cakes, three—some cakes tall and some cakes square, some cakes with wax paper–covered coins slipped between the layers. She believed in balloons and ribbon curls, and for a while, when her three children were small, she believed in accompanying the big day with something stuffy and homemade, something she'd crafted at who knows what hour on her trusted Singer.

My stuffed Humpty Dumpty sat (legend has it) atop the cake (was I three? was I four?), though there must have been a bit of Saran Wrap or foil between his egg-shaped behind and the frosting, for there, in that one place, are no telltale stains. The stains, the dirt, the years, are everywhere else—watermarks and split seams, a smile that has lost a stretch of lip, a lost ankle ribbon. Today this tattered Humpty takes its vaunted place in an old wooden cart carried forward from my husband's Salvadoran youth. Humpty is going nowhere in his cart.

As the years passed, I tried to equal my mother's gift—to find, in keepsake shops, Humpties intricate and interesting enough to surprise her, I do mean please her. I found, over the course of decades, just four ingeniously crafted Humpties, which I bought and wrapped and gave to her—it never mattered when or in which season. After she passed away, I brought her Humpties home.

My mother has been gone for seventeen years. Photographs don't return her to me as vividly as this minor collection of Humpties—these eggs in various stages of tumult. Lately, missing my mother, working through all the complications that defined our relationship, I've been pondering Humpty, this humble nursery rhyme character who, fallible and shattered, could not be pieced together again. Not by the king's horses. Not by the king's men.

I think of how my mother must have spent hours stitching her Humpty for me. I think of the hours I spent searching for Humpties for her. I think of how everything shatters in the end, but how love's first wish is to make what is broken whole again.

THIS IS YOUR PROMPT:

Write about a gift that you received that in some way defined your relationship with another. Where is that gift now (or where did it go)? What does it tell you about who you have become?

LETTER TO A STRANGER

Jennifer Leventhal

Dear Mother in the Waiting Room at MSK,

I've been thinking about you and your son for over a year. We were sitting on couches facing each other, me with my young adult daughter's balding head propped against my shoulder as she took a few bites of her egg-and-avocado sandwich. You with your teenage son's curly head nesting in your lap as he slept.

You smiled shyly, leaned forward, and whispered, "Where did you find that breakfast? I can't get him to eat anything." Suddenly, I felt validated, like maybe some of the random tidbits I'd learned over the past two excruciating years might actually be helpful to someone else.

"Eggstravaganza," I whispered with a little too much excitement. "It's a breakfast food truck just two blocks away, next to St. Bartholomew's Church on Park Avenue."

"Is it expensive?" you whispered back. I had to check myself before replying. It was an egg sandwich, and I would have paid anything if it brought some nourishment and a few minutes of pleasure to my frail daughter.

"I have an extra in the bag, and I don't want it to go to waste. Please take it."

Your eyes fell to the carpet, but you mumbled, "God bless you, thank you so much," as you reached for my lunch.

I looked away and tried not to listen when a social worker came and sat by your side, but that was impossible. I overheard her ask if you had any trouble getting to the hospital without a car, then suggest the Accessa-Ride program. She said she had made you an appointment with the Finance Assistance Office, who could help families who were uninsured. I stole a glance at your sleeping son, tall and lanky but with the face of a child, and I felt ashamed of all the times I had felt sorry for our family during this unending war against cancer.

It was and continues to be inconceivable to me that you had to face such an insurmountable battle without the resources I took for granted. I wanted to hug you and tell you three things—that you were doing your absolute best for your boy, that you were in the best possible place for his care, and that everything would be okay. But I sat motionless, unable to comfort you. I knew the first two were true, but not the third. None of us sitting in that waiting room—that club no one ever wanted to join—none of us could know if everything would be okay.

THIS IS YOUR PROMPT:

Write a letter to a stranger—someone imaginary, someone you met once, someone you only know from a distance. Tell them any and everything: when you first noticed them and what has happened since, how you'd like your day to start or to end, or what's been on your mind. Or tell them a story about a time when something difficult led you to an unexpected, interesting, maybe even wondrous place. Say whatever you want to say, whatever you think they need to hear.

CHAPTER 6

ON THE BODY

Our culture tells us that the body is a problem to solve. Youthful, thin, and shining is the ideal, and to attain it, we should just take this supplement, wear this waist cincher, or use that miracle face cream. Day after day, year after year, we chase this perfect state of being. The body must be constantly manipulated, kept up, and improved.

Yet at some point, life intrudes, unmasking the illusion we're being sold by the beauty and wellness industrial complexes. My liberation began in late summer of 2011. I was back in my hometown after two months in the hospital, sicker than ever. In anticipation of beginning a clinical trial, my doctors sent me home to rest and recuperate, to gain strength.

Returning to my old life in my hometown was dizzying. I was so physically changed—bald, browless, and lashless, my healthy size-six frame having shrunken to a double zero—that when I walked down the street, people stared. But I desperately wanted to hold on to some core sense of self, to that "normal" young woman I had been only months earlier. So one day, I made a special effort to look nice. Because it was hot and humid that morning, I left my bald head uncovered and put on a sundress, made myself up, and went to my favorite childhood hangout, the public library. I felt good until, as I emerged from a stall in the bathroom, a little girl pointed at me and screamed.

Her mother, who was standing next to her, was mortified, and I was shocked and unsettled, of course. But I didn't blame the little girl. I knew it was an honest reaction—likely the same one that all the adults around me felt, only they had learned it was not appropriate to point and scream. In the hospital, I had seen myself transform, watched as my skin turned translucent and became mottled with bruises and burst blood vessels from low platelet counts. As my hair fell out, I ran my hands obsessively over my scalp and stared at the clumps of lifeless locks between my fingers. I knew how I saw myself: as something monstrous. But the little girl's scream was the first time I realized that everyone else saw it, too.

When I went out after that, I wore a wig, dark and thick and wavy, so much like the hair I'd lost. I wore it when my family and I went to see the New York City Ballet at the Saratoga Performing Arts Center, an outdoor amphitheater at the edge of our sprawling state park. The heat was sweltering that day, and not long after the show started, I began feeling unwell. I tried to take deep breaths, to muscle my way through the nausea, but I soon realized I couldn't. I flew to the bathroom, though not quickly enough to make it into a stall. Instead I vomited into a trash can.

As I did, a group of young women primping in the mirrors started laughing. They clearly thought I had downed one too many wine coolers. I leaned against the wall, my scalp itching, sweat dripping from beneath my wig and down my face and neck, and felt a surge of rage. I wanted to tell them to go fuck right the fuck off. Instead, I ripped the wig from my head, and their sniggering immediately stopped. I never wore that wig again.

Over the next few weeks, my hair began growing back in duckling-soft tufts, and my eyelashes and eyebrows, too. I got stronger, and my doctors scheduled out my bone marrow transplant. Soon, I would lose my hair again. But rather than feeling traumatized by the transformation or trying to hide it from strangers' gazes, I decided to use it as an invitation to try wild hairstyles I never would have dared before. First, I bleached it, though I did it myself—which is a rookie mistake when you have dark hair and don't know what toner is. It came out the brassiest orange you've ever seen, so I went to a salon at the mall, where I had the stylist dye it dark again and shave the sides into a mohawk. Then I went to Magic Moon, the hippie shop in Saratoga that sells crystals and Wiccan spell books and patchouli and parachute pants, and I bought Manic Panic hair dye in a hue called purple haze. I rocked a punk-rock mohawk for the next few weeks.

A few days before I was admitted to the hospital for my transplant, I went to Astor Place Hairstylists, an iconic basement barber shop in the East Village. I planned to get a buzz cut as a preemptive strike against the induction chemo, which would leave me as bald and browless as before. My barber suggested taking it one step further by giving me hair tattoos. With his straight razor, he began carving spirals in the quarter-inch buzz. They looped like vines from my temples to the nape of my neck.

I have never felt more beautiful than I did walking out of that barber shop and, a few days later, into the bone marrow transplant unit. I was not reaching for some past self, trying to look how I did before. Rather than avoiding or hiding my new reality, I accepted it and made it my own.

It's a lesson I'd have to learn again and again. I had always been complimented on my hair and my full eyebrows and lashes. They were such a huge part of my identity, my femininity, my sexuality. When my hair did grow back, it was never quite the same—not as thick or lustrous—and I struggled to accept it, seeing myself as flawed, as less attractive. When our appearance doesn't sync up with the idealized notions, it's easy to default to binaries. As we do with sick and healthy, as with joy and sorrow, we sort our body parts and features and our entire selves into "beautiful" and "ugly."

Yet these categories are not objective truths—in fact, they're not objectively anything, which the poet Lucy Grealy spoke to so eloquently in her memoir, *Autobiography of a Face*. The book recounts her experience with Ewing sarcoma in childhood and the disfiguring effects of treatment that took half her jaw. "The things I went through were so blown out of proportion that I was allowed, in a strange way, to see past them," she said in an interview. She could interrogate societal messages about beauty in ways that wouldn't have been possible had she never gotten sick, had she never ended up feeling so far outside the standard beauty paradigm. It gave her a kind of psychological remove, where she could say, *Wait a minute, I have a reservation about this.* It was an enormous step to gain that distance, which allowed her to notice labels like *beautiful* or *ugly.* "Those are labels," Grealy said. "They're not actual things."

This is not to say that the bodily changes that take place—whether from an illness, an accident, or age—are not difficult to negotiate, especially when they are less superficial, or at least more layered. One of the changes that I struggled with in the aftermath of treatment was chemo-induced infertility and early onset menopause, which my medical team had not warned me about. No one had explained the full impact of cancer treatment on my sexual and reproductive health. I wasn't advised that I might benefit from guidance through this process, even though the hospital had a sexual health clinic. In fact, I learned the clinic existed only *after* I had written about the shock of going through menopause at age twenty-four in my *New York Times* column, when someone who worked at the clinic reached out and said I should stop in.

And so I navigated menopause in a void of information. It was bewildering and difficult, both physically and psychologically. I had all the symptoms, starting with hot flashes. I'd wake in the middle of the night soaked in sweat, tear off the covers, and run to the bathroom to dunk my head under a stream of cold water.

But as Mary Ruefle writes in "Pause," her lyric essay about this change in life, "You hear a lot about hot flashes, but hot flashes are the least of it, totally inconsequential in every way: you get as hot as a steam iron at odd moments—so what? The media would have you believe that hot flashes are the single most significant symptom toward which you should direct your attention and businesses their products, but when I think of menopause I don't think of hot flashes; I am not here to talk about hot flashes."

Instead, Ruefle talks about her cry-a-log, where she marked a tally for each time she cried in April of 1998. A three-day sampling: "Thurs Cxi, Fri Cxi *very bad,* Sat Cx4 *very bad.*" She talks about how menopause makes you want to upend your life—to take up a hopeless cause, to leave your partner, to walk to Canada, to sell your most valued possessions. "A kind of wild forest blood runs in your veins," she writes.

I read this essay when I was about a year out of treatment—right around the time I upended my life with that fifteen-thousand-mile solo cross-country road trip as a brand-new driver. I laughed and felt a flash of recognition, along with intense relief. Ruefle's words helped me understand that the things I had experienced were not personal flaws, but a common, shared experience, which was a crucial step toward making peace with the shifts in my mind and body.

Maybe even more important was talking about those changes with friends. The first time it happened was at a conference for young adults with cancer. I was attending with several of my cancer comrades, and one night in our hotel room, the subject of sex came up. One by one, we shared our experiences—how tender our bodies were, how the chemo and radiation had made sex difficult and even painful, how complicated everything felt since entering treatment.

Until then, I hadn't spoken of this with anyone. I was so isolated, so full of shame. Not only had I lost the things that the world deemed beautiful—my hair, my curves—but my body was diseased and barren. Not only did I feel undesirable, I felt like less of a woman. But talking about it was like sunlight pouring into a dark room, revealing that I was not alone, but surrounded by other humans in similar circumstances. To hear my friend Melissa—whom I thought of as the most beautiful woman in the world, and certainly no less desirable because of what she'd been through—say she felt the same things helped me see that the story I'd been telling myself was a fiction.

Our relationship with our bodies, like so many things, is ever evolving. As time goes on, we are given countless opportunities to deepen the practice of acceptance, to eschew binary thinking of beautiful versus ugly. I faced several such opportunities after my second bone marrow transplant, one being that this time around I ended up with a complication called graft-versus-host disease and had to be put on steroids for many months. Rather than losing forty pounds like I did during my first transplant, I gained seventy, and for a while, I couldn't recognize myself. I avoided mirrors and clothes with zippers. I felt like my body didn't belong to me.

Dissociating from my body is a familiar reflex. It's been a useful survival tool for me at many points, especially when I've been in great physical pain. It allowed me to enjoy time with friends, to travel, to laugh—to escape a corporeal reality that at times felt unbearable. Though my body felt awful, my mind didn't have to. However, dissociation is not a healthy long-term strategy. We often think of our minds and bodies as separate entities—a tempting dualism, but one with consequences. At my sickest, I was angry at my body for taking and not giving. I thought, *You're already occupying so much space.* The wider the divide between my mind and body grew, the more I wanted to cut my losses—to completely ignore my body and its never-ending list of needs. Eating well, exercising, investing in a new wardrobe that fit, would require work, which I didn't have in me. I didn't want to spend more money, more attention, more time. Taking care of my body felt like a waste of my already limited energy. I thought, *I already feel so awful. Why even try?*

Around then I encountered the work of the psychiatrist Phil Stutz, creator of "The Tools," which are simple techniques intended to help bridge the gap between insight and action. One of the tools is nurturing your life force, which is the part of you that can guide you when you're lost. According to Stutz, there are three levels of life force, layered in the shape of a pyramid. The bottom level—meaning the foundation—is your relationship with your physical body. Above that is your relationship with other people. At the highest level is your relationship with yourself.

There were a couple of reasons I found this interesting. The first was that, since getting sick again, my pyramid had been inverted. I had focused on trying to cope emotionally and on my relationships with others, but I had neglected my body entirely. The second was the idea that I didn't need to change my body, but my relationship to it. I realized I needed to care for it—and I mean the essentials here, like getting enough sleep and eating good, nutritious food—not to reach a number on the scale or to look a certain way in the mirror, but for my overall well-being.

So I began seeking out simple ways to feel good, to be reminded of pleasure, as a way of reconciling my body and my mind. I began washing my face each morning and applying an aromatic face oil—not just slapping it on, but really making a ritual of it. Then I combed my chemo fluff and applied lip balm. Caring for my body in a way that went beyond brushing my teeth and taking my meds felt like a small act of love.

These lessons in acceptance and integration were crucial to making peace with the changes in my body. But about a year after my second transplant, I realized that it was possible to take it one step further, and not just accept the changes, but find beauty in them. I had traveled to Mexico City with my husband—he was going to shoot a music video, and I was going for Frida Kahlo, whom I had long admired. As a teenager, I, too, had a unibrow and a shadow on my upper lip, and until seeing the film about her life, I wanted nothing more than to bleach and wax and otherwise erase them into oblivion. But Frida did the opposite and celebrated what could have been seen as "imperfections," from her unibrow and mustache to her physical ailments, the aftermath of a bout with polio in childhood compounded by a horrific bus accident at the age of eighteen.

At Casa Azul, her home turned museum, there's an exhibit dedicated to her clothes—a little side building full of her colorful dresses and traditional Mexican garments, her hospital gowns flecked with paint, her back braces and plaster corsets. There's a tall red lace-up boot; it's for the right foot, which toward the end of Frida's life had to be amputated. Across the toe, there's a piece of green silk embroidered with purple flowers and a yellow dragon. On the laces is tied a little silver bell, so that with each step, her amputated foot sang out as a song. It seemed like such a radical act: that rather than trying to hide her disability, she was calling attention to it, making it an object of art. Here again that lesson: What others might want to hide or obscure, she celebrated. "Everything can have beauty," Kahlo said, "even the worst horror."

A couple of months after my second bone marrow transplant, I was sitting on my back porch. I was as bald and brow- and lashless as I'd ever been. I heard the latch of our new neighbor's door click, and a little girl stepped out—the neighbor's daughter, I assumed. We hadn't yet met, and I wondered what she would think. We made eye contact, and I said, "Hi!" and she replied with the same. As she retreated back into the house, I wondered if my appearance had frightened her. Later, her mother told me unprompted that she had come in and asked, "Who is the very powerful princess next door?"

I couldn't help but compare it to that day a decade earlier at the library. Maybe my neighbor's daughter is just a really cool kid. Maybe it's that she grew up in New York City and sees far weirder things all the time. But I think part of the reason she reacted so differently was in the way that I carried myself. I was relaxed. I was comfortable. I was confident. I had made peace with my bald head, and more than that, had come to love it, even celebrate it.

In the pages that follow, you'll encounter the body in many forms. May these ten essays and prompts help you accept your body as it is. May they reinforce the connection between your body and your mind. And may they lead you to celebrate the corporeal in all its gloriously varied forms.

EMBODIED

Ruthie Lindsey

I walked around disassociated from my body for most of my life. When I was a senior in high school, I was hit by an ambulance going sixty-five miles per hour, and I broke the top two vertebrae in my neck. In the wake of that accident, everything my body was supposed to do was performed by someone or something else. A machine breathed for me. The nurses thinned my blood with little injections in my tummy. I was a robot with skin.

Almost a decade later, I was struck with debilitating pain. I eventually learned that the wire they used to repair my spinal cord injury had broken and pierced my brain stem. I spent the next several years bedridden, dependent on painkillers. I dissociated my mind from my body. My pain—the physical and also mental—was too much, too big. I thought it would swallow me whole.

But as my life unraveled, I realized I needed to learn to come back into my body. I needed to relearn joy, to trade morphine for small moments of beauty—a sunset, a field of wildflowers. It has been the hardest, most beautiful, healing act of self-love. And I know I'm not the only one. Many of us are walking around disassociated because of a variety of traumas. For many of us, our sweet little nervous systems are feeling shot, whether from the compounding effects of physical pain, unattended grief, or the dizzying changes in the world around us. One simple way to soothe ourselves starts with a few deep breaths.

THIS IS YOUR PROMPT:

Take a few deep breaths. Ground yourself in your body. Bring your attention to your sternum and your hands. Your legs and feet. Where do you feel electricity? Do you feel warmth or coolness? How is your heart? If you're experiencing an emotion, where does it show up in the body? What does the sensation feel like? Is there a color, a shape, or a temperature? How big is it?

Enter into your body as much as you can and then write about the experience—what you noticed, what you encountered, what you learned.

CURLING UP INTO A BALL

Alain de Botton

We cause ourselves a lot of pain by pretending to be competent, all-knowing, proficient adults long after we should, ideally, have called for help. We suffer a bitter rejection in love, but tell ourselves and our acquaintances that we never cared. We hear some wounding rumors about us but refuse to stoop to our opponents' level. We find we can't sleep at night and are exhausted and anxious in the day, but continue to insist that stepping aside for a break is only for weaklings.

We all originally came from a very tight ball-like space. For the first nine months of our existence, we were curled up, with our head on our knees, protected from a more dangerous and colder world beyond by the position of our limbs. In our young years, we knew well enough how to recover this ball position when things got tough. If we were mocked in the playground or misunderstood by a snappy parent, it was instinctive to go up to our room and adopt the ball position until matters started to feel more manageable again. Only later, around adolescence, did some of us lose sight of this valuable exercise in regression and thereby begin missing out on a chance for nurture and recovery.

Dominant ideas of what can be expected of a wise, fully mature adult tend to lack realism. Though we may be twenty-eight or forty-seven on the outside, we are inevitably still carrying within us a child for whom a day at work will be untenably exhausting, a child who won't be able to calm down easily after an insult, who will need reassurance after every minor rejection, who will want to cry without quite knowing why, and who will fairly regularly require a chance to be "held" until the sobs have subsided.

It is a sign of the supreme wisdom of small children that they have no shame or compunction about bursting into tears. They have a more accurate and less pride-filled sense of their place in the world than a typical adult: They know that they are only extremely small beings in a hostile and unpredictable realm; that they can't control much of what is happening around them; that their powers of understanding are limited; and that there is a great deal to feel distressed, melancholy, and confused about.

As we age, we learn to avoid being, at all costs, that most apparently repugnant and yet in fact deeply philosophical of creatures: the crybaby. But moments of losing courage belong to a brave life. If we do not allow ourselves frequent occasions to bend, we will be at far greater risk of one day fatefully snapping.

When the impulse to cry strikes, we should be grown up enough to cede to it as we did in our fourth or fifth years. We should repair to a quiet room, put the duvet over our head, and allow despondency to have its way. There is in truth no maturity without an adequate negotiation with the infantile and no such thing as a proper grown-up who does not frequently yearn to be comforted like a toddler.

If we have properly sobbed, at some point in the misery an idea, however minor, will at last enter our mind and make a tentative case for the other side: We'll remember that it would be quite pleasant and possible to have a very hot bath; that someone once stroked our hair kindly; that we have one and a half good friends on the planet and an interesting book still to read and we'll know that the worst of the storm may be ebbing.

THIS IS YOUR PROMPT:

Consider your relationship to crying. Do you indulge, or do you resist it? Find yourself feeling particular emotions around it—like shame or frustration, maybe relief or surrender? Write about any emblematic stories or feelings you have around crying and if you might benefit from a different perspective on a proper sob.

BODY LOVE/BODY HATE

Natasha Yglesias

I don't know a single person who doesn't have a complicated relationship with their body, or who hasn't been taught to dislike certain parts of it. In this way, dissatisfaction with our image and self-criticism are some of our most unifying commonalities. My own complicated self-image is so often my focus that many of my short stories were actually born from moments of frustration, sadness, or longing about my body. It was only once I began facing what made me insecure that I was able to learn more about these insecurities and unearth their roots.

Now when I create characters, I often find myself starting with the body, and I often pull from my own insecurities as inspiration. Does the character have flat feet or a downturned mouth? What are their hands always reaching for? How does gravity affect them? Have traces from their environment made themselves known on their skin or under their nails? Do they constantly pull at their clothes? What is their posture like?

While these moments of bodily consideration haven't exorcised the pain and toxicity from my self-view, they've given me the power to name and explore my discomfort more fully. They've illuminated how my relationship to my body affects the way I move and exist in the world, the way I connect with others, and my expectations for intimacy and acceptance. This learning and unlearning about my body has helped me understand myself and others better, which only enhances my writing and strengthens my character creation.

THIS IS YOUR PROMPT:

Write about discomfort or bitterness you've felt about your body. Don't be afraid to name it, to acknowledge its presence, and to try to discover its roots. Explore how your relationship to your body affects the way you move through the world and how it informs your relationships with others.

A PORTRAIT OF THE ARTIST AS A RIGHT FOOT

Bianca Bosker

A few weeks ago, frustrated by a story in progress that seemed to be stalling out, I forced myself to step away from my desk. I checked the fridge several times (excellent cure for writer's block) and checked Instagram several times (terrible cure for writer's block). I vacuumed. Ultimately, I ended up on my couch with what I discovered to be a terrific companion: my right foot. For maybe half an hour, my foot posed, very patiently, while I drew its portrait. I don't tend to spend a lot of time examining those five toes, but when I did—it was like exploring a new neighborhood in a new city, full of surprises and the thrill of discovery. The veins! The bumps! The mysterious hairs, nubs, and nails! An adventure.

Later, while reviewing notes for a book I'm writing, I came across a quote I'd scribbled in a notebook. It was advice from an artist: "In order to arrive somewhere that feels fresh and new, you have to break down what feels expected." I thought back to my foot, which I've seen every day for decades. But looking isn't the same as examining. And examining isn't the same as conveying. That exercise of translating—in, say, words or images—the essence of what we perceive can deliver us to someplace fresh and new, without ever leaving the couch. I experienced it, and I hope, now, it's your turn.

THIS IS YOUR PROMPT:

Draw a portrait of your right foot (or, if you prefer, the right foot of anything—a chair, a table, a pet) using whatever medium you'd like. After you finish, write a description of the foot as though it was a character you're introducing—its physical attributes, but also its personality and demeanor. Who is it? Where has it been? What does it want? What's it like?

CHAIRS

Lisa Ann Cockrel

I spend a lot of time thinking about chairs. They're such an elegant technology, a genius bit of engineering that gives us the power to levitate, to relax our bodies in midair. A chair doesn't defy gravity so much as mediate its demands—sometimes forcefully via a leather recliner, sometimes coyly via a cantilevered armchair. And sometimes that negotiation breaks down and you end up on your ass on the floor.

As a very fat person, I spend a lot of time thinking about chairs because I never take it for granted that I can sit down. Chairs are rarely made with bodies like mine in mind, and as a result, ending up on the floor is always a live possibility. I've broken chairs at a friend's dining table and at my own backyard birthday party and in a job interview. (I still got the job.) I've squeezed into seats in theaters and classrooms that left me bruised. I dig chairs and I am wary of them at the same time.

Chairs can hold us up or let us down. Likewise, they can bring us together or keep us apart. A chair's design might be the smallest unit of society's structure—in that one piece of furniture we find DNA that helps determine who gets to spend time in what spaces and at what cost. If you can't sit down, you have to keep moving on. If you can't sit down, you're not truly welcome. I think about this every time I sit on a city bench that has awkwardly placed armrests to make it impossible for unhoused folks to stretch out.

It's been years since I've broken a chair, not because I've lost any weight, but because I'm learning how to advocate for a literal seat at the proverbial table. And I hope that I'm getting better at advocating for other people, too. I hope I'm getting better at imagining bodies that are not like mine and stocking my world with all different kinds of chairs. Let's levitate together for a while. What could be better?

THIS IS YOUR PROMPT:

Picture the chairs that you sit in on a regular basis—at home, in public, comfortable or uncomfortable. Now pick one of those chairs and write an ode to it, considering the physical and emotional sensations it evokes. Does the lumbar support ease strain on your lower back? Does the chair remind you of a beloved grandparent? Does it have a great view? Try to make visible the dynamics of sitting you've gotten so used to that they're currently invisible.

TENDER AND STRONG

Nell Diamond

At thirteen years old, my body felt like an enemy.

I sat on the floor of my tub with the bright lights blaring and willed myself to look different. I hated the long, tangled hair, the skin so pale it showed blue veins, the flesh that hung over the waistband of my Miss Sixty jeans. I fought my body with celery and cold sliced turkey. I plucked and brushed and cried when she wouldn't bend. Humanity spilled out of me and I mopped it up hungrily, desperate to fit neatly into the world. The feeling continued throughout my adolescence, into adulthood.

Seventeen years later, I sat in a cold room on the Upper East Side and watched two dark circles appear on an ultrasound screen. Twins. "High risk," said the doctor with the cat eye liner. "This will be difficult." I walked along Seventh Avenue that afternoon and begged my body for forgiveness. I begged her to find the strength to bring me my babies.

For nine months, I multiplied, my cells dancing. My skin stretched to fit two brains, two hearts, twenty fingers and toes. By September, my organs huddled close, like lovers in the winter. I was round like a balloon, like a beach ball, like a planet spinning through time and space.

I watched my body shift and grow like a gardener tending to a rosebush. I fed her bread and butter and sweet, syrupy lemonade and plates of cucumbers dusted with salt. I held her close even when the vomiting felt endless, even when I had to sleep sitting up. Mostly I stayed out of the way and let her get to work. I trusted this sturdy thing with a mind of its own, these mounds of flesh and blood.

Together, we made it to October. On the day I gave birth I felt an otherworldly sense of purpose. I was so certain of my body's ability to power through.

In a room with twenty doctors and nurses, I closed my eyes and curled my spine and pushed with everything in me until I met my babies. Twelve pounds of life sprung into the air. When I held their sticky little bodies on my chest, I felt hot joy like a middle school fever dream. My body was open and raw and ravaged but she kept me breathing, kept me awake to feel the warm breath of my two babies on my neck.

Today I rejoice in the deep purple stretch marks on my hips and thighs, the black wiry hairs, the bones that still feel fragile and soft. My body is a tender thing and she forgave me for not trusting her.

THIS IS YOUR PROMPT:

Think about a time that you experienced a shift in your relationship with your body. What caused this shift? Did it last?

BREATHE OUT

Sarah Ruhl

One summer, I was in Maine with my mother visiting a friend. We were on the front porch eating dinner, talking about a family friend, a beloved Congregational minister who had recently choked on a piece of steak at a restaurant. Though the Heimlich was administered and the steak came out, she died in the hospital two days later.

We moved on to other topics, and I brought out a pistachio cake. My mom took a bite and started coughing uncontrollably. I looked at her, alarmed, then ran into the house and brought her a glass of water. She took a sip, then started wheezing and spitting and grabbed a Kleenex from a pocket in her sweater. My mind raced; should I try the Heimlich maneuver, which I'd never done on an adult before? My mother was coughing and gasping all at the same time. Then, suddenly, she spat out a small blue object; it was a piece of yarn from her sweater, which had pilled and made its way into a Kleenex she'd used to blow her nose. She must have wheezed that little piece of yarn into her throat. We all relaxed, and my mom drank some water.

Relieved, I joked about how you worry all your life that some dreaded disease might kill you, not realizing you were going to be undone by your own sweater. The killer sweater, we all said, laughing. But after the relief of laughter, my mother started coughing again. She stood up, and the coughs turned into terrifying wheezes. She could not speak or catch her breath. My friend said, "She's turning blue." Sure enough, she was the shade of a blueberry. I screamed for a doctor, knowing full well that in rural Maine there would be none running over to save us. Time seemed to stop as my mother's face turned purple and she gasped for air.

I hadn't done a CPR course in thirteen years and I didn't trust myself to do chest compressions. My mother was panicking. All I had at my disposal was my training in meditation, and I tried to find a little sea of calm under the rising tide of panic. "Mom," I said, putting my hand on her back. "Try to focus on your out breath instead of your in breath. If you can just exhale, it will relax your breathing. Just one long breath out." Miraculously, she heard me and started to exhale rather than gasping for an inhale that was hard to find. My mother's wheezing calmed. The purple began to drain from her face. She was taking in oxygen. Her face turned pink again.

Over the years, I've picked up various meditation techniques. One is the simple 5-7-5 technique; you inhale counting to five, then exhale counting to seven, and then inhale for five again. Exhaling for two seconds longer than inhaling relaxes your nervous system. When I learned the technique, I thought, *Wow, it's like the haiku in breath form—5-7-5 syllables*. I learned during the pandemic that haiku can be a form of journaling and a practice that can be done daily, with great benefit. I like to teach my students this 5-7-5 meditation technique and then have everyone write haiku immediately after.

THIS IS YOUR PROMPT:

Begin with a short meditation sequence: Close your eyes for a minute and count your breaths—on the inhale five, on the exhale seven. Then look around you and write in haiku form about whatever is most present with you. It could be what happened to you that day, what's going on outside the window, what is right in front of your face, or how your body feels in that moment.

For example:

A blue knit sweater
that almost killed my mother—
breathe out more than in.

MORE THAN SUSTENANCE

Jenny Rosenstrach

I got a text from my husband around three o'clock on a gray Wednesday in October. He was in his office. "Hospice called. I'm coming home now and will leave for Virginia soon after."

Virginia was where he grew up, where his dad had been living, and living with Parkinson's, for the past eight years. We had gotten this call a few times before, but that day, it felt more urgent. I cobbled together a babysitting plan for our two dogs—our kids are in college, so that was taken care of—packed a duffel bag with some jeans and running clothes, then went to the kitchen to figure out some sort of meal for the road.

I write about food—specifically dinner—for a living, which might make it easier to understand why the spice mixture (cinnamon, cumin, smoked paprika, curry) that I had been planning to use on a skillet shrimp for dinner was already mixed and waiting on the counter. I wondered if I should abort that plan and pack some peanut butter sandwiches. It seemed ridiculous to go ahead with this kind of recipe, to worry about spices and flavors, and even eating dinner, given what was happening. But it would only take fifteen minutes, so I started cooking—simmering water for five-minute couscous, sautéing the shrimp in a little butter, tossing in the spices, then dolloping yogurt and packing it all up in to-go containers I'd saved from a deli. I stacked them in a Trader Joe's shopping bag along with two cookies and a single cheap IPA for the passenger (i.e., me).

A few hours later, I found myself spoon-feeding my husband his shrimp dinner, making sure he had a little bit of everything in each bite, while he drove south on I-95. It was dark and starting to drizzle. We were almost in Delaware, the highway crammed with rush-hour traffic and trucks spewing exhaust. But "How Lucky Can One Man Get," by John Prine, was playing, and I weirdly felt a rush of gratitude. It wouldn't be an easy weekend; my father-in-law would die three days later. But in that exact moment, with that song playing, and that undeniably delicious shrimp-and-couscous dinner, I felt privileged to be there, doing my small part to take care of the caretaker.

That night, and countless other times, cooking made me feel useful, in control when things decidedly weren't.

THIS IS YOUR PROMPT:

When has cooking, or food in general, meant more to you than just sustenance?

I FALL IN LOVE

David Sutton

Just now, I've fallen deeply in love with the man in the curtain séparée adjacent to mine in the recovery area here at Cedars-Sinai Hospital. He's recovering from his third brain surgery. When he arrived here in recovery, he was moaning and sighing in pain, and confused by his uncomfortable catheter. Whenever he makes a sound or speaks, I reflexively look in his direction, but I can't see him. Instead, I see the beige curtain with a pattern, butterflies perched on vines.

I'm here today recovering from anesthesia needed to perform a spinal imaging test called a myelogram. My beloved, Mary Beth, and I are spending a bit of extra time in recovery, because my neurosurgeon wants to admit me directly to the hospital for tomorrow's surgery, and we must wait for a bed to be arranged. The facility is overstuffed with compassionate, highly skilled professionals. They have names like Noz, Kat, Jasper, Wouter, Tati, Rachel, and Marcel.

And now I've fallen in love with my neighbor's neurology nurse, whom I hear but never see, and who has just given my neighbor Dilaudid. She has taken away his pain and converted his moaning into singing. He's giving delightfully silly, improv-worthy answers to her neurological-assessment questions and to her questions about his needs. He hums while she asks, then he answers in a singsong voice.

Nurse: Do you want some ice?
Him: Is it Häagen-Dazs?
Nurse: Sure. Häagen-Dazs ice. (**Pause.**) What flavor is it?

Him: Gutter.

Nurse (later): Do you want some more gutter Häagen-Dazs?

Him: Yeah.

Nurse (later): How do you feel?

Him: Well, my head hurts. My hand hurts. And my pecker hurts. **(With delight):** That's all!

I am so deeply grateful. The condition I have is uncommon, to be sure, and it involves my spine and my brain. Beginning in 2007, it dogged me and made things difficult for five awful years while doctors tried to decipher my malady. At last they discovered a cerebrospinal fluid leak and made an effective repair.

Then I was well. An amazing decade of growth and happiness sped by. Whenever somebody would ask me how I was, I would answer "well" every time, conscious as never before of the depth and meaning of wellness, the grace involved in being in a position to say that.

Recently, the condition returned. I have been anxious.

But now we're on top of things. Mine is a simple, cleanly diagnosed condition with a clear path forward. My caregiver this time is the best there is. He has a sweet, dry, Dutch sense of humor and kind blue eyes.

My time frame for treatment is now. The recovery time is weeks, not months or years. My prospects, unlike my neighbor's, are for a full recovery, practically guaranteed.

There will be discomfort, to be sure, but it will be discomfort born like the beating of new wings against the walls of a holy chrysalis. Knowing this, having my love at my side, and imagining the next ten years make the pain much easier to bear.

THIS IS YOUR PROMPT:

Write about something you once took for granted but no longer do.

ODE TO AN OUTCAST PART

Melissa Febos

Sometimes I think about going back. I imagine reversing the film of my personhood, reeling the spool to find the single frame where it all changes. As though there would be one murky celluloid square in which my body was taken away from me. Not just my body, but all the pleasures that came through it. A hand reaching into the frame and snatching it all away—the sting of salt water on my skinned knees, the ache of a palm tendered by oak bark, the pelt of gravel against my calves as my bike flew downhill, the hum of my legs after running all day, my own voice ringing in a cathedral of pine trees, the perfect freedom of caring about only what my body could do and never how it was seen.

There wouldn't be just one frame, of course. It was so many things. The skinny girls splashed all over movie screens. The television set my mother tried to keep out of our house. The slippery issues of *Teen Magazine* that started arriving in our mailbox. That classmate at her pool party silently commenting on my precociously developed figure. The rich girl who pinched my thigh and pointed out how much thicker it was than her own.

I inherited a lot from my mother, though I first recognized my hands. We have long fingers, wide palms, and strong nails. They don't carry our ring sizes at mall kiosks. We shop for gloves in the men's section of department stores. We don't bother with bangle bracelets. In adolescence, it struck me as unfair because my mother was beautiful, with fine features and dizzying cheekbones. No one was ever going to be distracted from her face by her hands. But me? My hands gave me away. I was no petaled thing. I was not a ballerina. I was a third baseman. I was a puller, a pusher, a runner, a climber, a swimmer, a grabber, a sniffer, a taster, a throw-my-head-back laugher. I used my hands—they were marked by things and left marks. They would never let me become the kind of girl I had learned I should be.

The story of how I learned to love my hands is a long one, but suffice to say, it helped that I turned out to be queer. All the years of therapy helped. It helped to remember, as an adult, that my hands had been and still were the conduits of so much joy and connection.

Early in my relationship with my now wife, I once made some casually derogatory comment about the size of my hands and feet. She turned to face me, suddenly serious.

"Do you know what else has big hands and feet?" she asked me.

I shook my head.

"A baby tiger," she said. "They are very strong and nimble. They are excellent swimmers and climbers, in addition to being extremely cute."

It is true that I am loved now for exactly the things I have tried to erase in myself, but this isn't a story about love teaching me to love myself. It's not even about the decision to love myself. Loving myself has never been something I was able to do simply by deciding to. It is something I learned to do through intensive self-reflection. Through writing and making art. Through a close study of what brings me joy and gives my life meaning.

THIS IS YOUR PROMPT:

Write about your relationship to your hands. How have you thought of them, used them, or even abused them over the years? What about now?

CHAPTER 7

ON REBUILDING

There was a period of time only a few years ago that I was feeling rather unmoored. I was on the precipice of a number of big changes. I was trying to finish grad school, trying to finish my first book, and trying to figure out forever plans with my partner, Jon. Would we get married? And where would we live? Would we have kids? And how many rescue pups could I strong-arm him into adopting?

So I began calling my friend Hollye—or my "Mama Duck," a nickname that emerged naturally after she started calling me "Duckling," since I tend to toddle behind her, looking to her for direction and insight. Hollye was a pediatric hospice nurse in the early years of her career, and she has a clarity, a composure, and an all-knowingness that made her well suited to that work. She is unafraid to talk about the hardest things, which makes her the perfect friend to reach for when you're betwixt and between. I would call, and she would usually be out on a walk with her beautiful black Lab, Romeo, and we'd talk about all the variables and possibilities, about what was at stake, what could be lost or gained.

Hollye journals regularly, and she knew that I did, too. And at some point, she told me, "You really should try this journaling prompt I've been using. Write about a day in your dream life—not a holiday or a special occasion, but a typical day." She said it had changed her life.

I was a bit suspicious, I must say. It sounded a little hokey and too good to be true. But between my trust in her and my confusion about how to navigate these crossroads, I went with it. Each morning, I opened my journal and began writing about an ideal day some distance in the future. As I wrote, I found myself describing my would-be home over and over again: an old farmhouse with wide pine plank floors, a wood-stove, and a claw-foot tub. I would add on details, like that it was nestled on an acre of land with woods and walking trails nearby, and conjure its other inhabitants, like my two dogs—my road pup, Oscar, plus another scruffy rescue I had yet to meet—and our daily routine of going for a morning walk through trails in the woods, and how upon returning, I'd hunker down to work in my office: in my mind's eye, a tiny cottage in the backyard, where I could write in peace and quiet.

If you were to journal to Hollye's prompt—or I should say *when,* since it appears in the pages that follow—you might focus on other things, like your job, your friends and family, or what you do with your free time. However, I've been obsessed with the concept of home my whole life; from childhood, I drew pictures of my future home and wrote about it in my journals compulsively. Because my family moved around so much, my dream was to settle in one place and never leave.

But that sense of rootedness proved elusive for me, as I spent the first half of my twenties shuttling between my childhood home, hospital rooms, and borrowed apartments. The roving we did in my younger years had resurfaced in the most dramatic fashion. When I finally emerged from treatment and was in a position to seek out that stability, I struggled. Choosing a place to live, falling in love again, embarking on a career—these were things I desperately wanted, but the prospect of having them and then losing them terrified me. In my mind, relapse loomed large; it felt imminent. Again it was that old fear, *What's the point of setting a foundation, erecting a frame, investing time and attention and effort in building a life, only for the ceiling to cave in again?*

That indecision plagued me for about a decade. I poured myself into work, but I was the opposite of settled. On the counter in my kitchen, I had a blue frosted-glass bowl, and over the years, it had filled to the top with keys to various apartments and storage units, so that I looked like the world's most prolific building super—even though all I ever wanted was to have only one key.

Then came the pandemic, which made me a full-blown itinerant—but also led me home. What happened was this: I left New York City in the very early days of Covid, first for my parents' house, then to a cabin in the woods of Vermont. But in that remote part of the Green Mountains, the internet and cellphone service were practically nonexistent, and as the pandemic stretched on, Jon and I needed a more connected solution. We landed at a vacant artist's residency in the Delaware River Valley in late summer of 2020. We soon found we loved it there—both the residency, which was in a carpenter gothic house overlooking a moody cemetery, and the area, which was green and hilly, alternating between sprawling fields of corn and charming river towns. We walked Oscar along the towpath beside the river, frequented the town's quaint shops and restaurants, and began building community.

And yet, the thought nagged at me: *It's only temporary.*

I began doing Hollye's journaling prompt around that time—and let me tell you, I did it religiously. At the same time, I browsed real estate websites, looking at houses all around the area. Soon after, a friend introduced me to a local realtor, a retired New York City police detective named Barbara who loves dogs and houses as much as I do, and I began going to see some of those listings in person. We toured everything from a sturdy little cottage beside the river that was ultimately deemed a flood risk to a two-room schoolhouse that was listed as the erstwhile abode of a famous artist but also turned out to be a full-on hoarder's hamster nest (hundreds and hundreds of stuffed animals—some plush, others actually taxidermied) to an old converted creamery that was so charming I almost went with it but ultimately couldn't abide the compost toilet. We visited so many different houses that I began to worry that Barbara would think I was wasting her time. When I shared this, she said in her brusque New York accent, "Are you kidding? I love this shit. And I'm not in it for the money."

So we kept at it for months, me sleuthing on real estate sites, Barbara arranging a viewing and showing up in her little Volkswagen Jetta ready to love it or hate it with me. It was equal parts exhilarating and frustrating, as each house started out as promising, then turned out to be too big or too small or too much work or too budget busting.

One day, I came across a listing for a little red farmhouse—it had just gone up that morning. It was within our budget, sat on a grassy one-acre lot, and had a little cottage out back. I was on-site within a couple of hours. The first thing I toured was the cottage, which a previous owner had transformed from a potting shed into his ceramic studio. It was poorly insulated, with no central air or heating system, only a wood-stove, and the ancient glass in the windows was wavy and pocked with bubbles. I thought immediately, *This is it.* Then I toured the main house, and what did I find? Wide plank floors and a claw-foot tub in the bathroom. It also had a huge old hearth in the kitchen and a yard full of towering maples and elms and magnolias. I remember thinking, *This is a happy house.* I made an offer on the spot, and the seller accepted it in a handshake deal.

Immediately I set about scavenging for furniture in local thrift shops and on Facebook marketplace. I found a green velvet sectional for the living room, an antique spindle bed, some pilfered Tunisian rugs from my parents' attic for the bedroom, and some lovingly worn armchairs to nestle around the hearth in the kitchen, where I planned to sit and journal each morning in the predawn hours. Jon and I moved in just before Christmas. One of our first nights in the house, it snowed, and I awoke the next morning to shrieks of laughter. I peered through the bedroom windows onto a big sloping field across the road, and there I saw several kids all bundled up in their parkas, trudging up to the top of the hill with their sleds. A happy house indeed.

The last pieces of my day-in-the-life-of-my-dream vision arrived about a month later, when my brother called to say that his dog, Loulou, was struggling in the city in her newly blind state, and that she needed a new home—somewhere peaceful, somewhere quiet. I was already in love with her, so I didn't think twice. Around that time, my neighbors on the farm across the road came by to welcome us to the neighborhood with chocolates and a kind note. On it was a hand-drawn map of their property. It showed a series of trails in the woods; they invited me to walk the dogs there anytime I wanted.

I've thought about this a lot, and I want to go on the record and say that I don't believe this was a miracle of "manifesting"—at least not in the conjuring-something-out-of-thin-air sense. It was more that the prompt had allowed me to clarify for myself what I really wanted, so that I could recognize it when it arose. When I saw the house, I didn't hesitate. I was sure that it was the perfect place to begin this new phase of life.

Over the next year, I nested. At local antique shops, I found moody old oil paintings to hang above the hearth, and at a nearby nursery, I bought plants to nestle in the corners of the living room. When spring came, I got to work on the garden, trimming topiaries, lighting the footpath with solar-powered lanterns, and planting hydrangeas and boxwoods and beds of peonies and alliums. I felt so happy and settled and good. I was putting down roots—not just the geographical roots of a home, but with Jon, too. We began talking seriously about getting married and future-talking about kids and more dogs and maybe even some chickens. After years of holding back, fearing the ceiling would cave in, I was finally rebuilding my life.

The irony is that the ceiling did cave in just a few months later, and when it did, I didn't think, "Oh God, why did I do all of that?" It was traumatic, of course. When I learned the leukemia had returned, it felt like a sinkhole opened up and swallowed everything. Immediately Jon and I began clearing our schedules and packing and finding people to care for our dogs. I remember with elemental clarity the last time I saw Oscar, whom I left in the care of a dear friend; how he nuzzled his head into my chest, as if he understood what was coming. The last night we were home, we let Loulou sleep in the bed with us, then drove her the next day to the family who had agreed to care for her. I felt I needed to be cheerful and grateful, so that's the mask I wore that day, though I was utterly devastated.

The process of disassembling our lives took less than seventy-two hours. We gave keys to our neighbor Jody, and we left for New York City, where I would spend the next several months in and out of the hospital undergoing treatment. As we pulled out of the driveway, I looked back at our beloved little home and took a mental photo. I didn't know if I'd be back.

But as heartbreaking as it all was, I didn't feel rudderless like I did in my twenties when I first got sick. In fact, it was the opposite. Though my second bone marrow transplant was in many ways harder, healing came easier—because I knew myself and what I needed. Because as much as I had always wanted to be firmly settled, I learned to be at home in the in-between. Because I'd learned to endure the sorrowful times by noting the small daily joys. (Think dappled sunlight; think an afternoon on the couch with a heating pad and a good book; think falling asleep to the sound of my husband playing bluesy Beethoven on the piano.) Because I learned to counter my future fears by planting seeds for future joys—and I mean this quite literally. When I finally made it back out to the farmhouse almost a year later, it was to a garden bursting with flowers that I had asked my friend Sharon to plant, with the hope that I would still be alive to see them.

I've had many instances of forced rebuilding, after everything has been suddenly, dramatically, and completely razed, from the plans I had for my career to my romantic life to the literal regrowth of my bone marrow. But there are also moments when our internal compasses tell us it's time to change course—to leave something behind and build something new. "Destruction is essential to construction," as Glennon Doyle writes in *Untamed*. "If we want to build the new, we must be willing to let the old burn."

Rebuilding is not easy. It's tempting to maintain the status quo, to stay in a state of inertia. Rebuilding can be hard, exhausting, dirty work, not only because we know the grief of loss, but because we carry the imprints of those losses—both our own and, as discoveries in the field of epigenetics tell us, our ancestors', too. We don't start over with a blank slate; our lives are a palimpsest, carrying traces of what came before.

But to me, rebuilding unfolds alongside becoming. It is crucial, if we want to keep evolving and flourishing, to get rid of the things that are no longer serving us and make space for something new to grow. May the ten essays and prompts in the following pages give you the fortitude to do that. May they help you imagine and eventually inhabit even the most daring of dreams.

DAY IN THE LIFE OF MY DREAMS

Hollye Jacobs

A few years ago, I was professionally betwixt and between.

I was ready for a new chapter but found myself rudderless, not knowing which way to turn or how to proceed. I felt wobbly and uncomfortable in the unknowing. Throughout my life, I had always felt a magnetic pull to particular lines of work, from my time at Ralph Lauren to hospice nursing and grief counseling to writing a book about my cancer journey. Finding meaning in work had always come quite naturally, but suddenly the natural pull was gone.

In its absence, my reflex was to dive into bottomless despair. This involved self-criticism on a good day and feelings of worthlessness on a normal day. I had fully subscribed to this culture's edict that in order to be worthy, I had to produce, earn money, accumulate accolades, and jump through all the hoops. Living in this state created a vicious cycle that was wholly exhausting. I realized I had to put a plug in this energy suck.

I did this through an exercise that I call "A Day in the Life of My Dreams." Every morning, I poured myself a cup of coffee and sat down with my journal to write. I turned off my thinking brain and opened the door for my dreams to emerge.

From the time I started writing "A Day in the Life of My Dreams," my perspective brightened and my energy lightened. The stuckness that I felt evaporated. To my utter surprise and delight, I found that I began to have the exact experiences that just so happened to be in my dream life. As George Bernard Shaw wrote, "Imagination is the beginning of creation. You imagine what you desire, you will what you imagine and at last you create what you will."

THIS IS YOUR PROMPT:

Imagine yourself at some point in the future—maybe a year from now, maybe five, maybe ten—living the life of your dreams. This is a normal day, not a holiday or a special day; rather, it is a typical and perfect everyday. What do you see? What do you feel? What do you hear? What do you taste? Who is there with you in your dream day? Describe the day in present tense, from the moment you wake up to the moment that you go to sleep. Creation begins with imagination.

WHAT I LEARNED FROM THE ASTRONAUTS

Oliver Jeffers

There is a phenomenon known as the overview effect, where any human who has been far enough from the surface of our Earth tends to have the same shift in perception. In the first days onboard the International Space Station, astronauts take to pointing out their hometowns and cities, which shifts outward to their countries, then the rough continents that represent "home." Finally, a dawning realization plants itself firmly in their minds: This one object, floating in the cathedral of space, is home.

I grew up in the politically divided and violent city of Belfast, Northern Ireland. I know all too well the destructive patterns of an "us" and "them" mentality—how two opposing communities become insular and defensive, how their own identities become dependent on the existence of an enemy. "I don't know who I am, but I know who I'm not" all too often spills into violence.

Raised as a Northern Irish Catholic, I am somewhere in the middle of that turbulence of fortune. I've experienced much of the grace and advantage that come from being born into the body I inhabit. But I also come from a British colony—indeed the original British colony. For the best part of the twentieth century, Northern Irish Catholics were treated as second-class citizens in their own homeland.

But by the mid-1980s, the origin of all this conflict was lost on me. It had always seemed obvious that it was never a religious war, and by the mid-nineties, it wasn't clear that it had come from a class struggle, either. Partly because I'd been told some of the stories, partly because I hadn't been told others, and partly because I'd compared these stories with others far and wide, it seemed more like political terrorism on two fronts than anything else. Sophisticated gangsterism with good PR.

Years later, when I moved to New York City, I was shocked and hurt that no one on the other side of the Atlantic seemed to know or care about the divided and violent history of where I came from. But when I learned that British and even Southern Irish expatriates in New York were also broadly ignorant about our current status, I reached a new level of frustration. We were killing one another to be part of either a larger Irish or British identity, but outside the few hundred square miles of our province, no one seemed to care. What to take from that disheartening message?

Not much—until I started reading about astronauts.

I was researching for my book *Here We Are,* and I immediately recognized that the way they described looking at the Earth from space was the same as how I'd been talking about Northern Ireland from across the distance of the Atlantic Ocean.

The summer after my son was born, there was growing violence building back in Belfast. As I watched news footage coming from across the ocean and saw that, like when I was growing up, it was kids who were hijacking and burning buses, throwing petrol bombs, rioting with one another and with the police, I wondered what these teenagers truly knew of the eight-hundred-year-old conflict. The reality is they probably didn't know much. They'd simply inherited a story from their parents that was validated by their peers. They'd been told who to hate. This, I told myself, was not the story I was going to tell my son of where he came from. And as an artist, it was perhaps my biggest epiphany—that the most powerful thing we can do as civilized human beings is change the story. We can always, always, change the story.

THIS IS YOUR PROMPT:

Think of an inherited story that needs changing—in your own life, in your family, in your hometown, in your country. How was it told to you? How will you tell it differently?

I PACKED FOR SHIT THAT DAY

Nadia Bolz-Weber

When I answered my phone on a Friday morning in August 2021 and my sister said, "Someone killed Henry"—her son—my mind rejected the words. I knew what they meant individually; I knew what "someone" meant and what "killed" meant and what "Henry" meant. But together, they were indecipherable.

So I said, "No."

Reader, I'm not sure how many times in a row I said no, but it was many, many times. *No* is the only response my mind had to the words *someone* and *killed* and *Henry* all in a row. So my mind grabbed the biggest NO it could find, placed it between her hands, and tried to keep those three impossible words out.

It didn't work.

A couple days later, I was packing to fly to where Henry had been living—my husband and I were going to clean out Henry's apartment for my sister—and I realized that I no longer knew what to put in a suitcase. I am a seasoned traveler, and up until that moment, my mind had been really good at this task. She knew how many shirts to include, what size toothpaste is allowed, and where my toiletry case is. But this time, she failed. I failed. I packed for shit that day.

I guess one way to think of it is that I'd lost my mind. But another way is this: My mind had to take to the skies, it had to go circle the globe, and then dig itself a hole in which to rest in order to ever come back to me.

So, sweet reader, how do you grieve without losing your mind?

You can't.

The poor thing is undergoing a prolonged software update. Because it had understood the world one way—as one in which nephews aren't shot to death—and that world doesn't exist anymore.

It had a way of understanding a world in which your best friend doesn't suddenly betray you, or a world in which other people have cancer but not you, or a world in which your husband still loves you, and that world doesn't exist anymore.

So if your mind doesn't remember to pack underwear, or how to keep showing up for work, or the name of the person who cuts your hair, try and just be gentle with it. It will come back, but it and you will be changed.

No one escapes this, my friend—which sucks. But it's also a comfort, because you're not alone in the madness. And we who have also lost our minds with grief will overpack for you. Just in case.

THIS IS YOUR PROMPT:

Write about being gentle with yourself in grief. Maybe about a time you extended yourself grace. Maybe about a time someone else showed up and helped you pack (literally or figuratively). Maybe about a time you weren't gentle, but how you plan to be next time.

CITIES, SUMMER FORESTS

Ashleigh Bell Pedersen

In the winter of 2020, I was feeling celebratory. I was newly thirty-seven, I was considering moving from my decade-long home of Austin, Texas, to New York City, and I was pitching my novel to agents. Life was brimming with possibility. My New Year's resolution was—in all seriousness—to host more parties. That spring, of course, the pandemic arrived. And one day after Austin went into lockdown, I was diagnosed with breast cancer.

As a cancer patient, I relished each milestone: the halfway point of chemotherapy rounds, the MRI results that showed my tumor was shrinking. The afternoon of my last chemo infusion, friends and I met at a park with champagne. I felt bloated from all the IV fluids but overjoyed to celebrate the end of what I thought would be the hardest part of cancer.

After chemotherapy, however, I embarked on a year of surgery, radiation, and maintenance chemo infusions—and as I navigated the ongoing barrage of medical treatments and appointments, my emotions began to catch up with me. In the worst of chemo, I had rarely admitted (or let myself experience) my fear, sadness, or anger. I insisted on a positive attitude, plodding from milestone to milestone. But in the year that followed, I was knocked sideways by powerful waves of grief. It was the loneliest time of my life, and deeply frustrating. I had survived cancer only to feel further than ever from my old self, whose life had seemed so limitless.

As I approached my fortieth birthday this winter, the milestone invited yet another wave of grief. A third of my thirties, I suddenly realized, was spent first surviving cancer, and then its emotional aftermath. The revelation felt gutting. How could I lose such a precious window of time?

Then, days before my birthday, I discovered a poem.

In "It Is Difficult to Speak of the Night," Jack Gilbert describes his changing relationship to himself as he ages. The last lines read:

> I am forty, and it is different.
> Suddenly in midpassage
> I come into myself. I leaf
> gigantically. An empire yields
> unexpectedly: cities, summer forests,
> satrapies, horses.
> A solitude: an enormity.
> Thank god.

The poem arrived at just the right moment—as though from a friend who knew I could use a gift. I felt such kinship in Gilbert's admission of aloneness and wonder at his discoveries within it. What "cities, summer forests" await me as I navigate midpassage? What seeds are within me, longing to leaf gigantically?

THIS IS YOUR PROMPT:

What cities and summer forests await you? What seeds are longing to leaf gigantically?

TWELVE MINUTES

Linda Sue Park

Stuck sucks.

About ten years ago, I was pretty sure I had this writing thing figured out. I had published more than a dozen books for young readers and had a flourishing career teaching and speaking at writing conferences, workshops, and degree programs.

And then I got stuck.

For months.

By "stuck," I mean fingers completely frozen, motionless, the page as blank as my mind. Week after week, alternating panic and numbness. In desperation, I began reading dozens of accounts of how other creators dealt with writer's block.

One of the cures I stumbled on was the pomodoro method, where you set a timer for twenty-five minutes ("pomodoro" because of the iconic kitchen timer shaped like a tomato) and write without distraction for that duration, then take a short break. It seemed like a perfect solution. It wasn't asking me to write all day, or even for half a day.

Twenty-five minutes. I could do that.

Except, I couldn't.

I don't know how many times I tried. Even if I managed to get started, I could never get through the full twenty-five minutes. But there were hundreds of testimonials from folks—including luminaries like Elizabeth Gilbert—saying how well this method worked for them! Why wasn't it working for me?

I kept trying. Thinking that a shorter time period might help, I set the timer for twenty-two minutes, then twenty. Still no good. Then I started knocking off a minute at a time. Nineteen minutes . . . sixteen minutes . . . fourteen . . .

Finally, at twelve minutes, something strange happened. I typed for twelve minutes without stopping. I was stunned when my timer went off. Was it a fluke? I tried it again. And again. And again . . .

Twelve minutes was some kind of inflection point for me. Time after time, I found that I could write with focus and purpose for twelve minutes. And if things were going well, I would simply hit "restart" on the timer and do another twelve minutes. There were days when I hit that restart button four times in a row—meaning that I wrote for nearly an hour straight. But I could only do this by tricking myself—telling my brain that I was doing just twelve minutes.

In tandem with the twelve-minute sessions—and equally important— is that I give myself permission to write total crap. In fact, I encourage myself to do so, as in, "Let's go: twelve minutes of really terrible writing." The pressure is off.

I've since introduced this method to many people in my workshops. A typical comment: "You really can get something done in that amount of time!" Another, even more heartening: "This has changed my writing life."

Crucially, I can fit a twelve-minute writing session into almost any day. Traveling, in airports and on planes. At work events, between panel sessions. At home, when I'm mired in domestic duties, especially childcare.

For years now, I've written poems, picture books, short stories, and entire novels in twelve-minute sessions. I recently wrote a short essay using this method.

You just read it.

THIS IS YOUR PROMPT:

Set a timer and write for twelve minutes without stopping. The subject can be a work in progress, a story from your childhood, or a stream of consciousness. If things are going well when the timer dings, hit "restart" and write for another twelve minutes. Repeat as desired.

SURVIVAL SKILLS

Quintin Jones

As I sit here in this execution watch cell on Texas death row, with a camera surveilling my every move, I'm thinking about acceptance, and I'm thinking about survival. Years ago, I came to understand and exercise this power: "Change what you can. Accept the rest." Now, that last part doesn't mean that you give up. But by accepting things as they are, you in turn are able to gain a certain amount of control over said situation. You feel me?

I'm also thinking about how I ended up in this position, as well as where I came from and all that I endured and survived in my forty-one years of living here on earth, over half of it incarcerated. Growing up feeling unwelcome, unwanted, and unloved by my own parents. Dealing with mental and physical abuse at the hands of others, as well as at my own. Despite what I grew up feeling and believing about my own strength, I tend to shake my head and pat myself on the back for surviving so much for so long.

THIS IS YOUR PROMPT:

When was the last time you really noticed your inner strength? What were you doing or going through? Was there ever a time you realized you had taken your survival skills for granted?

THE RISK OF BLOSSOMING

Paulina Pinsky

Just because it's familiar doesn't mean it's good for you.

Last December, as I was driving from New York to New Orleans to spend Christmas with my fiancé's family, the man I was supposed to marry began yelling at me about his anti-natalist beliefs—that having children was unethical. I clung to the steering wheel fighting back tears.

I had heard his rant every single day of our seven-month engagement. It was familiar.

But for the first time in our two-and-a-half-year relationship, we were out of weed. I'd been a daily weed smoker for five years, and on day three without it, I was no longer comfortably numbed. And although his rant felt familiar, although I had told myself I was used to his rage, I could no longer convince myself that this was safe.

I was forced to see the truth: I had remained in an emotionally volatile relationship because I had convinced myself that what was familiar was safe.

But I no longer felt safe.

Suddenly I realized: What is familiar is not always safe.

I am now nine months sober. I'm no longer engaged and I'm happily living at home in Pasadena, California. Allowing myself to break with the familiar led to enormous, life-altering, and life-preserving change. I'm thankful that I believed I could try something new, that I deserved more—better. Even though I couldn't see what was ahead, my life has grown beyond my wildest dreams because I chose myself, because I chose change.

Now, I am connected to my intuition and how to listen to it. I no longer numb out, blunt, or destroy my gut instinct. I find daily comfort in my writing and in small nourishing acts like my skincare routine. I no longer allow familiarity to eclipse my judgment. I actively engage with what replenishes and revives me. I no longer stand for my own destruction. I am safe.

Familiarity is a form of comfort, but just because it's familiar does not mean it's not destructive.

I left because I was no longer afraid of discomfort. And I discovered that staying put was more uncomfortable than plunging into the unknown.

THIS IS YOUR PROMPT:

Ask yourself, *What feels uncomfortable to admit?* Is it a relationship gone toxic? A habit that's become unhealthy? An old story you're clinging to that's holding you back?

Then, without self-judgment, calling in compassion, go ahead and admit it.

BONUS PROMPT:

Create a list of small nourishing acts. Assign one for each day of the week.

THIS IS ME

Rebecca Rebouché

I recently went through a breakup. I felt engulfed by it, like a cloud of heartbreak surrounded me, and it was hard to imagine it would ever lift. But I kept telling myself, I'm more than this present experience—something we all have to remind ourselves of at times. When a cloud of uncertainty, fear, and loss hangs around us, it's hard to see forward or back, left or right.

A few years ago I was traveling solo around the Iberian Peninsula and spent three weeks on various islands in the Azores. On Pico, I rented a scooter, packed my little paint set, and spent a day exploring the volcanic landscape, navigating the mountains with a hopeless paper map and no cell signal. I went hours without seeing another human, and it was humbling how many times I got lost, how often I stopped among cows and horses to consult my map.

Then there were the moments where I was so high up in the mountains that the dense cloud cover settled across the ground, engulfing everything. When I entered a cloud, the fluffy white fog was so dense I could only see what was immediately in front of me. I slowed down and puttered through, hoping I wouldn't drive off the road.

I recorded many video diaries that day, all beginning with the words "This is me . . ." This is me lost again. This is me turning around. This is me stopping for a snack. This is me in a cloud. At the time, these diaries seemed silly, but now I cherish them because they remind me of a time I was alone, and lost, but in the middle of an adventure. They remind me that, as disorienting as it is to move through a cloud, emerging from it is thrilling. Suddenly you can see what was there all along but was shrouded. The unknown becomes known—the mountains and the ocean and the lush green fields all revealed in sharp and vivid detail.

THIS IS YOUR PROMPT:

What is the cloud that surrounds you now? Write about a situation or feeling that's so all-encompassing it's hard to see forward or back, left or right.

If you'd like, use the refrain "This is me . . ." to anchor yourself in the present moment and describe the experience in concrete detail.

NOT THERE, BUT HERE

Mariah Z. Leach

On December 30, 2021, the Marshall Fire burned our neighborhood near Boulder, Colorado, completely to the ground. While I was full of gratitude that my family and neighbors were safe, it wasn't easy to look at the ashes of the only home my three children had ever known. To realize that every object we had ever treasured—everyone's first Christmas ornaments, hand-sewn baby quilts, wedding rings, family photos—had all been reduced to nothing was devastating. It was raw. I felt a twist of pain in my belly. I could actually taste it in my throat.

Yet it was also somehow vaguely familiar, this feeling that everything was forever changed. Fifteen years earlier, illness had interrupted the trajectory of my life. Though it began in college, I made it almost all the way through my first year of law school before I got too sick to ignore it, and at the age of twenty-five, I was diagnosed with severe rheumatoid arthritis. I can't tell you how many times someone told me I was "too young" to have arthritis—meanwhile I was spending the second half of my twenties tethered to IV poles, learning how to stab myself with needles, dealing with chemo side effects (albeit at a much lower dosage than for cancer), and searching for a treatment that would help me "get my life back."

My life since the fire is sort of a blur, but flashes of memory are clear. Telling my small kids that absolutely everything was gone. (My seven-year-old cried about his stuffies, my nine-year-old cried about his books, my three-year-old couldn't understand why we never went home.) Desperately searching for nearby temporary housing with a thousand other devastated families. Visiting donation centers and leaning on our community for basic necessities like clothes, shoes, and toothpaste. Evaluating all our options and eventually making the heart-wrenching decision to relocate instead of rebuild.

But when the ashes of our old life had finally settled and we were able to begin anew, it occurred to me that we had weathered this storm and come out the other side more or less whole. Part of that, I realized, was that I had already been practicing resilience in the face of chronic illness for over a decade.

After my own struggles as a new mom with rheumatoid arthritis, I always wanted to write a book about pregnancy and parenting with chronic illness, but I think I was waiting for some sort of conclusion to my own story—as if I would magically hit some special point where my own life experiences would culminate into some resonant ending. But since the fire, I'm beginning to think that maybe the important thing isn't a "conclusion" at all. Maybe what I need to do is write about the journey and the inevitable ups and downs I have faced along the way. Maybe I will never get there; maybe "there" doesn't even exist. But the goal is simply to figure out how to thrive here.

THIS IS YOUR PROMPT:

Write about an unfinished journey—where you started, where you find yourself now, what you expected it to be like when you reached there, and how you can thrive here.

TO LIVE WELL

Hanif Abdurraqib

In the earliest part of the pandemic, I started a pen-pal group. All people who, like me, lived alone and lived alongside depression and/or anxiety. I didn't know the majority of them; it was an exercise in grace, both for myself and for others. I knew there were levels of isolation that seemed untenable, unsurvivable to me, and so they surely must be untenable and unsurvivable to others.

Our first-ever meeting was a Zoom call. Zoom calls had yet to become insufferable; it was still a delight to see people's faces in any capacity, even just lining small digital boxes. The first question I asked everyone was "What would you need in order to live *well* today?" In the throes of my worst depressive episodes, I have to shrink time. I have to survive in hours, sometimes minutes, occasionally seconds. And so, in the spirit of upsetting that, the idea was to tell me what you could get, right now, that would help you survive the whole day.

The answers were delightful and surprisingly simple: a bowl of fruit, a playlist made by someone who loves me, a phone call from a loved one, an animal eager for me to pet it.

It was refreshing. It was a reminder of what was within reach, and what remains in reach for many of us, even when we feel as though a bright feeling is too far away to touch. This isn't a fix-all, of course. The question grounds us in what we need, more than what we would like to see. Framing it this way distills the ask down to a plain sort of urgency, which can make the outcome more attainable.

I started writing about this, shortly after our first meeting, and it even inspired a series of poems. Maybe it will do the same for you.

THIS IS YOUR PROMPT:

What do you need in order to live *well* today? Make sure the answer is something concrete and within reach. What has kept you—or is keeping you—from what you need?

CHAPTER 8

ON EGO

I'm fascinated by stories of people who pick up a creative practice later in life. Many of us feel that, as time passes, as we get older, certain prospects are foreclosed upon. You turned right at the fork in the road, and you can't ever go back—your life must plod along that same path. As Robert Frost wrote, "Way leads on to way." But then I think of someone like Grandma Moses, the American folk artist who loved painting as a child but didn't have the time or means to pursue it. Grandma Moses lived a hard life. She went to work at age twelve, keeping house for wealthy families in upstate New York. Later, she married, gave birth to ten children, and worked the long hours of a farm wife. It wasn't until her late seventies, when her hands were too arthritic to embroider, that she returned to her favorite childhood pastime of painting. Over the next quarter century, until her death at age 101, she made over fifteen hundred works of art. In that time, she became a household name, and her paintings were printed on Hallmark cards and postage stamps and hung in hallowed institutions like the Museum of Modern Art and the Smithsonian.

Grandma Moses is an extraordinary example of a late-in-life artist—of course, not everyone who picks up a paintbrush in their golden years will garner such attention and acclaim. But stories like hers give me hope and a sense of possibility. I love the idea that you can reawaken dormant parts of yourself, parts that maybe you didn't even know were there. It reminds me that it's never too late to alter the course of your becoming.

Take, for instance, my realtor turned beloved friend Barbara, who at the age of seventy signed us up for a beginners' ceramics class. When I asked Barbara why ceramics, she was matter-of-fact: "Something to do." Barbara was accustomed to a busier pace than is typical in our sparsely populated neck of the woods. She lived most of her life in Manhattan— as a child in a tenement in Murray Hill; as an adult, in an apartment in the East Village, not far from where I was born and spent my twenties. Life in the city was buzzy, Barbara says, and it was lived in the streets— in parks, on ferries, in theaters, bars, and discos. So when she retired from her career as a police detective and moved to the countryside with her wife, Donna, she found the lifestyle slow and somewhat isolating.

A second career in real estate, however, gave her a foothold. She learned the area, and over the years, she met people, including a woman who owned a ceramics studio on the town's main street. Barbara hadn't taken an art class since high school. But she'd loved it, and she asked the studio owner if she could arrange a class with her friends—she imagined evenings together playing with clay, drinking wine, and enjoying one another's company. The owner agreed, though she quickly nixed the booze.

Despite that disappointment, in the fall of 2021, Barbara invited seven of us to join her in this eight-week course in hand-built clay. We met on Monday nights and began making pinch pots and bowls. Most of us struggled at first, but Barbara proclaimed herself the worst in the class. Her bowls kept collapsing, and when they did, she would roast herself in the most hilarious way. Finally she declared she was not going to make "another goddamn bowl"—which no one contradicted because no one contradicts Barbara. "My hands don't want to make bowls," Barbara said. "They want to make faces."

Looking back, it was an instinctive choice; Barbara was listening to her intuition. How often we ignore that voice that tells us what we want, what we need, what might bring us peace or comfort or joy. How often it's drowned out by other voices—by the chorus of societal expectations, by naysayers and critics, or by our own belief that we have to follow the rules, to be good, to be perfect.

So Barbara began sculpting balls of clay into human faces. And though our teacher tried to give her pointers and offered links to how-to videos online, Barbara didn't look to others. She taught herself by trial and error. Weeks passed, and her faces grew necks and ears; their eyes opened. And on top of the changes in her clay heads, she noticed a change in how she saw real ones. "From being a cop, I always watched people—mainly their hands, for self-protection," she said. "Now I look at their ears, their foreheads, the distance between their bottom lip and their chin, how far back their ears are, whether their nose is thin or fat.

"It's almost like you can't make a mistake when you're making a face, because there is such variety," she continued. "It doesn't matter what you make, because you're making somebody."

I felt the hair stand up on my arms when Barbara said this. It was thrilling in its sense of possibility—and the idea that you can't actually make a mistake? Pure liberation. That one thought, in one fell swoop, removes every roadblock and hindrance to creation—all the stymieing effects of perfectionism.

I admit that at another point in my life, I may have felt differently. I wouldn't have trusted my own intuition, rather than following the rules. Fettered as I was (and still sometimes am) by perfectionism, I might have thought, "If I'm not good at something, what's the point of even trying?" Rather than feeling a sense of possibility or permission, I may have resisted the idea that in art, there's no such thing as a mistake.

In fact, I likely would've come up with an excuse not to try at all. I'd have said, "That's great for Barbara, but I don't have time to take a ceramics class." And actually, that was my first thought when Barbara asked me. At the time, I was totally wrapped up in the cult of productivity. Each day I tried with all my might to get to the bottom of my to-do list, only to find myself with a longer list of to-dos. It got so that things that weren't even to-dos, like dinner with friends, started to feel like yet another thing to cross off the list. I was overwhelmed and exhausted. (I would soon learn that this was at least in part because my leukemia was back.) It would have been easy to say no and blame it on work deadlines and other responsibilities—on too much to do and not enough energy.

Recently I have been thinking about the stories that keep us from having an experience like Barbara's, stories like "I'm too busy." Like "I'm not going to be any good at that." Like "I'll never see this through, so I shouldn't even start."

Interrogating these stories, what comes to mind is the Buddhist teaching of the three poisons—attachment, aversion, and delusion, which are believed to be the root cause of suffering. By suffering, I don't mean physical or emotional pain, but how we interpret it, how our stories and beliefs can spawn a secondary, often psychological layer of affliction. It's how, rather than experiencing a simple pleasure, we become overly attached to it, then are tormented by desire and craving. It's when we think something will annihilate us—be it pain or unwanted change or abject failure—so we need to avoid it at all costs.

Often, attachment and aversion operate like flip sides of a coin: We cling to the familiar because we are terrified of the unknown. As for the third poison, delusion, it's a case of mistaken reality, of not seeing the world as it actually is. This can manifest in different ways, but it starts with our fear of impermanence. Everything is fleeting, all will pass away, but we want to insist on the opposite—that there is something that won't die. We think, *There has to be something permanent, something deep in our core that never goes away.*

According to the Buddhists, this is the source of ego, not in the sense of outsized self-esteem, but in the sense of being separate and individual, a solitary "me" rather than part of the larger fabric of consciousness and creation. In the same way the ego likes to split "me" from "them," the ego loves to break the world into dualisms and binaries, to label things as desirable or undesirable, perfect or flawed, good or bad—as a success or a failure. And what do those labels inspire? Here again we find ourselves in this loop, tormented by the push and pull of attachment and aversion. We're desperate to succeed, we're terrified to fail.

One simple antidote to this constant grasping and batting away is what the Buddhists call "the open palm." It means not holding too tightly to the things we want, and not pushing too hard against the things we don't want, but accepting whatever comes. It's one of those forever lessons, and it can take a whole lifetime to learn. For me, that figuring-out begins with a low-stakes creative practice—in a sketchbook, on a canvas, in the pages of a journal, or a Monday night ceramics class.

To date, Barbara has made seventy heads, and they're stunning—not because she has achieved some rarefied technical prowess, not because they embody some ideal of proportion or symmetry. It's in their organic energy, I think, and their vibrancy and variety. They share one common feature: They all gaze upward, as if transfixed by a meteor or flying saucer—something astonishing in the sky. Otherwise, they're all different. Some are glazed with rosy cheeks; others have lemon-yellow eyelids or the peachiest lips. Some have skin of ochre, several are a creamy mocha. One man is so ruddy he looks like a wind-worn old fisherman with a flask of whiskey in his boot.

Barbara was approached by a gallery that asked to put them in an art exhibit, but a requirement was selling them, and that was a deal-breaker. She won't sell them, not to friends (though I've begged plenty), not to anyone. "I enjoy looking at them," she said. "They make me feel good."

In *Big Magic*, Elizabeth Gilbert's book on creative living beyond fear, she writes, "Whether we make a profession out of it or not, we all need an activity that is beyond the mundane and that takes us out of our established and limiting roles in society (mother, employee, neighbor, brother, boss, etc.). We all need something that helps us to forget ourselves for a little while—to momentarily forget our age, our gender, our socioeconomic background, our duties, our failures, and all that we have lost and screwed up."

When Barbara took up ceramics, she was going through a hard time. Her elderly mother was facing the vicissitudes of age, and her younger sister was diagnosed with early-onset Alzheimer's. Making clay heads was relaxing and therapeutic—grappling with the clay, using her physical strength, letting her subconscious take over, being surprised by what emerged in the process. A fair number have bright red hair; one woman's locks fly back from her head like flames. "My sister has red hair," Barbara said. "I think, *Am I making my sister over and over?*"

Barbara doesn't know the answer, because no matter what—no matter whom she's thinking about, whatever plan she has—the clay heads seem to have their own will; they become who they will become. For Barbara, that's just fine. They all have a place on the shelf, even the ones she doesn't like as much. She holds them all in an open palm.

This is the value of a creative practice. It helps us forget our small self—our ego—and shed our self-limiting beliefs. It allows us to feel connected to our innate creative impulse, which connects us to all of creation. May the ten essays and prompts in the following pages clarify what you're resisting and why. May they help you elude the ego, slip the grip of attachment and aversion, and learn to hold both the cruel and the beautiful facts of life in an open palm.

DRAWING IN THE MARGINS

Anne Francey

Part of my practice as an artist is organizing community murals, where everyone—from people with no art experience to consummate artists—is invited to contribute a unique image. Over the decades that I've done this, I've become fascinated by how people relate to creativity and some of the patterns I've observed.

Sometimes I organize these murals in schools; and with teachers and staff, about 99 percent of the time they have hardly passed through the door when they declare: "I can't draw. Only stick figures." With principals, it's often worse. They retreat to their offices with the supplies and ask for extra time to make their contributions. One asked if she could make her image by tracing a logo. I'm always amazed at how resistant and even scared people can be. I always think: *Of course you can draw. You were just never shown how, or never encouraged to believe you could.*

With the kids, the delight in the process usually gets them going, but not always. Some start freely but soon lose confidence. After glancing at their neighbors' work, they end up replicating what they see, usually resorting to what's most generic—oh, the contagion of rainbows and smileys! Others will make one small mark, look at it, ask for an eraser, and get very upset before they've even tried. The ones who artistically thrive are those who accept whatever is happening on their small canvases, letting the paint talk to them and guide their imagination toward something they hadn't even planned. They simply trust that they *can*.

When it comes to my studio practice, I constantly experiment with new ways to get into a creative flow and to ward off the stiffness that comes with the fear of failure. I have a whole arsenal of tactics. It might be switching to a new routine. It might be setting simple rules and limitations. It might be observing minuscule events unfolding inside my studio—the sun hitting a painting just so and giving me a solution to a stubborn compositional problem, an insect landing on the windowsill. It might be having no routine.

More often than not, I find that the real stuff happens in the margins—meaning a free-flowing zone where the stakes are lower and I'm somehow able to tap into the essential. That often occurs in the morning, warming up with a small sketch, or at dusk, relaxing into a more playful mode because the workday is behind me. Or when I have such doubts about what I have created that I rework the whole thing in a fit of despair, thinking that there is nothing to lose—that's when I am at my freest!

Varying my approach helps relieve the pressure and muffles the "I can't" voice. Drawing in the margins frees me from my ego and unlocks that flowing creative mode where I just do.

THIS IS YOUR PROMPT:

Using whatever tools you'd like—pen, pencil, crayons, markers, watercolors—begin making marks in the margins of your journal. Let it be intuitive and expressive. Accept whatever is happening; resist the urge to judge. Let the marks spread and guide your imagination toward something you hadn't even planned. An accidental drop of your morning coffee onto the page of your diary could be your starting shape. The petals from a nearby flower, squeezed between your fingers and rubbed into the paper, could be your watercolor. For ten minutes, simply trust that you can.

THE FIRST READER

Sharon Salzberg

Years ago, when working on my book *Faith: Trusting Your Own Deepest Experience,* I had a great lesson in not being ego driven. I struggled writing that book. For one thing, it was about my own faith journey, including retelling the traumas of my childhood—my mother's death when I was just nine, my father's spinning off into mental illness. For another, I received a challenging directive from my editor. At one point, we were discussing obstacles to faith, and she noted that doubt was the opposite of faith. But that's not the case in Buddhism—as I told her, "Doubting, questioning, and insisting on knowing the truth for yourself are considered allies of faith."

"Well, what's the opposite of faith?" she asked.

"Despair," I replied.

"Then you'll have to tell a despair story," she said. I really didn't want to be that vulnerable and revealing. But I knew she was right.

On top of that, I struggled with the need to somehow redeem the word *faith* from its negative associations, like being silenced. But that lofty expectation led me to super-perfectionistic standards. I was afraid of not doing the subject justice, so I got abstract and philosophical. I was afraid of being too simple, so my writing got elaborate and felt phony. I became afraid of my choice of topic (several people had warned me against writing about faith) and kept second-guessing myself. I was stuck.

At one point I was talking to a wonderful writer, Susan Griffin, about my woes. She listened, then advised, "You have to stop thinking of yourself as the person writing this book, and see yourself as the first person who gets to read this book."

She was totally right. Seeing myself as "the author who has to make it completely perfect" led to terrible ego striving. When I thought of myself as the first person who gets to see the work, I was so happy. I stepped out of the way, let the writing flow through me, and felt blessed.

I still honor craft, and learning new skills in expressing myself more clearly, and being as present as I can be as I write. But when I am tempted to create from an ego-driven place, I remember Susan's comment. What in the end is most important is a heart-to-heart connection. If I can step out of the way and see myself as the first person getting to read the work, I find my own heart, and all things become possible.

THIS IS YOUR PROMPT:

Think of a situation where you are stuck or struggling—perhaps a creative endeavor, a family issue, a work predicament. Now shift from an ego-driven stance—where you are the one with all the answers, all the skill, all the responsibility to perfect or fix things—to a humbler stance of being a learner, a vessel, even a beneficiary. Can you describe the difference in how it feels? What does that shift make possible?

WILDERNESS OF CHILDHOOD

Diana Weymar

I grew up in the wilderness of Northern British Columbia in the 1970s. This line alone fills a book in my mind. I start by telling you what I didn't have: indoor plumbing, electricity, neighbors, plastic toys, pavement, a school, television, bedroom walls, visitors, playdates, a Christmas tree, Halloween, shopping trips . . . and the list is long.

And then you ask me how it was. (Sometimes with a concerned tone.) And I tell you that it was the best time of my life because I didn't know otherwise. There was nothing to compare. There was no one to compare myself to or any other sort of framework into which I had to fit myself. I just was. It was just me, my parents, a younger brother, a log cabin, a river, bears, fishing nets, mountains, moose, a wood stove, tools, a dog team, a few trips to the village or reservation, and chickens. (My best friend was a chicken until she was dinner.)

I find myself telling you about everything I did have because I didn't know what I was missing. Not just this. I also knew the sound of the river, the smooth wooden seat of an outhouse, the surface of a dirt path under bare feet, the busy network of ants beneath a stone, and the diamonds in the snow as it sprayed off the sides of a dogsled on a sunny day.

I would try to tell you about isolation, the wilderness, and that it was a time when I was never closer to both an imaginary world and the real world at the same time. Did I even know the difference? Did it matter? And I would end by telling you that I will always be looking for this feeling, this connection, and that the wild parts in me will look for the wild parts in you.

THIS IS YOUR PROMPT:

Where do you find the wilderness within yourself? Is it a new place or an old place? A physical place? A spiritual place? A place you remember or a place you forget?

THE MOUSE SESTINA

Ann Patchett

Creativity is a field so vast and open that sometimes I freeze up. (Deer. Headlights.) What can I write about? Anything? I do not wish for an infinite number of choices. It may sound counterintuitive, but sometimes I find creative freedom by venturing into the tightest spaces. I am by no means a poet, but I like to write poetry that's incredibly formal and restrictive. When I have to focus on counting syllables and cycling through a small number of words, it's almost as if I'm looking in the other direction and great ideas can walk right up to me.

Start with a simple haiku and see how it feels. Take a while to practice. If you like it, try a sonnet. There are lots of different kinds of sonnets to choose from. Try out a few and see what fits. My favorite form is a sestina. It's ridiculously complicated and fun. I can't tell you the number of times my sister and I have sat in a restaurant (back in the old days) writing dueling sestinas on the backs of paper place mats. She loves sudoku and I think it uses the same part of her brain.

I wanted to write something about mice, and so I wrote a sestina from the mouse's perspective. The point of it wasn't the poem for me, it was that I was trying to get into the mouse's head. As weird as it sounds, it works for me.

THIS IS YOUR PROMPT:

Pick out a poetic form and give it a try.

THE TURNS WE TAKE

Lidia Yuknavitch

I confess, I suffer from a bit of a savior complex, which I've been trying to recover from most of my adult life. I may have been influenced by early attempts to teach me about Catholicism, but more likely it was born of learning about Joan of Arc from my older sister. I was nine. She was seventeen. My sister's middle name, which she received when she made her confirmation, is Joan.

Joan of Arc, who heard voices and fought wars, mesmerized me. As a kid I found myself living through the domestic war zone of a house with an abusive father. After my sister left home for college, I waited around for a while in the hopes that some savior would show up, but no savior arrived. My sister left our story and entered her own. My mother drowned herself in alcohol. So I think I decided to swallow the Joan of Arc story whole—to take her into my body, like a communion wafer.

Growing up I felt most alive when I was alone, or when I was helping someone or something else. Baby birds who'd fallen from nests. Spiders who seemed to have lost their way and needed escorting back outside. Pinecones and rocks that needed me to fashion little beds made from small boxes filled with cotton. My friend who lived next door to me whose father left marks on her back. *Come for a sleepover at my house.* I'm not saying I was any good at saving anyone or anything. I just couldn't help myself.

The thing about people with savior complexes is this: In order to believe you can save someone else, you have to think you are somehow stronger than they are, or that you are performing a noble or righteous act, or that you are downright magical. As a kid I definitely believed I was magical, even if I didn't think very highly of myself. Somehow the story that formed in my body was: *Break rules, create fire, burn your way out of your father's house.* I hadn't yet figured out how to not burn myself up.

One of the many experiences that set me on my journey toward a savior complex readjustment happened after I was an adult, when I was on a road crew with ten men I'd never know beyond the six weeks of our shared labor. We'd all been convicted of crimes in the state of California, none of which included much jail time beyond a few days or weeks. This was not my first arrest, nor my last. (It has taken me a very long time to learn the difference between resistance for no good reason, which is just inverted rage, and resistance toward a larger purpose.) We were assigned community service, road crew in particular.

Men working. And me. A strange configuration. Up until that point in my life, men showed up either to fuck me or fuck with me. With these road crew men, I felt embarrassed. What was someone like me, a college professor, doing hanging out with them on the tracks? What funny little demon creatures our own egos are! Just like health problems, money problems, love problems, violence, or death, bad choices and mistakes come for all of us; it doesn't matter who you think you are. No one is ever really above or below anyone else. We're all just learning and forgetting and maybe relearning how to work together.

We were sent one day to move some railroad ties around. My work gloves were enormous. Ridiculous. My ability to lift half of a railroad tie? Equally ridiculous. I wasn't above anyone anywhere. To move a railroad tie, two people pick the thing up, one on each end, hoist it onto their shoulders, walk it to where it needs to go, and then toss it in unison. Except that every once in a while, a stray woman gets hit in both knees by an errant beam when she moves left instead of right to get out of the way, her knees popping completely out of joint, her body dropping to the ground all deadweight.

This could be a story about the violence of men. But it is not that story. Faster than you can say "men working," two men immediately flanked me on the ground like human body braces. Another man, who first muttered "jeez" under his breath, and then "all right then," squatted squarely between my legs and explained what he was about to do: pop my knees back into joint by giving them each a good whack. He said it was going to hurt, but only briefly. He spoke in that calm and direct man-way that a father—not my own father—might speak to a son. I could barely see him or any of them because my eyes had welled up with tears. I kept thinking, *No way am I crying in front of them.* But the tears spilled out.

One, two, three: The man popped my one knee back into joint, then the other, while the other two braced my body and the fourth—a lanky college kid, about the age of the college kids I was teaching at that point in my life—brought me a bottle of water. The two men at my sides hoisted me up, my arms over their shoulders. We all rested underneath a tree for a few minutes, the shade some kind of dumb small grace. After a while my legs felt like legs again, though my knees were swollen. Then we got back to work, although I was made to trim weeds with a dull set of loppers and the gigantic men's work gloves while the men I would never know traded stories in the air around me.

"Benny there got his foot caught in a thresher."

"Don once fell down a grain elevator, damn near suffocated."

"Remember when Ronnie got clipped by a car out on I-5?" They all laughed. "Thought we were gonna have to tourniquet his ass."

I stared at the group of men. None of them were saints or saviors. God only knows what went on in their regular lives. We may wish for heroes to exist who will swoop in and save us, as they do in epic tales and superhero movies. But the more we wish for someone to save us, the more we relinquish the most important human quality we all share— the ability to take turns helping one another. Holding space for those who struggle. Carrying water. Shoveling shit. Giving someone's body back to them. Tending to those who need care. Kissing children good night and sitting with them while they sleep, guarding their dreams.

Then, one of the men, the one who had "saved" me, said, "We take turns fucking up. We take turns getting it right. That's just how it goes, I guess." I don't know if it was wisdom or not, but it shot into my body just like the jolt he gave me when he popped my own knees back into joint. *Yeah,* I thought, *we take turns,* which is a truth I hope we can all learn, or we're done for.

THIS IS YOUR PROMPT:

Write about a moment when you learned an important lesson from someone you least expected—maybe even someone you felt superior to—after which everything changed.

SILENCE

Kimbra

The shows were going great, but some nights I felt empty. I was in total control, yet I still felt like a monkey, stepping onstage and doing the same tricks I knew so well. The fans were amazing, the shows were selling successfully, but I knew what would happen when I stopped singing. The audience would clap. I would smile. The next song would start. I would move. They would look. We would do what we've always done. Audience and Performer. Bow and stand. I was tired.

My show at the Sydney Opera House was fast approaching, and people kept asking me if I was excited. I would, of course, smile and say yes. But deep down, in that inner place of knowing, there was a resounding no. It was at this moment I knew something had to change. Music was my portal into the sacred. I could not let the demands of the music industry rob me of my gift and my service or let burnout rob me of my greatest joy. I lifted my eyes and asked the skies: *What would make me excited to play this show?* An interesting word emerged: silence.

I imagined the Sydney Opera House humming with the final vibrations of a song, the bass melting into the distance and the harrowing, serious arrival of silence. That certain, firm, loving absence that silence holds you in. I imagined listening to the builders who had laid every brick. That thick hum of human presence. That rich waiting. I called my band and told them of my plan. We created drones and sine waves to trigger in between songs and sketched out a new lighting concept that would help create an atmosphere of "holding."

The new show came together just in time. The night arrived; the lights went down. I walked onto the stage brave but prepared to flop. I issued an invitation to the audience: not only to withdraw their phones but also their applause between songs. We played our first, and as we finished, the sounds morphed into a long drone, like a meditation gong resonating through the house. Slowly the sounds disappeared. It was eerie. Now and then, a clap would cut the air and dribble through the blanket of silence. Awkward and clumsy, people would giggle, then settle into the void once more.

We pushed through the initial discomfort of such raw togetherness until that awkwardness subsided and the room became caring. Our curiosities swayed to one another. The artist was not creating the show; she was facilitating its arrival. We settled into our new role as one living organism. We felt held. We were resting together. All sound fell away, and together a sea of two thousand people bathed in an iridescent blue light came to complete stillness for six whole breaths after every song.

The applause at the end of the show was rapturous and glorious and so meaningful. It was cathartic for the audience, and it also fed me in new ways. I felt seen and known. I had shared my inner chaos and longing with these strangers. They had trusted me. We had held hands through the strange terrain, and now the rain was falling in the desert, and we were dancing under it together, celebrating the quenching of our thirst for deeper presence with one another.

THIS IS YOUR PROMPT:

Explore silence. Maybe set a timer for five minutes, or just sit in it for six long breaths. Do you resist it? Do you expand into it? Write about what happens in the waiting.

THE BADDER THE BETTER

Adrienne Raphel

Long before I started deep-diving into cruciverbalism (yup, that's the technical term for crossword obsession), I always sought out constraints in writing: the more rules to follow, the more hurdles to put myself through, the better. As a poet, I love complicated forms, like abecedarians (where the first letter of each line goes down the alphabet). I suffered from a touch of perfectionism, and working inside a structure was comforting—it offered a blueprint for an ideal.

But I remember vividly the first time a rule scared me. In a workshop, a professor told us: "Write a bad poem." My initial reaction was fear. What did that mean? Wasn't I supposed to be writing the best thing I could possibly write? Why would I want to go backward?

What I was really afraid of, though, was the messiness of it—the unwieldiness, the ugliness, the full-scale indulgence of imperfection. Accepting that I was not only going to fail, but that I *had* to fail, was revolutionary for me. I'd learned how to get a gold star, but I also had to learn who I was when there was no A to earn, no rules to tell me what to do, and no one, not even myself, who would look at what I'd made and say, "Good work."

THIS IS YOUR PROMPT:

Write a bad poem. What does a "bad" poem mean to you? Interrogate that. Is it a poem that sounds like a sappy greeting card, starting with "Roses are red," or "How do I love thee?" Maybe "bad" means something about form to you. A poem with too much rhyme in it, so every line is a singsong. Or maybe a bad poem has no form at all, so the lines wander across the page, maybe in your least favorite font (Comic Sans?), the tackiest color (neon purple?), or the worst pen (blunt Sharpie?).

Or maybe "bad" isn't about the shape or the quality of the writing at all, but about the content. A "bad" poem might mean saying the things you shouldn't say, or feeling the things you're not supposed to feel, or copping to your pettiest, dumbest, most embarrassing complaints. Let your "bad" self say the thing you don't let yourself say. If you want to swear, swear. If you want to write the word *NO* over and over for twenty lines straight, then—yes.

The badder the better. It might be so bad it's good.

LOOK DOWN, GET LOW, THINK SMALL

Joanne Proulx

One summer I was in a horrible boating accident that put me in a wheelchair for months. It was over fifteen years ago now and, perhaps oddly, what's stuck with me most from that time is how the slightest drop in elevation changed everything. Two feet down, I lived in a landscape of crotches, eye to eye with first graders, my face a licking post for the tongues of tall dogs.

During the long, unsettling early days of Covid, I had a similar shift in perspective. With cities shut down, theaters shuttered, and friendships cordoned off, I retreated to our family's cabin in the wilds of Ontario, Canada, where I began spending long hours in the forest. As a child I'd collected its stones, mosses, and mushrooms, built lush mini-worlds in shoeboxes, populated them with painted acorn people.

This time I took model-train people into the forest and got back down on my knees. Stuck a ¹⁄₆₄th-scale woman in a yellow dress into a thatch of broom moss and took her picture. Delightful. But soon I left the tiny people behind and let the forest floor tell its own story. Low down, in the knit of yesterday's pine needles, everywhere I looked, staggering beauty, so easy to miss while standing. Stumps like mossy castles, bright orange sea jellies on the bellies of fallen logs, puddles that held the whole sky. I swooned at the mushrooms. Their tininess. The whimsy of their caps. The spring of them in my hand, like rubber spun from silk. How they shot up overnight, untethered from the creep of the human clock. Soon I was in love with thousand-year-old lichens. Took videos of streams and cricks so I could listen to their babble when I left them behind.

I once walked through the world with such certitude, convinced by what lay before me. Now I know reality comes in layers, complex and delicious. Crawling around the forest floor has slowed me down, brought me closer to the earth, and made me somehow braver. How can our world be so scary when there's more beauty in a square foot of forest, more wisdom, than we'd expect in an acre? Humbled, heart opened, desirous, now when I step outside I look down, get low, think small.

THIS IS YOUR PROMPT:

Instructions for living a life:
Pay attention.
Be astonished.
Tell about it.
　　　　　—Mary Oliver

Climb a ladder. Or crawl across the kitchen floor. Drop to your knees in the forest, the garden, the guest room. Tell us what astonishes you about life at a different level.

REWIRING VIRTUE AND VICE

George Saunders

If a writer is good, I've found, almost any prompt will work. Assigning a prompt to that sort of writer is kind of like asking a great musician to "do something with" any three notes of the scale. And I'm not sure if, in my twenty-six years of teaching, I've ever come up with a prompt that would, for sure, produce a good story. I have a sense that, for a story to do its deepest work, it might want to result from a combination of some initial impulse on the part of the writer (a spontaneous self-prompt, if you will), plus that writer's particular mode of execution. It's in that combination of impulse plus execution that the magic happens, I think.

On the other hand . . .

A person's talent is like the ocean rushing in around certain rocks. The energy is inherent; the artist is just looking for something to interact with or even interfere with that talent—to challenge it, shape it, confine it (i.e., some rocks).

Usually, we make these confinements ourselves, by way of some initial "idea." We want to write about this or that; we've had this cool notion; we've witnessed some memorable event. These confine (restrain) us.

But I love the thought that, if we really want to know the true nature of our talent, we could just apply it to . . . anything. Something random, something that comes from outside of ourselves and is therefore untainted with intention.

Because intention, in my experience, can be limiting; intention is very close to "too-rigid idea of who we are, artistically." Because we have an intention, we may, in the process, turn away from sources of power that don't conform with our self-vision—and what a loss that can be.

So, if this sort of overdetermination is the enemy, a good random prompt can be our friend. What gifts do we have that might thrive free of our intention? Are there aspects of ourselves that are being neglected as we too rigidly serve that idea of who, artistically, we are?

So, here's a prompt, designed to disrupt your idea of who you are, and give you, perhaps, a slightly more generous vision of your capabilities.

THIS IS YOUR PROMPT:

To be done, ideally, in four stages:

STAGE ONE:

Think of someone—a type of person or an actual person you know—to whom you sincerely feel an aversion.

Now, write for, say, ten minutes, in that person's voice. Don't worry about writing a story or coming up with an inciting incident or any of that. Just try to find his or her voice. Try to become/channel that person sincerely. That is, don't load the dice against this person. Make the person smart, persuasive, self-aware, charming; the highest version of that person you possibly can. In other words, try to summon up this person from within yourself—find, in yourself, the micro traces of whatever it is that makes this person so repellent to you.

Let's call this "Person One."

(If this seems too daunting/general, pick out your person and then describe them trying to do some small task: choosing a pastry at a coffee shop, watering a plant, watching a cartoon on television, dealing with a car that won't start—give them something minor to do and then watch, and describe, them doing it.)

Once you've written for ten minutes, rewrite what you've done. Tighten things up—make the language better, the jokes funnier—make the thing corner more tightly, if you will.

Then take a break.

STAGE TWO:

Now, imagine someone that Person One is about to threaten or inconvenience or potentially harm.

This is going to be "Person Two."

Write, again for ten minutes, from the point of view of Person Two, before Person One has threatened/inconvenienced/harmed them. (Don't include Person One in this new bit of writing.)

Again: Make the highest version of Person Two that you can. If you can, give Person Two a few flaws or glitches—we don't want Person Two to be a plaster saint or purely a victim.

And now, again, revise what you've come up with.

Then: another break.

STAGE THREE:

Now: Cross the wires. Let Person One and Person Two interact. Invent a specific action Person One takes that will threaten/inconvenience/ harm Person Two. Make this action seem, to Person One, completely reasonable, even virtuous. It doesn't have to be anything world-changing. Maybe it's something as small as: Person One cuts in front of Person Two in line.

The main focus here should be on the action—who's standing where, who says what, and so on. Avoid the philosophical; err on the side of the real and active.

You might have to do some goofing around on the mechanical level— getting them into the same space and all of that. Do this loosely, with a very free hand. If you get stuck, have them both walk into the same café or post office.

Now you've got three bits: a description of Person One, a description of Person Two, and an interaction between them.

It should be fairly easy to rig those bits together into something vaguely narrative. (As an example, I might self-interestedly refer you to a story of mine, "The Falls," which was written pretty much in this way. You'll notice that there is a section of the story where I'm inside the head of the first character, and then I go into the head of the second—and then I, very mechanically, cause their paths to cross.)

STAGE FOUR:

The incident has happened. Now: Write *a reaction* to that incident from inside Person One's head.

Then from inside Person Two's head.

Be as accurate and openhearted as you can. Don't try to drive home any conclusion. Just say to yourself, "OK, I know Person One very well, and more sympathetically than when I first started, since, after all, I *created* Person One—so, what is Person One feeling right now?" Any answer is fine.

Ditto with Person Two. You made them. Where are they now, after this incident at the café or the post office or wherever? No holds barred. Person Two is going to be allowed—you are going to allow Person Two—a full range of human reactions.

—⧟—

Now, is the result of the above a story? Well, sort of. We met Person One, met Person Two, they crossed paths, some sparks flew, and then both Persons got a chance to react.

Could be worse, as a starting place.

On the other hand, possibly not—likely you, and the reader, can too keenly feel the moral-ethical scaffolding I've forced you to put in place.

But this prompt might be useful as, first, an exercise in voice. A chance to get outside of your normal habits, a chance to get better at communicating subtle shades of meaning by way of syntax and rhythm and phrasing. The main job, after all, is to distinguish between your two Persons (and voice is one vital way of doing that).

Second, there's an opportunity here, if you're up for it, to learn about what we might call your Internal Moral Positioning Habit. Did you find yourself siding with Person Two, against Person One? (That would be natural, since I set it up that way.) But (possible *stage five*): What happens if you reverse things? What happens if you go back and reverse things? Let Person Two (just as you've described Person Two in your existing *stage two* text) be the aggressor in *stage three*? To turn the tables on your initial sympathy to Person Two, and on your initial aversion to Person One?

In real life, most "bad people," in my view, don't see themselves as bad and, at least seen from inside their heads, are not easy to dismiss. So this exercise is a chance to rewire the usual way of assigning virtue and vice—to, through specificity (and rewriting!), break down those stolid categories (good/bad; aversion/attraction). In doing this, we learn about the world but, maybe more important, about our own habits of thought.

SIMPLIFY

Barbara Becker

My brother and I were sitting on the floor in our parents' living room, surrounded by piles of objects: the contents of their closets, paintings from the walls, stacks of books, pots and pans. Our task that winter weekend was to clear out the house to get it ready for sale.

It was a job neither of us relished. Both of our parents had died earlier that year, within weeks of each other. That, of course, made this project especially charged. It felt that every object we picked up was imbued with a memory of them, and we struggled to sort them into our neatly labeled boxes . . . "Keep," "Toss," or "Donate." I wasn't so sure I wanted to part with any of it.

Then I reached for my father's dog-eared copy of Henry David Thoreau's *Walden*. I opened right to a page heavy with underlining. There in the center of the page was Thoreau's exhortation to "Simplify, simplify." My father had even put a penciled star in the margin next to those two words. It seemed nothing short of a visitation from these two wise men, Thoreau and my dad: a reminder that by paring down the complexity of life—whether that be the material possessions or the clutter of unnecessary busyness—we will arrive at what's truly essential.

With this repeated word guiding me like a mantra, I turned back to the task with new resolve and a bit more ease. It has never left me since.

THIS IS YOUR PROMPT:

Simplify, simplify! If you were to let go of three things before bedtime tonight, what would they be? What would you gain by letting them go?

CHAPTER 9

ON PURPOSE

I was always a striver. In my younger years, I wore it as a badge of pride—something I now recall with more than a little embarrassment. At age twelve, I told my mom it was my last year to be "precocious," and it was time to "get serious." I threw myself into everything full force, from ballet to the double bass to writing. I filled journals with fictional stories and aspirations for the future, like an entry I made in the seventh grade called "Goals & Predictions." A sampling:

Be first bass in a high-class orchestra

Travel around writing philosophical and political messages on toilet seats under the name D. Seus.

Die and for a split second after, realize what I thought 'was'. . . isn't

Create a "bass suit" by cutting eye and leg holes in my double bass case

So maybe it took me a little while to refine exactly what "getting serious" meant, but certainly I had managed it by the time I got to college. I understood the sacrifices my parents had made that had paved the way for me, especially my dad, whose parents never learned to read or write, who was the only one of their seven children to leave his homeland of

Tunisia. It felt important to honor those sacrifices by making something of myself.

My only problem? I wasn't sure what that something was. I'd heard that old dictum: *Do what you love and you'll never work a day in your life.* Writing was that for me, but it didn't seem practical. From what I could tell, to become a writer, you had to get a job as an editorial assistant at a magazine with a salary far below a livable wage, or worse, an unpaid internship, then bide your time and hone your craft and slowly move up the ranks of the literary world—and that was the best-case scenario. I now understand that many of my classmates who took those positions had some supplemental support, like family money or a subsidized living situation. But back then, I was anxious and confused about how to make it work. It all felt very risky.

Senior year of college, I was still struggling to "find my purpose"—that well-meaning but loaded exhortation of school counselors and life coaches—and my anxiety about the future was reaching a fever pitch. This was in direct contrast to so many of my friends, whom I saw as sure-footed, quickly and confidently making plans. The ones who weren't moving to Manhattan to work at *Cosmo* for something like twenty thousand a year were signing lucrative multiyear contracts at consulting firms and investment banks. Or they were continuing on with graduate school, studying law or medicine or international policy. In my mind, everyone else had picked a path, one that came with a clear map plotting the route between where they were and their ultimate destination. I had nothing like that kind of clarity or certainty.

Graduation did not wait for me to figure it out; it arrived in the spring of 2010, along with thousands of well-wishing relatives and a slate of celebratory events. One was the baccalaureate speech, delivered by Amazon founder Jeff Bezos. In my cap and gown, I took my seat in the stained glass grandeur of the Princeton University Chapel; I listened as Bezos intoned from the pulpit. "Tomorrow, in a very real sense, your life—the life you author from scratch on your own—begins," he said. "How will you use your gifts? What choices will you make? Will inertia be your guide, or will you follow your passions?"

He told us we would be astonished by the discoveries humans would make in the years to come, by the marvels we would invent, from breakthroughs in clean energy to synthesizing life. To hammer home his theme of choice, he posed questions with dramatic alternatives: Would we follow the well-trod path, or would we be original? Selfish or service-oriented? Fragile or strong? He concluded with this: "When you are eighty years old, and in a quiet moment of reflection, narrating for only yourself the most personal version of your life story, the telling that will be most compact and meaningful will be the series of choices you have made. In the end, we are our choices."

Looking back, I'm not surprised that I was feeling near panic about my next step. The message coming from all corners was that real life was imminent, and each choice I made going forward mattered. I needed to find and pursue my singular purpose—one that was meaningful to me, had an impact on others, and also told the world, *I'm a person of value.* I needed to choose the correct path, preferably yesterday but by tomorrow at the very least. My eighty-year-old self depended on it.

Of course, that's not how things unfolded. Almost exactly a year to the day after graduation, I entered the hospital to begin chemo. And maybe this goes without saying, but when you've been given a 35 percent chance of long-term survival, it's hard to imagine yourself at eighty surveying your life, lauding all the pivotal, meaningful choices you made along the way. It seemed absurd and even hubristic to assume that kind of stability.

My diagnosis was a scales-falling-from-the-eyes moment, as if I was experiencing a version of my stoner-esque seventh-grade prediction: "Die and for a split second after, realize what I thought 'was' . . . isn't." All that pressure to find my purpose suddenly evaporated. The dominant question was not *What will I do with my life?* but *What do I need to survive today?* And the answer was simple. I needed my friends and family, a few quotidian comforts like a heating pad and my mom's rice pudding, and the creative outlet I had always relied on for company and counsel—journaling.

I journaled without any expectation of what those pages would become. Later, it happened that my journal became the source material for my *New York Times* column about the experience of illness in youth—but that felt incidental to the original creative impulse. When I launched Life, Interrupted from my hospital bed, I didn't think, *Oh, I've finally found my path!* It wasn't the first step in a grand plan, one that I intended to parlay into a successful writing career. Quite the opposite. I did it because I was about to undergo a bone marrow transplant, and the odds of survival were stacked against me, and I felt like I had nothing to lose. I simply wanted to share stories that were meaningful to me and that I hoped might be helpful to another young soul who felt as lost and lonely as I did.

Maybe without the forced pause of illness, I would have eventually found my way to the life I have now, the one I imagined as a young person—where I get to do creative work that pays the bills and is deeply fulfilling. But the truth is I'm not sure. So often our worth is measured based on what the writer David Brooks calls the résumé virtues—"those valued by the contemporary marketplace," like our alma mater, job title, salary, and accolades. Facing my mortality at such a young age reoriented my priorities from those résumé virtues to what Brooks calls eulogy virtues, "the aspects of character that others praise when a person isn't around to hear it: humility, kindness, bravery."

Here I'd like to regale you with some more wisdom that my friend Elizabeth Gilbert shared with me a few years ago. We were teaching a workshop, and a member of the audience asked how to navigate the tension she felt between fulfilling what she had been taught was her purpose as a woman, which was to be a good wife and mother—supportive of everyone else—and pursuing her own desires, like making art. Liz got visibly excited, then asked, "Can I give my purpose speech?"

Everyone nodded eagerly. She began with this: "The cultural message in a capitalistic, Protestant-work-ethic society is that you all have one gift that you are given by the universe. And your job in life is to find out what that gift is, and then to cultivate it, and then to become the best at it of anybody in the entire world, and then to monetize it, and then to expand it so that other people's lives will be changed by it. No pressure, but that's the fucking brief."

We were all still nodding. You can see it, can't you? A perfect distillation of commencement speeches across the land. "It's a brutal instruction manual," Liz said, and nothing like the messy, changeable, circumstance-thwarted, heart-driven experience of a human life. As a counterpoint, she told a little anecdote. She said that only a few months earlier, she was walking down the street in Venice Beach when she no-ticed a man at the top of a wobbly ladder painting an awning. She thought, *That doesn't look safe.*

And because Liz is someone who fears for the physical safety of just about everyone, and had nowhere to be, she stopped and held the man's ladder. A minute passed, then five, then ten. The man didn't look down, just kept on painting. Twenty minutes, then thirty. Liz thought, *This is a perfectly nice way to spend the afternoon.* Finally, she felt the ladder rumbling. He had finished and was coming down. After she saw that he was safe, but before he noticed her, she slipped away.

As Liz walked down the street, she thought, *That could have been the entire purpose of my life. As far as I know, in the great scheme of the universe, I was born and lived and died so that on that October day, I would be walking past the ladder and hold it, so that man, whose life was important for other reasons, didn't fall. And every single thing I've done in my life prior to that, or after that, was just killing time. I don't know.*

It's a wild thought experiment, one that I find so freeing, and not because I believe that was Liz's one purpose, or that her books don't mat-ter (because they do), or the wisdom she shares with all of us doesn't matter (it does), or her kindness and generosity to her loved ones is of no import (it is). I love it because it replaces that sense of certainty with curiosity. It's a gentler way in, to find purpose in the smallest and sim-plest of acts.

Today, if someone asked me, "What would you say is your purpose?" I'd probably say I have no idea. Another way I might answer that: I do not confine myself to a single purpose—it changes every day. I allow myself the freedom to be curious, to evolve, to grow tentacles that spread in all directions, to shift and adapt, to show up and be of service in the way only I can. But if I were to try to tease out the throughline between the moments in my life that I have felt most purposeful, I see that in those moments, I was aligned with my values and listening to my intu-ition. And I'm always striving for a closer alignment with those values and closer attunement to that intuition.

These days, purpose might look like taking extra care to swaddle my newest rescue pup, Lentil, who is elderly and hairless and always cold, in her favorite blanket. It might be taking the afternoon off, even though

I'm on deadline, to have a picnic with my husband on the riverbank because he's having a tough day. Or it might be painting watercolors, which makes me feel alive.

This may not be how one traditionally thinks of purpose, but for me, it's so much less pressurized, so much more humane. As Liz put it, "It might not guide you toward a life where you're going to monetize your talent and change the world and win a Nobel Prize. It just means that you'll have a nice life." Wouldn't that be something?

May the ten essays and prompts in the following pages help expand your sense of possibility around purpose. May they make you open and curious, more attuned to your own intuition and values. May they lead you toward a nice life, at the end of which someone might say, *You were kind. You were humble. You were brave. What a wonderful ladder holder you were.*

THE TO-FEEL LIST

Sky Banyes

We're all in search of purpose. For me, the form that took was fill-ing up my CV, my schedule, and my to-do lists. I was striving for achievements—and yet I never felt deeply fulfilled.

Three years ago, I started illustrating as a fun way to make sense of things. Over time, it became much more. With reflection, vulnerability, and the nourishing possibilities of pen and paper as my tools, I em-barked on an essential search for meaning. It's been a deep explorative dive, and what I discovered in the depths of every plunge were feelings. Even in everyday responsibilities such as work and family, I realized that the upstream of every "to-do" was actually a "to-feel": useful, financially secure, loving, loved.

Now, I consciously first focus on my *feelings*—instead of my *doings*—and allow them to guide my path. It has challenged the foundation upon which I'm building my life. The experience has been transforma-tive.

THIS IS YOUR PROMPT:

Write a "to-feel" list. Start by naming your deepest yearnings and aspira-tions. Then take a moment to reflect on each—to study your own feel-ing compass, teasing out the nuances of what each contains with more depth and specificity. You can make your list as a row or column, or lay them out in a fluffy brainstorming cloud. Feel free to use colors and to get creative.

Now, take a look at your list. Are your priorities, habits, and rituals serving these feelings? What steps can you take to honor the items on your "to-feel" list?

THE THING YOU CAN'T STOP DOING

Connie Carpenter Phinney

When I describe myself, I say I'm a humanist, feminist, artist, writer, scientist, entrepreneur, mom, partner, friend, and athlete. I am best known for the last one, having won the gold medal in road cycling at the 1984 Olympics in Los Angeles.

I actually started my career as an Olympian earlier than that. In the 1972 Olympics, when I was only fourteen, I competed in speed skating. Because of this, people often romanticize my story. They talk about my early talent—or how I married a fellow Olympian (Davis Phinney, bronze 1984), or how both our children became elite athletes.

They don't romanticize all the unknowns, the relentless self-doubt, the setbacks and injuries and countless failures. They don't focus on the fact that, as I stood at the start of an Olympic race, it was just me standing there. Knowing that I had worked hard, but never knowing: Was it enough?

When I was a kid, people asked my parents how they got me to work so hard. My mom's answer: "How do we get her to stop?" This was the 1970s, back when nobody was running like they do now, and I ran after dark through my neighborhood so no one I knew would see me.

For the last five years I've been sporadically working on a memoir trying to explain that part of me—that drive. I've written more than seventy-five thousand words, only to find myself thinking about starting over. As I age, I realize I'm still learning my own story, finding my voice.

I'm still reaching for the right words to tell my truth. My writing mentor says this desire to start over is the sign of a true writer. I think it's more that I'm still reaching, searching, and hopefully, still growing. I also think it might be that I value the work over the outcome.

So I'm wondering, what drives you?

THIS IS YOUR PROMPT:

Write about what drives you—not what you get paid for, not what others want you to do. Write about the thing you can't stop doing.

LEAVE YOUR NAME AT THE DOOR

Alexa Wilding

When my son Lou was first hospitalized for cancer, I'd stay up nights writing songs. The melodies kept looping in my head, as did certain lyrics, like the lines "red river run, red river run," while I stared at the East River and the red IV lines, the endless blood transfusions. The looping lines reminded me of spinning analog tape in a recording studio, my natural habitat—a land I could not have found myself farther from.

At the time, I was as afraid of losing myself as I was of losing my son. I didn't know how to share this fear with anyone, lest they think me a bad mother. The threat of erasure was only reinforced by the well-meaning medical team never calling me by my name. "Everything okay in here, Mom?" the nurses would ask. "Yep!" I'd lie, hiding the keyboard I'd borrowed from NYU Langone's Child Life Services under the rough hospital blankets. I knew it was protocol to just call me Mom, but I had a name, and how I longed to hear it.

Sometimes we moms would gather in the hallway with pretzels and Cokes. There was one dad, Brian, whose wife "couldn't handle it." We were fascinated by this absent mother. "She's not a real mom," Maria in room 902 would insist. But maybe she was more real than all of us for admitting that this was too much for a mother to bear.

As cancer caregivers, we had to leave our names at the door. And rightfully so; we were leading the battle to save our children's lives. Yet underneath our suits of armor were complex humans with deep desires, hopes, and dreams and a hunger for more than just our crises.

I satiated that hunger by working on my third album. Maria bought crystals online. Felicia liked to go on long runs along the river. Brian seemed to be obsessed with Mary, the night nurse. Some of us drank. There were affairs and other bad decisions, as one's head is not screwed on straight when one is terrified. While we cut one another slack, we feared the outside world would not.

A part of me is still pacing the hospital hall with my pretzels and Coke, even though it's been five years since Lou left treatment, even though he's thriving. Whenever I sing "red river run, red river run," or other songs from that time, I think of the parents I've met along the way. I say their names: Maria, Brian, Felicia. I hope they've forgiven themselves, as I have, for all the things we did to survive our children's illnesses. And I hope they allow themselves whatever they need to soothe their still-healing hearts.

THIS IS YOUR PROMPT:

Write about a time in your life when you struggled to hold on to your sense of self. What did you do to survive, and who helped you along the way? Were you able to forgive yourself for any missteps? Is the person you became in that moment of crisis still part of your identity?

FORKS IN THE ROAD

Jedidiah Jenkins

When looking back, a life tells a story. The chain of days string together into a narrative shaped by choices we make at pivotal moments, some large, some small.

In middle school, I was teased for having a girly voice. I was called a "fag" a few times but didn't know what it meant, only that it was bad. One kid—I still remember his full name the way we always remember a childhood bully's name—cornered me in the hallway and told me I was an "ugly fag." He was short, comically short, and it had turned him mean. I was six inches taller than he was but soft and rosy-cheeked and scared out of my mind. After he had seen my fear, happy in his power, he left me standing in the hall. I trembled and hot rage crawled up from my chest to my face. I wanted to become cruel like him. I knew I was smart and that if I used my words right, I could cut him into sashimi.

But as the anger flushed my cheeks, a thought appeared in my head: *What type of person do you want to be? A mean person or a nice person? If you are mean, you can hurt him back. If you are friendly, and funny, perhaps you can win him over, even make him like you.* I answered the question in my thoughts: *To be mean seems exhausting. I'd rather be funny and nice and show him that he should be kind to me and be my friend. I'll be so nice and fun that he'll regret being mean.* It was as if a demon and an angel were on my shoulders, and I chose the angel.

Here's another one. It was during junior year of high school, when we were all applying to college and daydreaming about what life would become. It just so happened that *Time* magazine had named the University of Southern California "college of the year." They had photos of beautiful grassy parks with kids playing guitar and frisbee, of college football and beautiful architecture. I'd never heard of it, but because of those photos, I made USC my first choice. If *Time* hadn't chosen that school, and had chosen another one, I wonder if my life would be completely different. If I would have planted my life in Chicago, or New York, or who knows?

Thinking of this makes me smile. So much of my life is either chance or some thought that sprung into my head as if from nowhere. It makes me grateful and curious about what it means to be alive, to have a life and be along for the ride. I am both the author and the reader of a fascinating story. One where this loss led to that triumph. This hope led to that disappointment. This longing to that love. With a little distance, and the knowledge that you survived what had once seemed difficult or even deadly, these moments can take on magical significance.

THIS IS YOUR PROMPT:

Identify two turning points in your life. Describe what led up to them, why you chose the path you did, and how they led to now.

LETTER FROM A BURNING BUILDING

Susan Cheever

Writers don't usually leave a lot of money when they die, but their estates can include big treasure. My father was an inspired and celebrated writer who hated to give me writing advice; he hoped I would have an easier life than he had. Still, his occasional slips have turned out to be solid gold. When, as a young writer, I was worried about taking a television job, he told me to go ahead. "A writer's life is an improvisation," he said. When I pressed him for technique, he suggested that I never use a dialogue tag. If the dialogue is strong, its delivery doesn't need to be described.

Best of all, I inherited the writing prompts that he used when he taught at Barnard and the University of Iowa. He asked his students to write a story linking six disparate objects; his student Allan Gurganus did this so well that his exercise ended up being published in *The Atlantic*. Over the years, I have added to the prompts my father left, collecting ideas from writers like Frank Conroy, Bret Anthony Johnston, and John McPhee, but the one I keep coming back to, and the one my father liked the best was this one: Write a letter from a burning building. What would you write if you knew it was your last chance to connect with another person? What would you write if you knew that you were writing your last words? Last words can change the world. An example: "I can't breathe."

What would yours be?

THIS IS YOUR PROMPT:

Write a letter from a burning building. You are trapped and will not be able to escape. No rescue. You know this is the last thing you will ever write. Whom will you write to? What will you say?

A DAY OF JUBILEE

Marcus G. Miller

My father once told me that success is the price of admission to the next challenge. He said this to me after he'd received high praise for leading a successful project at work, and at that moment, I could detect, but could not yet name, several emotional colors blazing out of his eyes. There was the simple crimson pride of a job well done, there was the effervescent azure ebullience induced by the promise of a bright future, there was the earthy-brown contemplation of a warrior taking a moment's rest, and there was black love. The love was black because he, in his blackness, was able to claim a level of victory that eluded so many men of his father's generation, and men of his own. And he could take that lesson, a life-affirming blueprint for managing success, and teach it—from the full weight of the experience—to his black son. The words were clever enough as an aphorism, but what was transmitted to me was the full spectrum of what it meant to him to say those words. It nearly brought me to tears.

And so, when considering Juneteenth, that shining golden day in 1865 when General Gordon Granger rode into Galveston, Texas, and proclaimed the freedom of the black women and men who were enslaved there, even though the Emancipation Proclamation had come two and a half years earlier; when considering their joy, and jubilee, and dancing, I hear the words of my father. I see the pink and purple and candied red of their celebration, and I see the long gray road ahead, through history, connecting them to the colorful eyes of my father, connecting them to me.

Let us hold labor and liberation in balance. Let us refuse to work without rest and reward, but also let us not eat, drink, and be merry, believing that tomorrow we will die. Let us mark every accomplishment with its deserved color, then let us not forget to look up at the ominous white snow-capped peaks of the mountains we must yet climb.

THIS IS YOUR PROMPT:

Who taught you about work? What lessons did they pass down to you? How do you balance your labors with rest and reward?

REAWAKENING YOUR ORIGINAL GENIUS

Martha Beck

"I have good news and bad news," said the researcher who'd just analyzed my brain scans. "The bad news is that you have ADHD. The good news is, it's treatable."

"Really?" I said. "I have attention deficit disorder? But . . . I have no trouble paying attention. Sometimes I pay so much attention to whatever I'm doing that I accidentally stay up all night."

"That's called hyperfocus," he said. "You pay too much attention to some things and not enough to others. You have what we call an 'interest-based' nervous system—you pay more attention to things that interest you than to things that don't."

"Wait," I said. "Do most people pay the same amount of attention to everything, whether they're interested in it or not? Good lord, how do they even decide what to have for breakfast?"

"No, no, no," he replied. "Most people can allocate their attention in a way that's *optimal*."

"Optimal for what?"

"Functioning in society. School. Work. I'm sure all that's been hard for you, but as I said, we can help."

I decided it would be obnoxious to tell him that I had three Harvard degrees and a job teaching business school. *Then again,* I thought as I drove away from the clinic, *I have no idea where those degrees are.* The physical paper ones, I mean. I know a lot of people frame them and whatnot, but that just didn't interest me.

I began thinking about the other things that didn't interest me. Maybe ADHD is what put me into a deep, involuntary slumber every time my accountant tried to explain tax law. Maybe my "disability" was the reason that, on several occasions, I've bolted from important meetings because someone said there was an animal outside: a moose in Alaska, a python in Singapore, a squirrel in New York City. An albino squirrel. I mean, wouldn't anyone leave a meeting to see that?

Apparently not.

On that drive I realized that I'd won a chunk of the genetic lottery: I was born with severe ADHD and an innate curiosity about everything taught in school. It was only after my diagnosis that I realized how awful school must have been for many of my classmates, sitting for hours, forcing their attention on things that bored or confused them.

In 1968, NASA funded a study to identify "creative geniuses." Researchers found that about 2 percent of adults fit into this category. But when they tested young children, a full 98 percent showed up as creative geniuses. The researchers blamed the school system for pushing, shaming, and punishing children out of their own interests and toward compliant behavior so that they'd eventually function well in factories and offices.

There's a high probability that something like this happened to you. I deeply believe that your essential nature is a creative genius. And I suspect you've been taught to ignore, repress, perhaps even hate this genius self. But it hasn't gone anywhere. You can still set it free.

THIS IS YOUR PROMPT:

Write about something you tried to learn even though it didn't interest you: a subject in school, a religious doctrine, a lecture from a coworker with the charisma of a turnip. Remember the feeling in your body when you focused on this thing, how it felt when you forced yourself to pay attention to it. Notice the sense of having to push forward as if you're walking uphill.

Now write about something you did enjoy learning about. It may have been a skill, your first love, or a car you longed to own. Remember what your body felt when you learned about it or thought about it in idle moments. Notice that you feel almost magnetically pulled toward it: Your eyes, ears, and other senses give it primary attention.

What in your life today feels like a "push"? What feels like a "pull"? For ten minutes today, choose to go away from something that feels like a push and toward something that feels like a pull. If you do this consistently, you'll feel your original genius awakening, guiding you, expressing itself. If people disapprove, do it anyway. Become the genius you've always been.

THE WORLD'S MOST UNENDING PROMISE

Maggie Doyne

I've spent the last seventeen years completely surrounded by children. I'm part of a team that runs a residential care home in midwestern Nepal, as well as a community-based school for children living in poverty, a women's empowerment center, a health clinic, family development programs, and safe homes. There is rarely a day that goes by that I don't interact with a few hundred kids—fifty of whom I live with, two of whom are biologically my own.

Like most humans, I struggle at times with mental health. To stay hopeful, to stay sane, to hold on to joy despite the sadness, suffering, violence in this world, is a constant battle. My greatest wish is for a world where every child is safe and loved, and my biggest trigger is seeing children suffer. But over the years, during some of the darkest days and most difficult moments, I started to notice something: When I look into the eyes of a child, it's almost impossible for me to feel anything other than hope. While my brain churns in fear and doom scrolls on my phone, I look down and see a three-year-old holding a perfectly smooth stone in their hand, in awe and wonder. They ask me to keep it safe in my pocket. As my mind wanders and worries, a six-year-old stops me, points to the sky, and says, "Maggie mom! Did you SEE THE MOON?!"

There is nothing more magical to a child than their first wiggly tooth, or finding the perfect hill to roll down (over and over), or tasting their first marshmallow. They always spot the ladybug, the fluttering orange butterflies, the dandelion that's one little puff from bursting. Their questions are my favorite part. After hearing the birds sing, they ask, "But why do they always sing in the morning?" Why this? Why that? But how?

Children have been my greatest teachers. They are anchored in the present, in wonder. There are so many times I wish I could just bottle up the joy, the innocence, the purity, the sanctity of children. That's what it is—children feel sacred to me. They're our world's most unending promise.

THIS IS YOUR PROMPT:

Write about a time a child taught you about, or reminded you of, something important in life.

BRAZENFACE

Tatiana Gallardo

I remember the first time I heard the word *brazen,* in English class. I was twelve, timid, and struck by the meaning of the word and its power. *Bold and without shame.* It felt like something I could never be: audacious, capable of doing whatever, without worry. Taller than my entire class and most of my teachers, I was scared to stand out any more than I already did. I had grown comfortable in the corner. There, I could soften myself and my size. I preferred to be quietly creative and studious rather than loud and large.

With age, I became more confident about my height, thankfully—but I never dared to be brazen about my dreams. When I turned twenty-four, I still felt the twelve-year-old me's fear. I had graduated college, gotten the job I hoped for, felt generally happy, yet I felt like I was still in the corner: afraid to speak up, to take risks, to pursue what I most desired—which was to shamelessly share my creative work with the world.

As I entered 2022, I wanted to push myself to overcome fear in every aspect of my life: professionally, personally, creatively. But I needed fuel. I needed inner strength. I needed to be, somehow, brazen. So I started letting the word I most remembered inspire me rather than haunt me. Every time I was about to do something scary—heart pounding, chest tightening, the worst-case scenario flashing before me—I'd tell myself: *Just put on your brazen face.*

At first, I started saying it as I geared up for small moments of courage, like killing a spider or telling someone no. Just put on your brazen face. Then, the mantra appeared as I braced myself for bigger, scarier moves toward my dreams. Like pitching an essay. Publishing an illustrated story. Leaving my job to focus on my creative work. Just put on your brazen face, Tati. There's conviction in the command, but I say it with gentle love. It's a reminder that I am capable of courage. That I can summon my secret strength.

Aside from the subtle straightening of my spine, my appearance doesn't change when I put on my brazen face—my face quite literally looks the same. But internally? There's a wave of composure. A rush of confidence. A release of the brazen that's always been there, ready to break through.

THIS IS YOUR PROMPT:

Write about the word you wish to embody. Where did you first learn it? What does it mean to you? Who does it allow you to become, what does it allow you to do?

THE LAST PAGE

Jonathan Miles

I've never written a novel or a story without first knowing the ending. This seems to be an uncommon method, at least among writers of my acquaintance, but not unheard of. I think it was the novelist Richard Russo who likened his writing process to throwing a pebble into a pond—the pebble being the ending—and then swimming around to find it. One of my heroes, Katherine Anne Porter, always wrote her last page first and then worked toward it. "I know where I'm going," she once told an interviewer. "How I get there is God's grace."

THIS IS YOUR PROMPT:

Write the ending to your story. By this I don't mean your physical end, your deathbed scene, no—that's creepy. Rather, try to imagine the moment at which the plot threads of your life are tied together, when the arc of your story resolves. Where will you be and who will be with you? What dreams will you have realized? What mysteries might you finally have solved? What will you deem your greatest achievements? And what do you fear might still be left undone or unsaid (because, remember, all great endings are slightly ambiguous)? Write the last page of your story, the pebble in the pond silt. And then after, with God's grace, start swimming.

CHAPTER 10

ON ALCHEMY

My family and I spent our summers on the road when I was a kid. My father was a college professor, my mother an artist, and at the end of the school year, we'd rent out our house for two months and use those funds to travel. We usually visited family in Tunisia or Switzerland, but we sometimes explored new places, like the summers we spent riding chicken buses and camping on beaches in Central America. On such trips, everyone was required to pack light: only one backpack each.

There was a kind of joy in that constraint; it freed us up and forced us to discover new things. We often stayed at youth hostels, and when I needed something to read, I'd pull a volume from the shelf in the common room. If it was good, I'd pass it along to the rest of my family, and we'd form an inadvertent book club. In Tunisia, the only books in English I could get my hands on were classic tomes like *Anna Karenina*. I remember lying on the floor reading for hours. Because there was nothing to distract me—no wifi, no TV, no modern comforts—I finished it in about three days.

What we bring with us—and where, and when, and why—often seems self-evident, needing no exploration. But in fact, our must-haves point to what we value, not just in the material sense. They offer clues about who we are, where we are in life, even our hopes and dreams. This is something I came to understand after reading Joan Didion's title essay to her collection *The White Album;* in it, Didion included her essential packing list for reporting trips. It went like this:

To Pack and Wear:

2 skirts
2 jerseys or leotards
1 pullover sweater
2 pair shoes
stockings
bra
nightgown
robe
slippers
cigarettes
bourbon
bag with:
    shampoo
    toothbrush and paste
    Basis soap
    razor, deodorant
    aspirin, prescriptions, Tampax
    face cream, powder, baby oil

To Carry:

mohair throw
typewriter
2 legal pads
pens
files
house key

Didion said this list enabled her to pack without thinking. But she also knew that the objects themselves held meaning, that together they told a story. "This may be a parable," she wrote, "either of my life as a reporter during this period or of the period itself."

When I was preparing to enter the hospital for a multiweek stay for my second transplant, I began thinking about the essentials, in every sense of the word. I asked myself: *What do I need? What will see me through?*

Many of the things that made it onto my packing list were practical, like lip balm and moisturizer, along with the softest socks, sweatpants, and hand-knit caps for when I'd lose my hair. Others were for making my surroundings more beautiful. As an antidote to the harsh fluorescent lights, I got some candles—not real candles, of course, but some very convincing fake ones made of actual wax softly scented of vanilla, with the most flame-like flickering LED wicks. (They were so convincing that when the nurses peered into my room from the hallway, they panicked, thinking I was about to set the whole joint ablaze.)

But the most important items I packed were those meant to ignite a creative spark. I bought a gray felt diaper caddy, and I filled it with everything I could think of as a kind of choose-your-own creative adventure: novels, art books, and sketchbooks; into the pockets, I tucked pens and colored pencils, paint brushes and watercolors. I also brought journals, of course. Journaling had saved me during my first transplant as much as the treatment itself. Maybe that sounds bold to say, but it's true. It was in those pages that I first began learning that survival is its own kind of creative act.

So, I packed four journals in the diaper caddy—all for different purposes. One was for medical notes, to record fluctuations in my body, test results, and notes from the doctors' rounds. Another was titled "Observations from the Nurses' Station," a kind of reporter's pad for jotting down character sketches, overheard conversations, and little anecdotes: the cafeteria worker who offered to go to the coffee cart and get me an iced chai latte once, then again and again and again; the day my friend Behida called me from the sidewalk below my hospital room, and when I came to the window, did a solo Lindy Hop without any regard for the gawks of passersby; or the night my nurses had my husband, Jon, prank call their boyfriends pretending to be an elderly Brooklynite named Ernie who was desperate for a glass of milk. The third journal was for writing letters to Jon. We weren't always able to see each other every day, and to stay connected, we promised to continue our long-standing practice of writing to each other when apart, then snapping a photo and texting it to each other. The fourth journal would hold all the things I couldn't say out loud.

I placed the diaper caddy on my bedside table, within arm's reach, and I put it to use that first night in the hospital when I woke in the middle of the night, anxious and addled and full of fear. But to my surprise, I didn't reach for my journal and pen. Instead, I found myself painting a surrealistic portrait, where a semi-autobiographical figure dozed peacefully in a hospital bed nestled in the limbs of the tree outside my window, behind it the Manhattan skyline and a star-strewn sky.

I hadn't painted since childhood, when I used to mess around with acrylics and pastels in my mom's attic studio after school. Returning to painting was thrilling but strange. It would soon become essential. Only days after I made that first painting, I was put on an IV drip of potent pain meds that blurred my vision, making it difficult to write. So I continued painting those pseudo-self-portraits: a young woman receiving a blood transfusion with a giraffe as her IV pole, or swimming in cobalt waters surrounded by narwhals and other sea creatures, or teetering on a watermelon beside an elephant rearing up to pluck a blood orange from a heavily laden tree. In the dream logic of my watercolors, my hospital bed had become a flying carpet taking me on an apocalyptic journey through Book of Revelation–esque scenes. On the canvas, I could transport myself far beyond the confines of my corporeal reality. I could defy circumstance, collapse space and time.

Each day, a new painting emerged, and my mom hung them on the wall beside my bed, transforming that cold, sterile chamber into a fantastical gallery. My nurses began lingering in my room, asking questions about them, delighting in the colors and shapes, eager for the next apparition to appear. The hospital staff who came to change my bedding or take my vitals found excuses to stay; one woman told me that she loved the energy in my room and looked forward to coming to clean the floors. But more than brightening the space, they were for me a kind of visual diary, a record of each day I'd survived there and the fears I was facing and defanging one brushstroke at a time.

Looking back on that time, it feels almost fated—like so many things were leading me to those paintings. Maybe a better way to say it is that it felt deeply intuitive. I had studied the long lineage of artists and writers, from Ludwig van Beethoven and Marcel Proust to Frida Kahlo, who in the midst of illness and upheaval alchemized isolation into creative solitude, who used their limitations as a springboard and turned their circumstances into fodder for new creative pursuits.

I also had friends who had modeled this for me, like Melissa Carroll, the brilliant painter I'd met a decade earlier in that same hospital during my first bout with leukemia. She was in treatment for a recurrence of Ewing sarcoma, and she had switched from painting portraits in oil to self-portraits in watercolor. In the final weeks of her life, her vision became blurred from medication, like mine did, but she continued conjuring human silhouettes enveloped by colorful auras. Her earlier portraits were all craft and precision, a specific individual perfectly rendered. In her last paintings, the effort at human likeness has disappeared. These are figures in transition. They seem to be reentering the cocoon and at the same time breaking apart and blooming. They are otherworldly.

I have always loved the word *alchemy*. I love how it sounds on the tongue, with its melding of Arabic, Greek, and French influences pointing toward how in human hands (and mouths) everything shifts and changes. Even more so, I am inspired by the idea that it's possible to transmute something base, something considered worthless, into something precious, like gold. It appeals to me on the material level but also on a higher level: as a fusion or reunion with the divine.

I was once speaking to the theologian Nadia Bolz-Weber, and I confessed to her that I didn't grow up in a religious household, so I hadn't ever really prayed until the first time I got sick. I told her that on my first night in the transplant unit, I got down on my knees and began haggling with a higher power, bartering good behavior for survival, as in, *If you let me live, I'll be less selfish.* I found myself making my own kind of Pascal's wager—*If you let me live, I'll believe in you.* Nadia's response was so comforting. "You pray when you need it," she said. "The most powerful prayers are born of despair."

That's how I feel about art born of desperation. Sometimes the most powerful forms of creative expression come from a savage place, from urgency. To express what you need to express, you grab whatever tools are within reach, and you make it happen.

I recently encountered an astonishing example of this kind of urgent conjuring in a letter written by a man named John Binkley to his late wife, Sherrie, who had just died of cancer after three long years in treatment. They had been married for nearly half a century, and he'd been her devoted caregiver through it all. He was understandably bereft, and what gave him solace in the months following her death was writing letters to her.

"Dear Pook," he writes. "I'm still on this side. As you, safely ensconced on the other side, well know." He tells her about a note that his oncologist friend received from a ten-year-old patient after the boy had died of a brain tumor. The boy writes as if from the beyond, thanking his doctor, encouraging him, telling him, *Pet your dog for me!*

"Children possess the ability to create a new reality where there was none before," John writes.

He composed one letter after another to his late wife—to keep her alive, to stay connected to her across the gulf of spacetime. Over the course of nine months, he penned forty-six letters, and it gave him such light and connection and purpose.

In that time, his own health began to fail. And about a week before he died, he showed the letters to his two daughters. "Forty-six," one of them said. "Wasn't that the number of years you knew Mom?"

"Oh, that wasn't intentional," John replied. "I just wrote until I felt like I had finished."

Call it a coincidence if you like. But as humans, we are meaning-making machines and relentless seekers of patterns, rhythms, and rhymes. Not only do they feel like signs, but we find beauty in them. In turning to the page, John alchemized his grief. He transformed the loss of the love of his life into continued companionship. When he died shortly thereafter, he left his daughters a record of that utterly beautiful conjuring they themselves could turn to for comfort and connection.

This kind of alchemy is available to each of us. You only have to tap into that mystical, propulsive, seemingly divine trait that exists in every human: creativity. That is not to say it's easy, or that there aren't moments of terror. You can't help but feel vulnerable when everything has changed, when things are beyond your control. But I know from experience that when I hide from whatever plagues me, it's like the mice: the darkness spreads and multiplies. It's only in alchemizing the terror of the unknown into the magic of the unknown that I remember what's essential. Whether you choose to journal or write letters, draw or paint, may these final ten essays and prompts help you transform what perhaps seems of little value into precious gold—or a sidewalk Lindy Hop.

ACROSS THE GULF OF SPACETIME

John Binkley

March 6, 2023

Dear Pook,

I'm still on this side. As you, safely ensconced on the other side, well know. At least that's the way I picture you. Only two long months since we were in the same room. I'm still having difficulty accepting that I can't communicate with you the same way.

It must be synchronistic that I'm reminded of my neuro-oncologist friend Paul reading me the letter he'd received from a ten-year-old patient.

Dear Dr. F.,

If you are reading this note, it means that the tumor won, and I am now in heaven . . . I appreciate how well you take care of me. You seem to really care, and you have sad eyes. I think you are a "real" person . . . Please never feel like you failed if a child dies . . . You will go to heaven some day and all your cancer kids will have hugs waiting.

Pet your dog for me!

Your friend,
S.

How did that little boy transport himself through spacetime and imagine himself speaking to his doctor from the other side? If he can do it, I can. Right? The way he moves from present to past tense and then back to present and future exposes his ambiguity about where he is in time and what is real. I experience the same fluidity of time with you. Past, present, who knows—future? Where I am spatially when I encounter the energy you created during your lifetime is irrelevant. Am I courageous enough to embrace it, whatever the form, or am I afraid that I may be ridiculed for engaging with a force that no one understands? I have never been afraid to be contrarian in the past. Why start now?

I'm writing to keep you alive. Perhaps that's presumptuous. Maybe I'm only believing in the possible. I've spent a lifetime pushing that dream. You gave me so much love for forty-six years that it has fueled my recovery from the loss of your companionship. You changed my life. From the start. And these past three years, we drew even closer to each other as the insatiable cancer attempted without success to consume the best in each of us. We defeated it. We two became an inseparable team, determined to beat back the disease and preserve your indomitable spirit for every instant possible. Over time, two distinctly different personages melded from my perspective into one seamless identity. Two became one. We fought as one. Love required no words. Hope and all of love's dividends appeared as needed and crossed tired boundaries with unfamiliar ease.

Now we need that child's confidence that we can continue to communicate across the ultimate divide. Picture that ten-year-old child imagining himself to the other side and conjuring up what he wanted to say to his doctor. I don't even know how to label such a feat. But he's thrown down the gauntlet to me.

If a child can transport himself across the gulf of spacetime, surely I can. Rational thinkers define spacetime as any mathematical model that combines space and time into a single continuum. I want a spiritual variation on the same phenomenon: a dimension which permits a party on one side or the other to transcend whatever boundaries might obstruct the commingling of two spiritual entities. What is refreshing about children is that they don't bother with justifying or reasoning; they just leap from one reality to another and expect adults to follow them without questioning. Children possess the ability to create a new reality where there was none before.

Damn the skeptics. Crush the fences. Transcend the static, whatever the interferences, to enable us to carry on the teamwork. The oneness. I don't need to understand it to embrace it. To live by it. To profit from it. There are no rules. No barriers. No tracks in the snow on this one.

Be patient, Sherrie, with my learning how to do this. Show me once more that tolerance that has marked our forty-six years together, from the beginning.

I love you.

Pook

THIS IS YOUR PROMPT:

Damn the skeptics. Crush the fences. Transcend the static. Transport yourself across the gulf of spacetime.

Write a letter to someone you love who is no longer on this side. Communicate across the ultimate divide.

THE ENCHANTED

Rene Denfeld

I was leaving the prison where I worked as a death row investigator exonerating innocents and administering to the guilty. I remember that day vividly: the spring sunshine, the ducks in a skein across the sky, and the voice I heard as I made my way to my car, keys in hand.

The voice spoke clearly in my ear, as if he were a real person: *This is an enchanted place.*

I turned around. No one was there. There were just the tall walls and decrepit guard towers of the prison—built in 1866, a stone dungeon—and me, standing alone, the smell of despair still lingering on my skin.

I followed that voice all the way home, and that night, I began working on my first novel, *The Enchanted.* I had always wanted to write a novel but felt fettered with the usual fears: I wasn't educated in the right way, and people wouldn't want to hear what I had to say. The voice brought a sense of direction and gave me hope. If a prison could be enchanted, I could be enchanted, too: I could be a source of enchantment.

It was the beginning of a whole new life for me. Not just books and awards and the trappings of success, but something deeper, and far more important. I got in touch with the absolute joy and enchantment of life, from the worst places we can find ourselves, like that death row prison, to the most sublime moments of hope. I began tying the threads of my life together, and for the first time, they made sense. They made poetry.

The enchantment of it all.

Whenever rage or anger or despair threatens to drag me down, I remember the enchantment, and this keeps me going.

When we see enchantment in one another and ourselves, the world blows wide open. Suddenly, change is possible. Love grows where there was none.

THIS IS YOUR PROMPT:

Find a special spot in which to write. It might be outside, in nature, or in your favorite chair. But the beauty of the enchantment is that all you need is the four walls of your own mind—a world can grow there. If you like, take a special object. I have a collection of rocks and feathers I've found in my wanderings. Anything that connects you to a sense of magic will help.

Now, sit quietly, and ask the voice inside of you—your very own special voice, which no one else has—to tell you about the enchantment. Who inside you speaks in that voice, and what do they have to share with you? What enchants them? What enchants you? Write it down.

WRITING AS EXORCISM

Puloma Ghosh

So much of my impulse to create art has always been about giving form to the thoughts that haunt me and releasing my obsessions. It can be as simple as making a character eat a meal I've been craving, or as complex as turning a recurring nightmare into a short story.

It's been this way for as long as I can remember. When I was a child, I wrote stories that imitated the books I loved reading over and over. As a teenager, I drew pictures of people who resembled my crushes. As a young adult, this took a darker turn, manifesting in strange artwork that mirrored my own tumultuous thoughts. We often chide ourselves for becoming too fixated on any one thing, especially if it invokes a strong emotion. But art—the creation of words, images, music, etc.—is a safe and private place to let out your ghosts, beautiful and ugly.

There are nights when I can't sleep unless I've exorcized whatever is inhabiting my thoughts on paper. But once it's out, I can see my obsession for what it really is and have a conversation with it, which helps me connect to the *why* behind my preoccupations. Only then can I gain a better understanding of myself—the hopes and fears and passions that drive me—and recognize the context for my creative work.

THIS IS YOUR PROMPT:

Write to exorcize what's haunting you. Write about whatever it is you can't get out of your head—a person, a place, a fear, a fictional scene, a memory from your past, a fantasy for your future. Allow yourself to think obsessively and shamelessly about only that one thing for as long as it takes to get it down on paper.

SOMETHING THEY CAN'T DO ALONE

Hanif Kureishi

Since an accident left me without the use of my arms or legs, I have never been so busy. Last night at around nine, I watched a few minutes of *The Glass Onion,* which I enjoyed. Then I lost connection and everything went dark. I fell asleep, woke at one, and was conscious for the rest of the night. I had many ideas, but since I can't use my hands and make notes, I had to shout them at my poor son Carlo, who was trying to get some sleep. This is how I write these days; I fling a net over more or less random thoughts, draw it in, and hope some kind of pattern emerges.

On the writing of my book *Shattered,* which Carlo is helping me with, it has become clear how pleasurable it is to write with someone else. We work from ten every morning until one and get about five pages of editing and rewriting done. We are cutting, reshaping, and expanding the dispatches, keeping them in the present tense and arguing over improvements. It reminds me of working on plays and movies with directors and dramaturgs, where there is plenty of amusing gossip about politics and sport, even as you work. It is consoling to work alone as a writer, but it is a blast to have companionship and banter.

My wife Isabella's grandmother, a screenwriter who wrote many films—*The Leopard* and *Rocco and His Brothers* for Luchino Visconti and *Roman Holiday* for William Wyler—said in an interview that the best way to write comedies was to work with others, since you can test the humor as you go. The internal critical voice, the one that tells you that you are no good, is muted when there are others to cheer you along.

Music and cinema emerge out of creative alliances, from the Beatles to Miles Davis, Alfred Hitchcock to Robert Altman. Would we have heard of Lennon or McCartney if they had never met? Maybe the most important thing an artist can do is go to school with the right people, or have the ability to recognize a compatible talent. An artist can then do something they can't do alone.

THIS IS YOUR PROMPT:

Write about someone—a family member, friend, or creative collaborator— who silences your inner critic. What do they allow you to do that you can't do alone?

A SUNDERING

Salman Rushdie

For many years now, I have taught a nonfiction graduate seminar at New York University. In several of the books we read and discuss, a common theme emerges. People in a peaceful community—often a remote, rural place—are suddenly confronted with a calamitous intervention into their lives. Two examples of this are Truman Capote's true-crime novel *In Cold Blood*, and Svetlana Alexievich's *Voices from Chernobyl*. Capote has said that when he first read about the murders of the Clutter family in Holcomb, Kansas, a small town at or near the very center of the United States, he was more interested to discover the effects of the murders on the people of Holcomb than he was in the crimes themselves. Meanwhile, Alexievich, for obvious reasons unable to examine the site of the exploded Chernobyl nuclear reactor itself, and unable to talk to all those first responders who died in the effort to shut it down and make it safe, talks instead to the survivors and constructs the story of the horror through their traumatized voices.

Capote arrived in Holcomb, accompanied by his childhood friend Harper Lee, to find a community mired in mutual suspicion. Until the arrest of the actual killers, who were strangers from far away in search of money, the townspeople of Holcomb mostly assumed that the murderer was one of them. They began to eye one another with distrust and even fear. Some Holcomb people moved away. The town no longer felt safe.

The Chernobyl survivors found themselves treated with fear by their fellow countrymen, much as the survivors of the Hiroshima and Nagasaki nuclear bombs had been treated in Japan. People didn't want to come near them, let alone marry them or bear their children. And many of them decided that the only way forward for them was to return to their homes near the reactor, knowing full well that radioactivity levels in the region were off the charts, so they would be drastically shortening their own lives by going back.

We all have a picture of the world, an idea of what is real, inside which we live. Sudden disaster—the death of a loved one, the loss of a vital job, a murder, a meltdown at a nearby nuclear reactor—breaks that picture and we have to try to reconstruct it, or something like it, or something completely different.

I myself have had such an experience, when I was attacked by a man with a knife in August 2022 and almost killed. It has taken me a year and a half to deal with the physical and psychological consequences of that attack, and perhaps I haven't fully dealt with it even now.

THIS IS YOUR PROMPT:

Write about an event that changed your world, or the world of someone close to you; that forced you to reexamine your beliefs. Or, do it as fiction. Imagine a peaceful suburban community disrupted, one morning, by the landing of a flying saucer in the town square. In fact or fiction, write about an event that disrupts reality, and the human consequences of that event.

GREYHOUNDS

Crow Jonah Norlander

I'm an honest person. Most of the time, at least. The truth is good, but sometimes it's inconvenient, awkward, or boring. Like when I'm out walking my greyhounds and tourists on their way to the beach stop me to ask, "Are those greyhounds?"

If I could sell a joke, I'd say, "They're pugs—these are their Halloween costumes." The tenth person to ask, "Are they friendly?" might be surprised to hear about my dogs' hallucinatory disorder that causes them to perceive petting hands as irresistibly delicious rabbits. "Chomp chomp," I'd say, shrugging an insincere apology.

"Are they retired racers?" No! After all but two states voted to outlaw racing, I opened up my own black-market offtrack betting operation in the next county over, where I have hired goons ready to break the knee-caps of anyone who asks too many questions.

How could I possibly know that this particular canine admirer is on the board of PETA? That the very next day she will bring to bear the full force of their power barging down my front door?

Finding no illegal dog-racing activity, they nonetheless pass judgment: I take my dogs for granted and undermine their ability to brighten others' days. Given the state of discretionary authority, oversight, and funding, I'm not sure what to expect. But it turns out that they think I'm worth saving. They want to rehabilitate me! They assign a caseworker to observe.

She arrives looking vaguely Montessori in her muumuu. Is that a stitched bunny emblem on the breast? Could that be a uniform? She's calm, firm, and authoritative. She finishes sentences with a leading lilt but walks like she's packing something. PETA doesn't believe in guns, do they? I'm an animal, too, I deserve to be treated ethically.

After gradually getting used to her being around, I revert to my usual ways. She watches me shoo the dogs away after a perfunctory pat. On a walk, she stops me: "Why so soon to tug their sweet snouts away from some luscious scent?" This hypothetical clinician might be overboard with the poetics, but she makes a good point. She has more to say. "Are you genuinely in a hurry? Or do you seek power and control in relationships as a means of overcompensating for an upbringing made precarious by poverty, addiction, and divorce?"

Wow, okay, easy now. But again, she's not wrong.

"Do you begrudge these beautiful creatures their affection for and dependence upon you? A dynamic of your own design?" She has me imagine my life without dogs, and then a world in which gardeners guard their flowers and trees greedily absorb birdsong.

Point being: Blessings should be a delight to share.

Now they can't shut me up. Everyone, look at my handsome dogs! Yes, they're related!

And they'd absolutely love a rub.

THIS IS YOUR PROMPT:

Think of a time you were reluctant to tell the truth. Consider what it would've looked like to lie instead. Then indulge the fabrication to its logical—or illogical—end.

BREAKTHROUGH IN DESPAIR

Cleyvis Natera

When my husband and I decided to start a family, I'd been writing fiction for the better part of a decade. While in my MFA program, I'd written one novel that had failed. I'd quickly turned my attention to another project, a book I initially found easier to write, which made me confident I was guaranteed to succeed in publishing it.

Yet life has very few guarantees. As the years passed, the book became more complicated and difficult to write; the story seemed to slip through my fingers. Eventually I became so disappointed by the heartbreak of rejection that I left this other book to the side. There were other ways to have a meaningful life, I told myself—after all, I had a thriving career as an executive in corporate America, I was a new wife, and I wanted to be a mother. I repeated it often, especially when I felt the book and its characters tugging at my imagination.

There is no way to describe the way despair can alter our sense of reality. During some routine pregnancy tests, my husband and I found out our first child, a son, would be born with a dangerous blood disorder, sickle cell anemia. It was a terrifying disease; I'd seen my older sister suffer from it since childhood. I was determined to do all I could to prevent my child from experiencing such pain.

After my son, we were blessed to have a daughter who was a perfect bone marrow match. But the blessings during that time in our lives are difficult to calculate. The first bone marrow transplant failed to engraft. After many difficult conversations, we decided to try again. Then, only days after the second bone marrow transplant, while we rested and played silly games in a light yellow hospital room, our son's appendix burst. It was a dire situation. He had no immunity, so the surgery could be fatal, but the appendicitis might also end his life.

We lived suspended for three days while the doctors treated our son with antibiotics. Each day extended before us endless and sepia-colored. I remember not sleeping. I remember trying to eat and having the sensation that everything tasted either of cardboard or too salty. I remember having a thirst that overwhelmed me, that wouldn't go away no matter how much water I drank.

I found myself oddly dissociated from my life, and I felt my mind drifting to the characters in my long-untouched novel time and time again.

But suddenly I had an unexpected understanding: The fear of losing my child brought into stark relief the losses my characters had suffered. It also made clear an error I'd made—attempting to write about gentrification, womanhood, about grief, about displacement from the self, the community, without talking directly about love. This was the breakthrough I didn't realize I needed.

My son recovered from the appendicitis after those terrible three days. A few weeks later we learned his second bone marrow transplant was successful. He emerged sickle-cell-free, ready to rejoin the world after many months of isolation, with his health and an endless curiosity that blooms and blossoms as he gets older.

The breakthrough I experienced in that moment of despair injected life into a story that might very well have remained buried. *Neruda on the Park* was born out of the deepest moment of despair I've known as a parent, as an artist, and as a human. Every time I hold my book it sparkles with all the love and grief I lived through to earn the right to write it.

THIS IS YOUR PROMPT:

Write about a time you had a breakthrough in despair. What did you learn? What did you do with that knowledge?

ON ANTI-BLESSINGS

Kate Bowler

We have days that sparkle, days lit up by fireworks. Nothing can be ordinary, because we have stumbled into some kind of magic. An evening that unspools. A day that seems to wait for our decisions. We feel blessed to be, for a split second, at the center of the universe.

And then we have days of undoing. There is an undoing that is pulling apart every plan. We have the creeping sense that nothing can or ever has been right. The future has disappeared over a horizon we can never reach.

I am a historian who studies the language we use for those moments of magic, that deep luck that makes us wonder if it's divine. It's the language of blessing. But so often our culture mistakes the language for a kind of shellacked certainty that good things should always happen to good people. So on the days like fireworks, we take to social media and proclaim ourselves #blessed. And on days of gentle or ungentle tragedy, then what can we say?

The ancient meaning of the term *blessing* can be beautiful and instructive for naming that strange mix of awful and lovely experiences in our lives. A blessing is a form of spoken poetry about the divine. It's an incredibly positive form of speech, but it's not simply "reframing." (We don't need to say, *Oh, never mind. Tragedy is great! I love it. This is my new mind-set practice!*) We might use blessing as a kind of act that scholar Stephen Chapman calls "emplacement." Calling something blessed can let us say: This goes here, that goes there. This is beautiful. This is awful. And all of it can be called true.

I started using that language especially on days when I was getting chemotherapy. There were moments of unspeakable sadness. And there were moments of surprising joy. Like I am sitting in the basement below the basement in a hospital in Atlanta, a place so comprehensively without light that I began to joke with the nurse that someone would have to be a vampire to work here. And then the nurse, every Wednesday, begins to agree. He strokes my vein before taking out the needle. He pretends to shrink from any light outside the door. He asks if I have any "extra" blood he could have for his own purposes. And I realize, *Oh, this is it*. The beautiful and the terrible right up next to each other, each setting the other in relief, is the only way I would notice blessing at all.

THIS IS YOUR PROMPT:

Think of a time when you felt especially unlucky. The opposite of #blessed—the "anti-blessing," if you will—but then you noticed something beautiful, funny, anything that sparkled. Write about holding the tension of both the deep terrible and the fairy dust feeling.

THE SACRED CENTER

Jasper Young Bear

In my tradition, our story of creation is one that takes four days to tell.

Often people think this is a quaint little story, but it's not. It's a sacred truth, and at its center is this most crucial concept: that you are the universe, that everything the creator went through, you've gone through, too.

Most people struggle with this. Most aren't ready to accept that they are the sacred center. But it's an important shift to what's called whole-to-part thinking, where all the dichotomies of the universe are cast aside. Where there is no male and female, no black and white, no political divide.

When you use whole-to-part thinking, the sense of self is much deeper, more expansive. In our sacred ceremonies, we play this out starting as a baby, when we get an Indian name. In this ceremony, they put us in the center of the universe and have us turn to face all directions. When we get named, we are the light. We are the beginning. We are one with time and space. We go forth, and we vibrate with our names, attracting what others have instilled, attracting what is already inside of us.

Right now, people feel trapped by the systems. The current political system. The distribution of land. People don't feel like they have enough. They don't get to see a rolling river; they can't go pick juneberries, plums, or chokecherries, which all grow wild here where I live, or go fishing in Lake Sakakawea. There's nowhere they're told how nature and community can be in harmony.

But we can create a new world—we must create a new world. All it takes is a mustard seed of faith. We must believe that we are not separate, we are not John or Amy or Ken. I am not Jasper Young Bear. I am the creator, and believing that I am the creator is the only way I can do this work. It's the only way I have the strength to say, "How dare you hurt the earth? How dare you hurt my people? How dare you hurt each other?"

If there is any time that God is listening, if there is any time to pray, it's now.

THIS IS YOUR PROMPT:

Imagine you are the center of the universe. Imagine that you are the creator. Imagine that your power and your prayers have no limit. Imagine all things moving and in motion and all things static and sitting are affected by your prayer. What would you change? What is your prayer?

GESTURES FROM THE SOUL

Behida Dolić

The year after my son died, I watched my dreams fall, one by one, like autumn leaves leaving their branches bare and without any color. This was the hardest year of my life, and I became obsessed with fragile things that persevere in the harshest conditions. In my darkest days, I began creating little pieces of art that no one but me would ever see—little gestures from the soul.

During rainstorms, I opened a window and arranged the sheer white curtains in exactly the right position so I could see them ripple as I lay in bed at night. I wrote joyful memories on hundreds of little scraps of paper, then stacked them to form an arch that, I imagined, was preventing my bedroom wall from falling in on me. Using twine and tacks, I pinned the outlines of shadows to the wall before they disappeared in the passing afternoon light. I painted in watercolors on my window, then watched as the rain washed them away. I placed flowers in a frigid lake and watched them freeze beneath the ice, like grief trapped, no place to go.

These were my ways of tethering all of the little pieces of my soul left behind; of remembering what it felt like to love and be loved, to be safe. These impermanent pieces of art reminded me of times when I was not lonely. They whispered in my ear, "Everything will be all right. You, too, will persevere."

There are endless forms these conceptual, ephemeral pieces can take. Some examples:

Make ten-second films. Download an app on your phone that imitates a vintage super 8-mm camera, or a 16-mm camera. Then, overlay a beautiful piece of piano music that touches your soul.

Close your eyes, and let your body fall into movement. Into poetry in motion.

Write one sentence or word on a corner of a page, perhaps in your favorite book. Fold it over. Write one every day until the book is swollen with folded corners. Your soul carefully placed on a page that someone, someday, hundreds of years from now, will pick up and think, *My goodness. I wish I had known this person. I would have loved her so much!*

These gestures from the soul don't require an immense amount of energy to complete. But they can mend your life back together, tether you to happiness, make you feel free.

THIS IS YOUR PROMPT:

Make a piece of impermanent art. Create a little gesture from the soul, something free. You can choose one of the prompts above, or dream up your own. Then write about what you created, how it made you feel, how it will live on.

AN ENDING AND A BEGINNING

In late July 2024, I was working on the final pieces of this book, puzzling over what to say in the epilogue. *How do I tie all the threads together?* I wondered. *How to wrap this all up with an elegant bow?* But before I could put pen to paper, I got a call that reminded me life doesn't work that way. It was from Dr. G, my oncologist. I'd had a routine bone marrow biopsy earlier that week, and I knew what he was going to say before he said it. Immediately I asked if the leukemia was back again. He replied, "I wish I had better news."

My disease is aggressive, and I knew that an eventual relapse was likely. Still, I was shocked. I was just over two years out from my second transplant, and I expected I'd have longer before I got such a call. More than that, I don't feel sick. All spring and into summer, I worked from sunup until sundown painting watercolors in preparation for my first art exhibit. In early July, I traveled to Europe to visit family and attend a few shows my husband, Jon, was playing, and the long flights and time zone changes barely fazed me. I even started lifting weights each morning, hoping to fortify my body after all it's been through. I truly feel stronger than I have in years. Yet, here I am.

A few days ago, I found the tiniest newborn creature in the middle of my lawn. Pink and hairless, seemingly only hours old, it was the most vulnerable being I'd ever beheld. I thought at first it was a mouse, but upon closer examination, I realized it was a squirrel. A plumber had come by to do some work, and he said I should toss it into a bush, and its mom would either find it or not—either way, nature would run its course. I was horrified at the thought. This was a tiny, precious life, and I had to at least *try* to save it!

My brother, Adam, was visiting, and I recruited him to help with Esquire, as I started calling the little guy. We googled "how to care for a newborn squirrel," found a website with a long list of dos and don'ts, and followed the instructions. First we placed Esquire beneath a nearby tree and played a soundtrack of squirrel distress calls that were supposed to lure the mother in and help her find him. But by nightfall, the mother hadn't shown up, and the website advised against leaving him out, as he'd be vulnerable to predators and the night chill. So we brought Esquire inside, put him in a shoebox lined with the softest towel, and placed it on a heating pad.

Throughout the night, I got up about once an hour to check on him. Each time, I approached the box with so much trepidation—it was as if my own life depended on Esquire's making it through the night. When I woke up and found he was still breathing and, more than that, he'd started squeaking, I felt such a tender sense of hope. Adam and I drove him to the local animal sanctuary, where he's being cared for in the company of baby raccoons and fawns and robins. When strong enough, he'll be returned to the wild.

It's been ten days since the phone call from Dr. G. In a few hours I start a heavy-duty course of chemo. I spent all weekend trying to prepare for what's to come—which is to say, trying to control everything within my control. I have washed all the laundry, organized the closets, and cleaned the bathrooms. I bathed my three dogs and vacuumed the rugs, and yesterday I got on my hands and knees and scrubbed my kitchen floor. My beloveds have been keeping themselves similarly occupied. Jon canceled his upcoming tour dates, reached out to in-the-know contacts about cutting-edge therapies, then called our friend Jonny Miles, a brilliant writer and also a talented cook, to ask if he could deliver some meals during chemo week. Adam took it upon himself to do all the odd jobs around the house that needed doing, replacing lightbulbs, putting new batteries in the fire alarms, and watering the garden.

Yet I know that no matter how clean my house is, how many anti-cancer casseroles I have in the fridge, or how many vulnerable creatures

I rescue, it will not change my circumstances. Our toiling will not change the fact that the path ahead is full of uncertainty, that there will be many obstacles, both known and unknown.

So today, I did one last thing to prepare. I selected a new journal and cracked its spine. On its opening page, I wrote the following lines as a reminder of the alchemy I know so well:

I reach for the page like I reach for prayer: to plead, to confess, to commune, to remember that all is not chaos, all is not lost.

I reach for it like a reporter's pad: to record something overheard, something glimpsed, some stray thought I don't want to forget.

I reach for it like a friend: for company, for counsel. I tell my journal what knots I'm in, and together we untangle the threads. I murmur my dreams and together we arc toward them.

I make of this writing a ritual: to mark the thresholds, to traverse the valleys and the peaks, to honor the space between no longer and not yet.

The journal is oceanic. It is capacious. It is memory, reverie, distillation. It teaches me to pay attention, to see the world anew, to re-arrange the pieces, to play.

The journal is tabula rasa and terra incognita. It is a mirror for the self—past, present, and future—and a portal onto the not yet known. It is refuge: a hiding place, a searching place, a finding place. It's where I go to know myself, to uncover the unlived lives within me.

Here I create myself. Here I write my way through.

This may be the end of *The Book of Alchemy*, but as with most endings, it's also a beginning. This practice is ongoing because life is ongoing. The journal allows us to navigate life's waters, be they turbulent or calm, and to learn to hold the paradoxes—the beautiful and cruel facts of life—in an open palm.

So stop looking for reasons not to do it. Open your journal. Pick up your pen. Return here as many times as you need to. Keep going.

ABOUT THE AUTHOR

SULEIKA JAOUAD is the author of the instant *New York Times* bestselling memoir *Between Two Kingdoms,* which has been translated into over twenty languages. She wrote the *New York Times* column and Emmy Award–winning video series Life, Interrupted, and her essays and feature stories have appeared in *The New York Times Magazine, The Atlantic, The Guardian,* and *Vogue,* among others. She is also the subject, along with husband Jon Batiste, of the Oscar-nominated documentary *American Symphony*—a portrait of two artists during a year of extreme highs and lows. A visual artist, her large-scale watercolors are the focus of several upcoming exhibitions. She is also the creator of the Isolation Journals, a weekly newsletter and global community that harnesses creativity as a tool to navigate life's interruptions.

Newsletter: theisolationjournals.substack.com

suleikajaouad.com

Instagram: @SuleikaJaouad

facebook.com/suleikajaouad

CONTRIBUTORS

HÉDI ABDEL-JAOUAD is a professor emeritus of French and francophone studies at Skidmore College and also my dad. The editor of *CELAAN,* a journal dedicated to the promotion of North African literature and art, he is the author of
numerous articles and books, including *Browningmania: America's Love for the
Brownings* and *Limitless Undying Love: The Ballad of John and Yoko and the Brownings.* (The working title for my next book is *Hédi's Browningmania: How My Father's Obsession with Robert and Elizabeth Barrett Browning Has Ruined Our Family
Dinners for the Last Two Decades.*) Inspired by his own 100-day project, he is writing a memoir of his childhood in Tunisia, *Until the Sahara Blooms Again.*

HANIF ABDURRAQIB is a poet, essayist, and cultural critic from Columbus,
Ohio. His nonfiction includes *They Can't Kill Us Until They Kill Us,* the *New York
Times* bestsellers *There's Always This Year, Go Ahead in The Rain: Notes to A Tribe
Called Quest,* and *A Little Devil in America,* which was a finalist for the National
Book Award and winner of the Gordon Burn Prize and the Andrew Carnegie
Medal for Excellence in Nonfiction. He is the author of two full-length poetry col-
lections, *The Crown Ain't Worth Much* and *A Fortune for Your Disaster,* which won
the 2020 Lenore Marshall Prize. Hanif is also a recipient of a MacArthur Fellow-
ship.

AZITA ARDAKANI is a philanthropist and social entrepreneur. She is a student of
nature's principles as a means to inform economics, social organizations, and design. The founder of the creative impact agency Lovesocial, she is currently in the
pursuit of the relationship between inner life and outer ecology to meet the challenges of these times.

SKY BANYES is an artist, writer, and physicist engineer who believes all feelings
are valid and valuable and strives to discover beauty and healing through everyday
experiences. She is the author and illustrator of *The Little Book of Silver Linings:
Finding Joy in the Toughest Times.* Although she calls Paris home, she has gathered
a worldwide community on Instagram.

JON BATISTE, my beloved partner in life and creativity, is an Oscar, Emmy, Golden Globe, and five-time Grammy Award–winning musician from Louisiana. He earned a BA and an MFA from the Juilliard School, spent years playing music on subways and throughout the streets of New York City with his band Stay Human, then served as the bandleader and musical director of *The Late Show with Stephen Colbert* from 2015 to 2022. He has released seven studio albums, including *We Are,* which won Album of the Year in 2022, and *World Music Radio,* which draws inspiration from his mission to create community and expand culture through the power of music.

MARTHA BECK, PHD, is a bestselling author, coach, and speaker. Her books include the *New York Times* bestsellers *Finding Your Own North Star, The Joy Diet, The Way of Integrity,* and most recently, *Beyond Anxiety: Curiosity, Creativity, and Finding Your Life's Purpose.* The author of over 150 magazine articles, including almost two decades of monthly columns for *O, The Oprah Magazine,* she has been called "the best-known life coach in America" by NPR and "one of the smartest women I know" by Oprah Winfrey.

BARBARA BECKER is the award-winning author of *Heartwood: The Art of Living with the End in Mind.* She is a mom, a perpetual seeker, and most recently a breast cancer survivor. As a hospice volunteer in New York City, she has shared time with hundreds of people at the end of their lives and sees each as a teacher.

MICHAEL BIERUT is a partner in the New York office of the international design consultancy Pentagram, a founder of the website Design Observer, and a teacher at the Yale School of Art and the Yale School of Management. His clients have included *The New York Times,* Saks Fifth Avenue, and the New York Jets; as a volunteer to Hillary Clinton's communications team, he designed the *H* logo for her 2016 presidential campaign. He has published a monograph on his work, *How to Use Graphic Design to Sell Things, Explain Things, Make Things Look Better, Make People Laugh, Make People Cry and (Every Once in a While) Change the World* as well as a collection of essays, *Now You See It.* Elected to the Alliance Graphique Internationale and the Art Directors Club Hall of Fame, he was awarded the profession's highest honor, the AIGA Medal, in 2006.

JOHN BINKLEY was a playwright, political activist, and television producer, writer, and director. In 1977, he moved from California to Houston, Texas, where he met Sherrie Matthews; they were married six months later. John penned forty-six letters to Sherrie after her death in December 2022 before he followed her to the other side in October 2023. A complete collection of the letters will be published at a future date.

NADIA BOLZ-WEBER is an ordained Lutheran pastor and the author of three *New York Times* bestselling memoirs: *Pastrix: The Cranky, Beautiful Faith of a Sinner*

& Saint, Accidental Saints: Finding God in All the Wrong People, and *Shameless: A Sexual Reformation.* She writes and speaks about personal failings, recovery, grace, and faith and always prefers to sit in the corner with the other weirdos. You can keep up with her recent writing in *The Corners* on Substack.

BIANCA BOSKER is an award-winning journalist and the *New York Times* bestselling author of *Get the Picture: A Mind-Bending Journey Among the Inspired Artists and Obsessive Art Fiends Who Taught Me How to See.* She is also the author of the *New York Times* bestseller *Cork Dork,* which has been praised as the *Kitchen Confidential* of wine. She writes regularly for *The Atlantic,* graduated from Princeton University, and currently lives in New York City.

JENNY BOULLY is the author of six books, including *Betwixt-and-Between: Essays on the Writing Life, The Book of Beginnings and Endings,* and *The Body: An Essay.* She attended Hollins University, then earned an MFA in creative writing from the University of Notre Dame and a PhD in English from the City University of New York. A 2020 Guggenheim Fellow in General Nonfiction, she teaches at Bennington College.

KATE BOWLER, PHD, is a four-time *New York Times* bestselling author, award-winning podcast host, and professor at Duke University. She wrote the first history of the American prosperity gospel—the belief that God wants to give you health, wealth, and happiness—before being diagnosed with stage IV cancer at age thirty-five. While she was in treatment, she wrote two *New York Times* bestselling memoirs, *Everything Happens for a Reason (and Other Lies I've Loved)* and *No Cure for Being Human (and Other Truths I Need to Hear).* The host of the podcast *Everything Happens,* she lives in Durham, North Carolina, with her family and continues to teach do-gooders at Duke Divinity School.

I met **AURA BRICKLER** through her husband, Bret Hoekema, who died in 2021 after nearly a decade of unrelenting cancer and treatment-related complications. As tender and honest a human as there is, Aura works as a social worker with the Chicago public schools. With the help of modern medicine, Aura and Bret were able to welcome Evie Maeve into the world in 2017. Aura says their daughter is "a radiant light beam, and by far their best accomplishment."

ARDEN BROWN lives on a farm in central New York with her dog, Oban, and her cat, Coco, among other animals and humans, too. She spends her free time reading and playing the violin. She wrote "Mrs. R—" about her fourth-grade teacher.

ANNIE CAMPBELL learned storytelling at the dinner table—the only time life stood still in a diplomat's family—then she spent forty years teaching children to be passionate about their lives as writers and readers. She lives in Richmond, Virginia, with her husband, Ben. She wrote "I Have Been Eating Figs" after listening to a conversation I hosted for the Isolation Journals where I talked about being a third-culture kid.

SUSAN CHEEVER is the author of sixteen books and dozens of essays. The stories of her father, the writer John Cheever, are the subject of her book *When All the Men Wore Hats: Cheever on Cheever.* The winner of a Guggenheim Fellowship, Susan has written for many magazines and newspapers, including *The New Yorker, The New York Times,* and *Newsday,* where she contributed to winning a 1997 Pulitzer Prize for breaking news. Cheever has taught at Yale, Sarah Lawrence College, Brown University, and Bennington College, and is currently a faculty member at The New School in their MFA program. She also serves on the board of the Yaddo Corporation and the Author's Guild Council.

LISA ANN COCKREL is a writer, editor, and event curator whose own creative writing explores the interplay between social bodies and individual bodies, with a specific focus on fat bodies. Currently an acquisitions editor for Eerdmans, she was previously the director of programs for *Image Journal,* director of the Festival of Faith and Writing, and managing editor for Brazos Press. Lisa Ann also holds an MFA in creative nonfiction from the Bennington Writing Seminars.

STEPHANIE DANLER is a novelist, memoirist, and screenwriter. She is the author of the international bestseller *Sweetbitter* and the memoir *Stray;* she's also the creator and executive producer of the *Sweetbitter* series on Starz. She is based in Los Angeles.

ALAIN DE BOTTON is the author of more than a dozen essayistic books, most recently *A Therapeutic Journey,* that have been bestsellers in thirty countries. He's written on love, travel, architecture, and literature and has been described as penning a "philosophy of everyday life." Alain also founded and helps to run the School of Life, dedicated to a new vision of education. Born in Zurich, Switzerland, he now lives in London.

RENE DENFELD is the award-winning, bestselling author of four novels, *The Enchanted, The Child Finder, The Butterfly Girl,* and *Sleeping Giants.* A *New York Times* Hero of the Year and a recipient of the Break the Silence Award, she is a former chief investigator for public defenders and has worked hundreds of cases, including exonerations and helping rape trafficking victims. She lives in Portland, Oregon, where she is the happy parent of kids from foster care.

NELL DIAMOND is founder and CEO of Hill House Home, a fashion and lifestyle brand that brings beauty and joy to everyday rituals. Founded in 2016 as a direct-to-consumer bedding and home business, Hill House Home went viral with the 2019 launch of their cult-favorite product, the Nap Dress.® Led by the values of quality, comfort, and design integrity, Nell has been named to *Inc*'s Female Founders 250 list, *Fast Company*'s Most Innovative Companies list, the *Business of Fashion*'s "500" List, *Marie Claire*'s Power List, and more.

BEHIDA DOLIĆ grew up in a small village in southern Bosnia, among kilim weavers and furniture builders, where "handmade" was a way of life. Fleeing war, she moved to the United States in 1998 and went on to study art in San Francisco and Florence, Italy. Since 2011, she has been the owner of Behida Dolić Millinery in Hudson, New York, where she sells handmade hats and her own line of women's clothing. A cancer survivor, Behida also paints, sculpts, dances, writes, and makes ephemeral art. She is currently working on a memoir.

MAGGIE DOYNE has dedicated her life to educating children and empowering women in Nepal. She is co-founder and CEO of the BlinkNow Foundation, author of *Between the Mountain and the Sky,* and the subject of a new documentary film of the same name. The BlinkNow Foundation provides an education and a loving, caring home for at-risk children in Surkhet, Nepal. The foundation also provides community outreach to reduce poverty, empower women, improve health, and encourage sustainability and social justice.

LENA DUNHAM is an award-winning multihyphenate. The author of the *New York Times* bestselling essay collection *Not That Kind of Girl,* she is also the creator of the HBO series *Girls,* for which she was nominated for eight Emmy Awards and won two Golden Globes, including Best Actress. She was the first woman to win the Directors Guild of America Award for directorial achievement in comedy. Lena is also the writer, director, and star of *Tiny Furniture,* which won an Independent Spirit Award for Best First Screenplay; she has since written and directed the films *Sharp Stick* and *Catherine Called Birdy.* She's also a host of the podcast *The C-Word,* which examines the stories of women that history loves to call "crazy."

MELISSA FEBOS is the author of four books, including the nationally bestselling essay collection *Girlhood,* which won the National Book Critics Circle Award in Criticism; the memoirs *Whip Smart* and *Abandon Me;* and a craft book, *Body Work.* Her fifth book, *The Dry Season,* is forthcoming from Knopf. The recipient of a 2022 Guggenheim Foundation Fellowship and a 2022 National Endowment for the Arts Literature Fellowship, she is a professor at the University of Iowa and lives in Iowa City with her wife, poet Donika Kelly.

LIANA FINCK graduated from Cooper Union in 2008 and has been making cartoons ever since. The recipient of a Fulbright, she has published several books, including *Passing for Human,* a graphic memoir; *Let There Be Light,* a graphic novel; and *You Broke It!,* a children's book. Her cartoons appear regularly in *The New Yorker* and on her wildly popular Instagram page, which has one of my favorite bio lines. In reference to requests about her cartoons, it says, "You may tattoo for free."

ANNE FRANCEY is a visual artist whose studio practice includes painting, drawing, and ceramics and who has exhibited in the United States, Switzerland, and Tunisia. She is the recipient of several grants from the New York State Council of the Arts for creating community murals in schools and public spaces. She was named a Fulbright Scholar for 2021 in Tunisia, where she led a participatory art project called 1,001 Briques. She is also my mother, and my first and forever teacher on the subjects of curiosity, experimentation, creativity, and beauty.

TATIANA GALLARDO is a marker-wielding writer and illustrator. Her newsletter, *Brazenface,* chronicles her adventures in facing fear—like giving up alcohol, wearing head-to-toe orange, and most recently: finally mustering the courage to begin again.

PULOMA GHOSH is the author of the short story collection *Mouth.* Her work has appeared in *One Story, CRAFT, Cake Zine, BoTM's Volume Ø,* and other publications. Puloma has served as a teaching fellow at Bennington College and received a scholarship from Tin House Writers Workshop. She was born in Kolkata, grew up in Massachusetts, and now lives in Chicago.

ELIZABETH GILBERT is the author of ten books of fiction and nonfiction—most famously her 2006 memoir, *Eat, Pray, Love.* Her TED Talk on creative genius is one of the twenty most viewed TED Talks of all time, and her book *Big Magic* has helped untold numbers of readers—myself included—choose lives of curiosity over fear.

JOHN GREEN is the author of the #1 *New York Times* bestselling novels *The Fault in Our Stars* and *Turtles All the Way Down,* as well as the essay collection *The Anthropocene Reviewed.* He was the 2006 recipient of the Michael L. Printz Award, was a 2009 Edgar Award winner, and has twice been a finalist for the *Los Angeles Times* Book Prize. Along with his brother, Hank, John is involved in a number of video projects, including vlogbrothers, their YouTube channel where they promote intellectualism and try to better the world, including raising millions of dollars to fight poverty in the developing world and planting thousands of trees; and Crash Course, where they teach science and the humanities to more than ten million subscribers.

MARIE HOWE broke poetry open for me. She is the author of five collections of poems, most recently *New and Selected Poems,* as well as *What the Living Do* and *Magdalene.* She has received fellowships from the National Endowment for the Arts, the Guggenheim Foundation, and the Academy of American Poets. She was the Poet Laureate of New York State from 2012 to 2014 and is currently the Poet in Residence at the Cathedral Church of St. John the Divine. She lives in New York City.

HOLLYNN HUITT is a writer and the community manager for the Isolation Journals. She holds a BFA in writing from the Savannah College of Art and Design and an MFA in fiction from the Bennington Writing Seminars. She has stories published in *Stone Canoe, Hobart, PANK,* and *X-R-A-Y.* She lives in an old farmhouse in central New York with her family and many animals, which she writes about on her Substack, *far away.*

PICO IYER is the author of seventeen books that have been translated into twenty-three languages, including *The Half Known Life, Aflame,* and *The Art of Stillness.* He has been a constant contributor for more than thirty years to over 250 periodicals worldwide, including *The New York Times, Harper's Magazine,* and *The New York Review of Books.* His four recent talks for TED have received more than eleven million views.

HOLLYE JACOBS, RN, MS, MSW, is a resilience coach, nurse, speaker, and author. As a coach, Hollye supports and empowers people as they navigate life's inevitable challenges and transitions with strength, confidence, and compassion, and she shares practical strategies to help people find clarity, purpose, and a path forward. Diagnosed with breast cancer in 2010, she writes about her experience in her *New York Times* bestselling book, *The Silver Lining: A Supportive and Insightful Guide to Breast Cancer.*

OLIVER JEFFERS is an artist, author, and activist working across a number of fields using a number of mediums. He grew up in Belfast, Northern Ireland, where he studied at Belfast School of Art at Ulster University. Primarily known for his picture books for children, his work has been translated into forty-nine languages and has sold nearly fourteen million copies worldwide. An internationally recognized painter, sculptor, and speaker, Oliver's work, with its simple and accessible beauty, encourages people everywhere of every age to reconsider how they see a world that is radically changing, and, armed with perspective and hope, to reexamine their role in how it will be shaped for future generations.

JEDIDIAH JENKINS is a professional adventurer, travel writer, and environmental advocate who, after leaving his job at age thirty, bicycled from Oregon to Patagonia. He is the *New York Times* bestselling author of three memoirs: *To Shake the Sleeping Self, Like Streams to the Ocean,* and most recently, *Mother, Nature.*

QUINTIN JONES spent more than half his life on death row, where he passed the time reading books, writing letters to pen pals, and doing a thousand push-ups each day. In the spring of 2021, I worked with a bevy of lawyers and advocates on a clemency plea to save Quin's life, and with the help of the Isolation Journals community, shared his story widely; a change.org petition for clemency received nearly two hundred thousand signatures. When Quin was executed by the State of Texas on May 19, 2021, there were no media witnesses, a first in the modern death penalty era. Quin's last words to me were "Keep doing the good work."

JILL KEARNEY is a producer of communal spectacles, a curator, and a former journalist and film executive. After graduating from Harvard with a degree in English and creative writing, she worked in Hollywood as a creative executive at Francis Coppola's Zoetrope Studios, then as West Coast editor of *American Film* and *Premiere* magazine. Later she produced literary, music, theater, and dance events in an old dairy barn in Bucks County, Pennsylvania, then founded ArtYard, an interdisciplinary arts center in Frenchtown, New Jersey, where she currently serves as executive director.

A National Book Award finalist, **BETH KEPHART** has published some forty books in multiple genres, from memoir and fiction to picture books and poetry. She is a paper artist and also an award-winning teacher at the University of Pennsylvania. Her essays have appeared in *The New York Times, The Washington Post,* the *Chicago Tribune,* and elsewhere.

Known for her writing on addiction and recovery, mental health, and relationships, **ERIN KHAR** is the author of the memoir *Strung Out* and the popular advice column Ask Erin on Substack. When she's not writing, Erin is probably watching *Beverly Hills, 90210.* She lives in New York City.

KIMBRA is a New Zealand–born songwriter, musician, producer, and adventurous performer. Her 2011 debut, *Vows,* was certified platinum in Australia and New Zealand; that next year, "Somebody That I Used to Know," a duet with Gotye, topped *Billboard*'s Hot 100 chart, was the bestselling song of the year in the United States, and earned her two Grammy Awards. Since then, she has toured with artists ranging from the Roots and David Byrne to Beck, Son Lux, and Jacob Collier. She has released four more albums to date: *The Golden Echo, Primal Heart, A Reckoning,* and most recently *Idols & Vices, Vol. 1.*

MICHAEL KORYTA is a *New York Times* bestselling author whose work has been translated into more than twenty languages, adapted into major motion pictures, and has won the *Los Angeles Times* Book Prize. A graduate of Indiana University, he previously worked as a private investigator and journalist. He also writes novels under the pseudonym Scott Carson. He lives in Bloomington, Indiana, and Camden, Maine.

HANIF KUREISHI is a playwright, screenwriter, filmmaker, and novelist. He is the author of dozens of works, including the Oscar-nominated screenplay for *My Beautiful Laundrette.* His novel *The Buddha of Suburbia* won the Whitbread Prize for Best First Novel, and his novel *Intimacy* was adapted as a film that won the Golden Bear Award at the Berlin Film Festival. Awarded the CBE for his services to literature and the Chevalier de l'Ordre des Arts et Lettres in France, his works have been translated into thirty-six languages. He also writes the newsletter *The Kureishi Chronicles.*

KIESE LAYMON is a professor of English and creative writing at Rice University and the author of three books: *Long Division,* which won the NAACP Image

Award for Fiction; *How to Slowly Kill Yourself and Others in America;* and *Heavy: An American Memoir*—a book I admire so much I've read it at least a half-dozen times. The recipient of a Radcliffe Fellowship at Harvard, Kiese was awarded a MacArthur Fellowship in 2022. He hails from Jackson, Mississippi.

MARIAH Z. LEACH is a writer, patient advocate, and mom of three living with rheumatoid arthritis. After learning firsthand how challenging and lonely it can be to face pregnancy and motherhood with chronic illness, she founded Mamas Facing Forward, a website and support group for women with chronic illness who are or want to become mothers.

ELIZABETH LESSER is the author of several bestselling books, including *Cassandra Speaks: When Women are the Storytellers, the Human Story Changes; Broken Open: How Difficult Times Can Help Us Grow;* and *Marrow: Love, Loss & What Matters Most.* Co-founder of the internationally recognized Omega Institute, which hosts workshops and conferences on wellness, spirituality, creativity, and social change, she is one of Oprah Winfrey's Super Soul 100, a collection of a hundred leaders who are using their voices and talent to elevate humanity.

A former magazine editor and communications consultant, **JENNIFER LEVEN-THAL** is a caregiver adviser with the Patient and Family Advisory Council for Quality (PFACQ) at Memorial Sloan Kettering Cancer Center. She lives in Rye, New York, with her husband, Eric, and their doodle, Hudson. She is the proud mother of Alex and Danielle, a talented painter who introduced herself to me in a New York City café while she was in cancer treatment, and who passed away in 2021 at the age of twenty-seven. Jennifer's essay was written in response to the very first Isolation Journals prompt, which I sent out on April 1, 2020.

SARAH LEVY is the author of *Drinking Games,* a memoir in essays exploring the role alcohol has in our formative years and what it means to opt out of a culture completely enmeshed in drinking. She is a graduate of Brown University, and her work has appeared in *The New York Times, The Cut, Vogue, Time, Marie Claire, Cosmopolitan, Glamour,* and *Bustle,* among other publications. She lives in Los Angeles with her husband and son.

RUTHIE LINDSEY is the author of the memoir *There I Am: The Journey from Hopelessness to Healing.* A Nashville-based speaker and coach, she helps people become endeared to their own lives, souls, and bodies. Her message is one of strength and resilience and the power of telling a new story through radical self-love and compassion.

NATHAN LOWDERMILK is a surfer and the founder of Native Surf School on the Outer Banks of North Carolina. He has more than a decade of ocean rescue experience and deep, hard-won knowledge of waves, which he shares with students between the ages of five and eighteen. Nathan also spends part of the year as a guide at Two Brothers Surf Resort in Popoyo, Nicaragua.

MARIE MCGRORY is a cancer survivor and a visual storyteller. She is an innately curious human who spent years as a photo editor at *National Geographic.* Most recently, she joined TED in their work accelerating climate solutions. She is happiest when she is out enjoying nature or bringing people together for thoughtful celebrations. And she absolutely loves giraffes.

NORA MCINERNY is the author of five books, including *No Happy Endings* and *Bad Vibes Only,* and the host of *Terrible, Thanks for Asking,* a podcast that lets people be honest about the hard things in life. She's also a remarried widow raising a beautiful blended family with her current, very much alive husband.

LAURA MCKOWEN is the bestselling author of *We Are the Luckiest: The Surprising Magic of a Sober Life* and *Push Off From Here: Nine Essential Truths to Get You Through Sobriety (and Everything Else),* and the founder of the Luckiest Club, a global sobriety support organization. Laura has been published in *The New York Times,* and her work has been featured in *The Atlantic, The Wall Street Journal,* on *The Today Show,* and more. She lives outside Boston with her daughter and writes the newsletter *Love Story.*

TAMZIN MERIVALE is an Irish artist, writer, and mentor currently based in Europe. Tamzin creates unique Soul Sign Energy Portraits, guiding clients through an immersive experience to unearth their powerful selves, their incomparable light, and their strength. Her mission is to hold space for greater empathy and understanding, as these are the true enemies of prejudice and judgment.

JONATHAN MILES is the author of the novels *Dear American Airlines* and *Want Not,* both *New York Times* Notable Books, and *Anatomy of a Miracle.* A former columnist for *The New York Times* and a continuing editor for a wide range of national magazines, he recently joined my husband, Jon Batiste, on his Uneasy Tour, playing the harmonica and banjo and whipping up the occasional pot of gumbo for the band. A former longtime resident of Oxford, Mississippi, he currently lives in rural New Jersey.

Born in New Jersey, **MARCUS G. MILLER** took up saxophone at age nine and was playing professionally in his teens. A graduate of Harvard University with a degree in mathematics, he worked for a short stint at a hedge fund before moving to New York City to pursue music. He has performed at the Obama White House, Madison Square Garden, Coachella alongside Jon Batiste, and Carnegie Hall. Recognized as an Artist of Distinction by the state of New Jersey and the first Artist in Residence at the Brown University Physics Department, he is now music director at Grace Farms and records and performs with his group, IWM.

DEBBIE MILLMAN is a designer, educator, curator, host of the long-running, award-winning podcast *Design Matters,* and the author of seven books on design and branding. Debbie co-founded the world's first graduate program in branding at the School of Visual Arts in New York City in 2010, and she is also president emeritus of the American Institute of Graphic Arts (AIGA)—one of only five women to hold the position in the organization's hundred-year history. She was awarded a lifetime achievement award from AIGA in 2019.

FERNANDO MURILLO, a San Francisco resident, is passionate about hospice care. During his five years working in the prison hospice at California Medical Facility, where he was incarcerated, he was trained to provide compassionate end-of-life care for geriatric and terminally ill patients in a correctional setting. Now, as the program manager at the Humane Prison Hospice Project, Fernando trains incarcerated peer caregivers to provide better care for terminally and seriously ill individuals within the carceral system.

CLEYVIS NATERA is an award-winning novelist, short-story writer, essayist, and critic. She is the author of the debut novel *Neruda on the Park,* which was a *New York Times* Editors' Choice and was awarded a Silver Medal by the International Latino Book Awards for Best First Book of Fiction. The recipient of awards and fellowships from PEN America, the Vermont Studio Center, and Bread Loaf Writers' Conference, among others, Natera studied literature and creative writing at Skidmore College and holds an MFA in fiction from New York University. Her second novel, *The Grand Paloma Resort,* is forthcoming from Ballantine Books.

CROW JONAH NORLANDER lives in Maine with his family of humans and hounds. His fiction, poetry, and interviews have appeared in *BOMB* magazine, the *Los Angeles Review of Books, FENCE,* and *New World Writing.* He is also the co-editor of *HAD.*

LINDA SUE PARK is the author of many books for young readers, including the 2002 Newbery Medal winner *A Single Shard,* the *New York Times* bestseller *A Long Walk to Water,* and most recently, *Gracie under the Waves,* a novel for young readers about a girl who loves to snorkel. The founder and curator of Allida Books, an imprint of HarperCollins, she serves on the advisory boards of We Need Diverse Books and the Rabbit hOle museum project. She also established the website Ki-Booka to highlight children's books created by the Korean diaspora.

ANN PATCHETT is the author of nine novels, including *Bel Canto; State of Wonder; Commonwealth; The Dutch House,* which was a finalist for the Pulitzer Prize; and *Tom Lake.* She has written four books of nonfiction, including one of my very favorites of all time, *Truth & Beauty,* about her friendship with the writer Lucy Grealy. The recipient of numerous awards and fellowships, including a National Humanities Medal, the PEN/Faulkner Award, and a Guggenheim Fellowship, she is also the owner of Parnassus Books in Nashville, Tennessee, where she lives with her husband, Karl VanDevender, and their dog, Nemo.

ASHLEIGH BELL PEDERSEN is the author of the novel *The Crocodile Bride* (a *New York Times* Editors' Choice) and assorted nonfiction, most recently in *Garden & Gun*. She lives in Brooklyn, where she also paints, acts, and struggles to teach her sweet dog, Ernie, better leash manners.

Psychotherapist and bestselling author **ESTHER PEREL** is recognized as one of today's most insightful and original voices on modern relationships. Fluent in nine languages, she helms a therapy practice in New York City and serves as an organizational consultant for *Fortune* 500 companies around the world. She is the author of two *New York Times* bestsellers, *Mating in Captivity: Unlocking Erotic Intelligence* and *The State of Affairs: Rethinking Infidelity.* Esther is an executive producer and host of the popular podcast *Where Should We Begin?* and her celebrated TED Talks have garnered more than twenty million views.

CONNIE CARPENTER PHINNEY is an entrepreneur, author, artist, and an Olympic speed skater and cyclist who won the gold medal in cycling at the 1984 Olympics. She attended UC Berkeley, where she rowed crew and majored in physical education with an emphasis on exercise physiology, then earned her master's in exercise science from the University of Colorado–Boulder. She is also the cofounder and a board member of the Davis Phinney Foundation for Parkinson's.

PAULINA PINSKY is a writer, educator, and figure skater based in Los Angeles. She received her MFA in creative nonfiction from Columbia University and studied improvisational and sketch comedy at the Second City Conservatory in Chicago. An Ernest and Red Heller Fellowship recipient at MacDowell in 2021, she has been published in *Narratively, Columbia Journal,* and *HuffPo Women,* among others. She is the co-author of the teen guide to consent *It Doesn't Have to Be Awkward* and also writes the newsletter *newly sober.*

MOLLY PRENTISS is the author of *Old Flame* and *Tuesday Nights in 1980,* which was long-listed for the Center for Fiction First Novel Prize and shortlisted for the Grand Prix de Littérature Américaine in France. Her writing has been translated into multiple languages. She lives in Red Hook, New York, with her husband and daughters.

JOANNE PROULX is a writer and photographer whose critically acclaimed debut novel, *Anthem of a Reluctant Prophet,* won Canada's Sunburst Award for Fantastic Fiction. Her second novel, *We All Love the Beautiful Girls,* was named one of a hundred best books by *The Globe and Mail* in 2017. She's currently working on her third novel, *There Will Be Swimming.* A graduate of the Bennington Writing Seminars, Joanne lives, writes, and teaches in Ottawa, Canada.

CARMEN RADLEY is a writer and the managing editor of the Isolation Journals. A graduate of the University of Texas and the Bennington Writing Seminars, she's currently writing a memoir about her hometown of Sour Lake, Texas, an early-twentieth-century oil boomtown where her family has worked in the oil field for more than a century. She lives in Austin.

ADRIENNE RAPHEL is the author of *Thinking Inside the Box: Adventures with Crosswords and the Puzzling People Who Can't Live Without Them; What Was It For*, winner of the Rescue Press Black Box Poetry Prize; and *Our Dark Academia*. Her essays and poetry appear in *The New York Times, The New Yorker, The Paris Review, Poetry*, and many other publications. Born in New Jersey and raised in Vermont, Adrienne is a graduate of Princeton University and holds an MFA in poetry from the Iowa Writers' Workshop and a PhD in English from Harvard University.

REBECCA REBOUCHÉ is a painter, writer, filmmaker, and entrepreneur known for her large-scale paintings of allegorical family trees. A Louisiana native, Rebecca's work is fed by the rich artistic history of New Orleans and the myths and mysteries of the city's surrounding forests and waterways. She has been featured in *The New York Times, Garden & Gun, Anthology Magazine*, and *The Great Discontent*.

JENNY ROSENSTRACH is a food writer and cookbook author. Her *New York Times* bestselling book, *The Weekday Vegetarians*, is about a vow she and her family made that goes like this: Eat less meat, sort of. You can find her work in various national publications, including *Cup of Jo, Real Simple*, and *Bon Appétit*, where she was a columnist for seven years, and in her newsletter, *Dinner: A Love Story*.

RAVEN ROXANNE is an abstract and impressionist painter. Raised on the Florida Gulf Coast by a family of artists who encouraged creativity from an early age, she studied painting at Auburn University. She is drawn to themes of nature, femininity, community, and family, and uses natural elements such as nests, flowers, and birds to explore the nuances of these ideas. She lives in the heart of the historic district of Charleston, South Carolina, with her husband, Thomas; son, English; daughter, Sunday; and rescue pup, Willie.

SARAH RUHL is a poet and playwright. Her plays include *In the Next Room, or The Vibrator Play*, which was a Pulitzer Prize finalist and Tony Award nominee, and *The Clean House*, also a Pulitzer Prize finalist, and winner of the Susan Smith Blackburn Prize. She is the author of the memoir *Smile*, a poetry collection, *Love Poems in Quarantine*, and the co-author of *Letters from Max*, a deeply moving portrait of her friendship with the poet Max Ritvo, whom I met in treatment and, like Sarah, loved oceanically. A recipient of a MacArthur Fellowship and the Steinberg Prize, she is currently on the faculty of the Yale School of Drama and lives in Brooklyn with her family.

SALMAN RUSHDIE is the author of fifteen novels and one collection of short stories. He has also published five works of nonfiction, including his most recent memoir, *Knife*. He is a member of the American Academy of Arts and Letters and a Distinguished Writer in Residence at New York University. A former president of PEN America, Rushdie was knighted in 2007 for his service to literature.

SHARON SALZBERG is a meditation pioneer, world-renowned teacher, and beloved author. A co-founder of the Insight Meditation Society, she has written thirteen books, including the *New York Times* bestseller *Real Happiness*, now in its second edition, and her seminal work, *Lovingkindness*. Her popular podcast, *Metta Hour*, features interviews with thought leaders from the mindfulness movement and beyond.

GEORGE SAUNDERS is the author of twelve books, including the novel *Lincoln in the Bardo*, which won the Booker Prize, and the story collections *Pastoralia* and *Tenth of December*, which was a finalist for the National Book Award. He has received fellowships from the Lannan Foundation, the American Academy of Arts and Letters, the Guggenheim Foundation, and the MacArthur Foundation. He teaches in the creative writing program at Syracuse University and writes the newsletter *Story Club*.

RACHEL SCHWARTZMANN is the author of *Slowing* and the creator of Slow Stories, a multimedia project that explores living, working, and creating more intentionally. Her essays and interviews have appeared in *BOMB* magazine, *Coveteur*, *Literary Hub*, and *TOAST* magazine, among other places. A member of the Isolation Journals community wrote in to tell me that she believes Rachel's essay and prompt were the equivalent of four hundred dollars' worth of therapy.

DANI SHAPIRO is the author of eleven books, most recently the novel *Signal Fires*, which was named a best book of 2022 by NPR, *Time* magazine, and *The Washington Post*, and the memoir *Inheritance*, which was an instant *New York Times* bestseller. Dani is also the host and creator of the hit podcast *Family Secrets* and the co-founder of the Sirenland Writers Conference in Positano, Italy.

Hailed by NPR as "one of America's defining voices of freedom and peace," **MAVIS STAPLES** is a once-in-a-generation artist whose impact on music and culture would be difficult to overstate. She's both a Blues and a Rock & Roll Hall of Famer; a civil rights icon; a Grammy Award winner; a National Arts Awards Lifetime Achievement recipient; and a Kennedy Center honoree. She marched with Dr. Martin Luther King, Jr., performed at John F. Kennedy's inauguration, and sang in Barack Obama's White House. She's collaborated with everyone from Prince and Bob Dylan to Arcade Fire and Hozier, blown away festivalgoers from Newport Folk to Glastonbury and Lollapalooza, and graced the airwaves on *Colbert, Austin City Limits*, the Grammys, and more.

GLORIA STEINEM is a writer, lecturer, political activist, and feminist organizer. She has spent decades traveling worldwide as an organizer and lecturer and is a frequent media spokeswoman on issues of equality. She is particularly interested in nonviolent conflict resolution, the cultures of Indigenous peoples, and organizing across boundaries for peace and justice. She lives in New York City.

MARGO STEINES is the author of the memoir *Brutalities*. She holds an MFA in creative nonfiction from the University of Arizona, where she teaches writing. Her work has appeared in the *New York Times* Modern Love column, *The Sun,* and elsewhere. A native New Yorker, she lives in Tucson, Arizona.

ANGELIQUE STEVENS lives in upstate New York, where she teaches creative writing, literature of genocide, and race literatures. She holds an MFA in creative nonfiction from the Bennington Writing Seminars and an MA in literature from SUNY Brockport. "Ghost Bread" will appear in her book of essays, forthcoming from Simon & Schuster.

ASH PARSONS STORY is a photographer, writer, and mother. Her work has appeared in the *HuffPost, American Photo Magazine,* and *Real Simple Weddings.* An alumni of the 2019 Thread at Yale program through the Yale Journalism Initiative, Ash has taught at workshops and creative retreats and been a filmmaker, a community volunteer, and a vital part of creative collaborations all over the world for the last eighteen years. I write to her prompt "Just Ten Images" at least once a week.

LOU SULLIVAN is a two-time pediatric brain cancer survivor, tap dancer, and fedora enthusiast. He lives in upstate New York with his parents, his twin brother, West, and their rescue pup, a black standard poodle named Oscar Wilding. His mother, Alexa Wilding, is a writer, musician, breast cancer survivor, and advocate.

DAVID SUTTON is a photographer, writer, builder, singer, and songsmith based in Evanston, Illinois. He's written and photographed two books about building cigar box guitars and has an album called *From Gold to Brown to Blue* (with Friedel Geratsch). For the past thirty years, he has operated Sutton Studios, photographing the deep and meaningful relationships people have with their pets.

NOOR TAGOURI is an award-winning journalist, producer, and speaker. She has told critically acclaimed stories in every medium, from radio and print to documentaries and brand campaigns. The founder of At Your Service Media, a production company telling representative stories as a form of service, she is also the creator of the investigative series and subsequent course *REP: A Story about the Stories We Tell,* which explores the concepts of representation and objectivity in media.

Born and raised in Southern California, **NAFISSA THOMPSON-SPIRES** earned a PhD in English from Vanderbilt University and an MFA in creative writing from the University of Illinois. She has attended the Callaloo Writers Workshop, the Tin House Workshop, and the Sewanee Writers' Conference as the Stanley Elkin Scholar. She is the author of the short story collection *Heads of the Colored People,* which was long-listed for the National Book Award, and she is currently working on her debut novel.

JIA TOLENTINO is a staff writer at *The New Yorker,* the author of the *New York Times* bestselling essay collection *Trick Mirror,* and a screenwriter. She grew up in Texas, received her undergraduate degree at the University of Virginia, and earned her MFA in fiction from the University of Michigan. In 2020, she received a Whiting Award, as well as the Jeannette Haien Ballard Prize. Her work has also appeared in *The New York Times Magazine* and *Pitchfork,* among other places.

NATALIE WARTHER graduated summa cum laude from Northeastern University and earned an MFA in poetry from the Bennington Writing Seminars. Her most recent work has been published in *Wigleaf, Hobart After Dark (HAD),* and *SmokeLong Quarterly,* and her short-story collection in progress explores the strangeness of female domestic life. Natalie lives in Los Angeles.

LINDY WEST is the co-host of the comedy podcast *Text Me Back* and the author of the newsletter *Butt News* (which gets my vote for best newsletter title ever). She has published three books: *Shit, Actually: The Definitive, 100% Objective Guide to Modern Cinema,* the *New York Times* bestselling memoir *Shrill: Notes from a Loud Woman,* and the essay collection *The Witches Are Coming.* Her next book, *Adult Braces,* is forthcoming from Hachette. A former contributing opinion writer for *The New York Times,* Lindy is a writer and executive producer on *Shrill,* the Hulu comedy adapted from her memoir, and a writer and producer of the independent feature film *Thin Skin.* She lives on Washington State's Olympic Peninsula.

DIANA WEYMAR is an artist and activist. She grew up in the wilderness of Northern British Columbia, studied creative writing at Princeton University, and worked in film in New York City. She is the creator and curator of Interwoven Stories and the Tiny Pricks Project, both of which are open for public participation, and the author of the book *Crafting a Better World.* Her work has been exhibited and collected in the United States and Canada.

ALEXA WILDING is a writer, musician, and mother of twins. After a decade as a singer-songwriter (called "the neo–Stevie Nicks" by *The New York Times*), she received her MFA from The Writer's Foundry in Brooklyn, New York. Her work has appeared in *Departures, Cup of Jo,* and *Parents.* She writes the newsletter *Resilience,* where she shares her journey as both a two-time cancer mom to her son, Lou, and in a recent plot twist, an early breast cancer survivor herself. Alexa lives in Tivoli, New York, with her family and is working on a memoir and new music, too.

RHONDA WILLERS is an artist with a diverse art practice that includes ceramics, mixed media, drawing, painting, and time-based installations. The author of the book *Terra Sigillata: Contemporary Techniques,* host of the podcast *The Artist in Me Is Dead,* and former president of the board of directors for the National Council on Education for the Ceramic Arts (NCECA), she lives and works in rural Elk Mound, Wisconsin, with her husband, three children, and cats.

NATASHA YGLESIAS is a queer Cuban American editor and writer based in California's Bay Area. A graduate of Sarah Lawrence College and the Bennington Writing Seminars, she's the co-author of the *New York Times* bestseller *Raising Antiracist Children: A Practical Parenting Guide* with Britt Hawthorne. Her fiction has appeared in *Third Point Press, Waypoints Magazine,* and *Malasaña,* and elsewhere. She's also the author of *The Anime Tarot Deck and Guidebook.* When she's not agonizing over the written word, you can find Natasha in her garden, her dog, Lyra, by her side.

JASPER YOUNG BEAR, whose Indian name is Red-Headed Woodpecker, is a member of the Mandan, Hidatsa, and Arikara Nation. He is from the Hidatsa Water Buster Clan on his father's side and the Arikara Bear Society and Arikara Medicine Lodge on his mother's. He is the founder of the Running Wolf Wellness Center and Cultural Survival School.

LIDIA YUKNAVITCH is the bestselling author of seven books, including the novels *The Book of Joan* and *The Small Backs of Children;* the memoir *The Chronology of Water,* which was a finalist for a PEN Center USA Award for creative nonfiction and won the Oregon Book Award: Reader's Choice; and most recently the memoir *Reading the Waves.* She earned her PhD in literature from the University of Oregon and is the founder of the Corporeal Writing workshop series in Portland. She is also a very good swimmer.

LATONYA YVETTE is a storyteller, writer, community builder, and steward of the Mae House. She writes on style, family, and culture at *With Love, L,* and is the author of *Woman of Color, The Hair Book,* and *Stand in My Window: Meditations on Home and How We Make It.* She lives in Brooklyn with her two children, River and Oak.

ABOUT THE TYPE

This book was set in Garamond, a typeface originally designed by the Parisian type cutter Claude Garamond (c. 1500–61). This version of Garamond was modeled on a 1592 specimen sheet from the Egenolff-Berner foundry, which was produced from types assumed to have been brought to Frankfurt by the punch cutter Jacques Sabon (c. 1520–80).

Claude Garamond's distinguished romans and italics first appeared in *Opera Ciceronis* in 1543–44. The Garamond types are clear, open, and elegant.